D1406693

SCRIPTURES

ARTURO MARCELO PASCUAL

SCRIPTURES

SACRED WRITINGS OF THE WORLD'S RELIGIONS

Konecky & Konecky
72 Ayers Point Rd.
Old Saybrook, CT 06475

Translated from the Spanish by Sean Konecky

This edition published by arrangement with Editorial Océano, S.L.

ISBN: 978-1-56852-820-5

Printed and bound in China

For the one and only María Muñoz,
the boisterous Paco
and, Ana, the most beautiful of all.

Contents

Introduction

Sacred Books

Archaeologists have discovered rocks and cave walls with paintings dating to at least forty thousand years ago. These are now looked upon as sacred spaces. A religious impulse seems to underlie the hunting scenes, fabulous animals, effigies of gods and geometric figures that seem to offer accounts of the creation of the world long before the appearance of materials that can be read by historians.

Millennia later Egyptian priests and scribes depicted in hieroglyphics the voyage of the soul into the afterlife on the walls of tombs and sarcophagi. But this symbolic language was of only limited expressiveness and practicality, as it entailed memorization of hundreds of different characters. Sometime later the seafaring Phoenicians invented the alphabet to facilitate commercial transactions. Soon writing became the single most important means of transmitting and storing information. In different parts of the globe there gradually emerged a corpus of writings said to be inspired by divine powers, dictated to exceptional individuals looked upon as apostles, prophets or saints, and often mediated by angels or other divine intermediaries.

Sacred literature has a historical and a normative character, often including both elements in various combinations. Sometimes the language used is cryptic or metaphoric, imbued with hidden meanings. In some cases its interpretation was the responsibility of a priestly class. The earliest books predate printing. They were set down in manuscript form in scrolls or later in codices, often in languages that are now long extinct. The transmission of these texts usually involved translation. In the passage from one language to another, ideas can change. Sometimes fragments of ancient works resurface and need to be taken into account.

The books that have had the greatest influence on modern life originated in Asia. The Bible and the Qur'an emerged in the ancient Near East, Hindu and Buddhist texts in India, Taoist and Confucian texts in China. Of all of these, the book that has had the most profound influence is the Bible. All of Western civilization is founded upon its basic premises and worldview. Western powers colonized the world, carrying the Bible with them. They imposed their commercial and industrial systems, promising to raise the indigenous people's standard of living, while at the same time imposing dictates on the private lives of individuals. Often the two went hand in hand.

Without religion and canons of sacred literature, civilization as we know it could not exist. Religious texts and the passions they arouse have led to much bloodshed but sublime artistic creations as well. On the other hand the ambiguity of their metaphorical language necessitates hidden keys of interpretation that allow them to survive the vicissitudes of history. In this way they can adapt to changing circumstances. At any given moment, power or money may seem to replace the God who dictated the sacred text, but its internal coherence guarantees its continuing influence upon the faithful.

It is precisely the ambiguous nature of sacred literature that permits it to be interpreted in many different ways. Its words have been used to proclaim war and make peace, to enslave and emancipate. In the Far East religious texts admit to widely different interpretations of the divine plan for the individual and a tolerance for differing belief systems. The concept of reincarnation encourages disdain for material wealth, since the aim of human existence is cast as liberation from attachment to the material world. The downside is a society in which everyone has to accept his or her place in the established order. Despite this, Far Eastern societies are seen to be adopting new paradigms and joining in the pursuit of material well-being.

In this book, we offer a wide-ranging consideration of the most important and historically significant examples of sacred literature, in antiquity as well as in today's world, as we are convinced that humanity is above all the product of the spiritual disquietude that goads it into reaching for explanations of its existence and destiny.

Teo Gómez

Christianity and Gnosticism

The Bible

For Judaism and Christianity, the Bible is divine revelation, containing those truths about the natural and the supernatural order that God conceived as necessary for human salvation. The study of history limits itself to examining the formation, over a period of millennia, of a vast assemblage of sacred texts in the land of Canaan, a territory that extends through modern-day Israel, Lebanon, Syria and Jordan. The Bible as we know it is the product of a long cultural process. The word itself comes from Ancient Greek (*byblos*), used to refer to any form of writing, whether as a scroll or as a codex. The Bible is the bestselling book of all time. It arose from the historical experience of the Jewish and Christian societies of that time.

▲ *God creates sun and moon in this engraving by Raphael representing the stage of creation related in Genesis 1:16. Traditionally Christianity has portrayed God as a powerful old man with a long white beard.*

◀ *Cover of an ancient Bible.*

> *In the beginning God created heaven and earth.*
>
> Genesis 1:1

▲▶ *Lucas Cranach,* Adam and Eve, *1526, Courtauld Gallery, London. Adam is just about to be seduced by Eve into taking a bite of the forbidden fruit.*

The Biblical World

When dealing with the origins and development of the Bible, historical truth and sacred history do not always coincide. It is thought that the first Hebraic tribes arrived in Palestine (Canaan) around 1500 BCE. According to the Scripture, God promised the land to the patriarch Abraham and his descendants. Abraham's grandson Jacob went down to Egypt with his twelve sons, eponymous founders of Israel's twelve tribes. These events are recounted in Genesis.

Around 1250 BCE, the tribes that had settled in Egypt returned to Palestine and confronted the inhabitants of the land. According to the Biblical account, Moses guided the people across the Sinai desert after freeing them from Egyptian oppression. This story is told in Exodus along with the recital of the prodigious signs and wonders: the ten plagues that Yahweh visited upon the Pharaoh, the crossing of the Sea of Reeds, the provision of manna and the tablets of the Law that established the covenant between God and Israel.

▲ *Michaelangelo,* Moses, *1513–1515, Church of San Pietro in Vincoli in Rome.*

Once settled in Canaan, the Israelites established the monarchy, which reached its apogee around 1000 BCE with David, the conqueror of Jerusalem and all of the other Canaanite cities, and his son Solomon, famed for his wisdom and who married the pharaoh's daughter. It was during this golden age that the extensive oral traditions that had accumulated since the time of the patriarchs was set down in writing to form the grand tapestry of sacred history. Leviticus, Numbers and Deuteronomy were added to Genesis and Exodus, resulting in a heterogeneous collection of law and an account of the Israelites' wanderings. These five books constitute Torah of

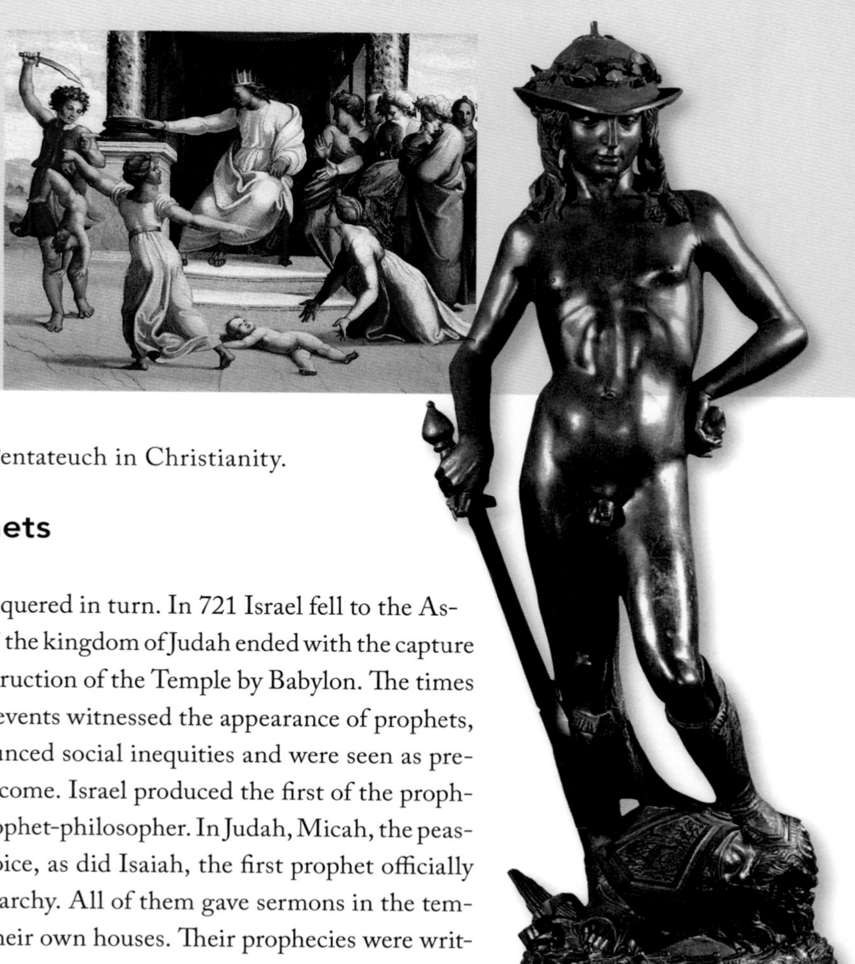

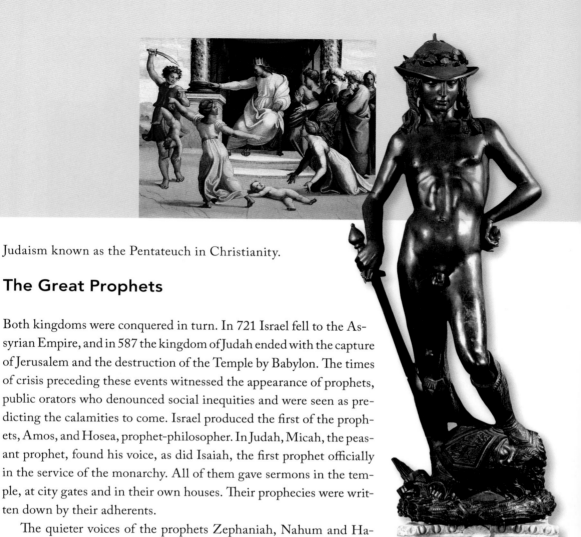

Judaism known as the Pentateuch in Christianity.

The Great Prophets

Both kingdoms were conquered in turn. In 721 Israel fell to the Assyrian Empire, and in 587 the kingdom of Judah ended with the capture of Jerusalem and the destruction of the Temple by Babylon. The times of crisis preceding these events witnessed the appearance of prophets, public orators who denounced social inequities and were seen as predicting the calamities to come. Israel produced the first of the prophets, Amos, and Hosea, prophet-philosopher. In Judah, Micah, the peasant prophet, found his voice, as did Isaiah, the first prophet officially in the service of the monarchy. All of them gave sermons in the temple, at city gates and in their own houses. Their prophecies were written down by their adherents.

The quieter voices of the prophets Zephaniah, Nahum and Habakkuk were eclipsed by Jeremiah, the highpoint of prophetic power, not only in his poetry, but in the sweeping nature of his condemnation of existing authorities and his annunciation of the destruction of the Jewish people in the days leading up to the Babylonian conquest. This was followed by the exile of the Jewish people to Babylon, which lasted from 586 to 538 BCE. During these dark days the prophets held their peace. The priest Ezekiel relayed his intense visions of God's majesty, as well as powerful admonitions and condemnations of the idolatrous perversions of Israel and Judah. During this time the enigmatic prophet Daniel, to whom the book that bears his name is attributed, is said to have had his apocalyptic visions.

▲ *Donatello,* David, *ca. 1440, Museo Nazionale del Bargello.*

▲◄ *Raphael,* Judgment of Solomon, *1509–1511, the Vatican. One of the most memorable episodes in the Old Testament.*

▲ *Francesco Hayez,* Destruction of the Temple *(detail), 1867, Gallerie dell'Accademia, Venice. The Romans razed the Jerusalem temple in 70 CE.*

▲ *Pieter Breughel,* The Tower of Babel, *ca. 1565, Museum Boijmans van Beuningen, Rotterdam. The Biblical author probably conceived of the tower along the lines of the Babylonian ziggurats.*

Religion as Law

In 539 BCE, the Persian emperor Cyrus II conquered Babylon and authorized the return of the Jews to Judah, which became an autonomous province of his empire. New prophets arose with the end of the Babylonian captivity and resettlement of the Holy Land. Haggai, Zechariah and Malachi spoke of the rebuilding of the Temple, while Obadiah, Joel and Jonah predicted calamities in Edom and Palestine and the fall of Nineveh.

From then on the prophetic voice was no longer heard. The last books, Ezra and Nehemiah among them, were historical, dealing with the establishment of the community and administrative matters. Along with Chronicles (also called Paralipomenon), they provided a political framework for Jewish society. The Torah became the ultimate authority for the life of the people.

By now the bulk of the Jewish scriptures had been completed. Still to come were the poetic writings of the Song of Songs (also known as the Song of Solomon), the narrations of Ruth and Esther, the wisdom texts such as Job that confront the problem of human suffering head on, the skepticism of Ecclesiastes and the desolation of Lamentations. These concluded the ensemble of the writings that constitute the Hebrew scriptures, twenty-four books in all.*

Authors and Compilers

For many centuries it was believed that the authors of the Old Testament were the patriarchs, prophets and kings who appear in the Biblical narrative. A prime example is the unquestioning acceptance that the Torah is the Word of God received by Moses on Mount Sinai. In the eighteenth century, theories based upon the critical examination of the documents arose to challenge this doctrine. In fact it turns out that in almost no cases were the actual authors those traditionally credited.

Noting the wide differences in style, lexicon and doctrine not only among the five books, but within each book itself, scholars have concluded that what is known as the Pentateuch is the product of a long process of the combination and redaction of different oral and literary sources dating from long after the time of Moses. The same holds true for the Psalms of David. The authors of most of them are not known, even though they may well have been composed in the days of the monarchy. As to the works of Solomon, they are believed to have been written about a century after his death. It may well be that some of the prophets elaborated part of the texts that bear their names during the Babylonian Exile. Other cases are instances of the widespread tradition in antiquity of attributing literary works to famous authors to enhance their credibility.

The Vatican Council of 1965 declared: "For Sacred Scripture is the word of God inasmuch as it is consigned to writing under the inspiration of the divine Spirit ..." As we have pointed out, sacred history is different from scientific history. The Bible is the work of generations of editors, compilers, sages, apostles and disciples who fervently transmitted oral traditions, and recognized testaments and foundational texts over the course of centuries, resulting in a true encyclopedia of the sacred, a holy library.

▲ *Rembrandt,* Moses Smashing the Tablets of the Law, *1659, Gemäldegalerie, Berlin. In his anger at the people's worship of the Golden Calf, Moses destroys the tablets given to him by God.*

> « …and God called the light day and the darkness night. »
>
> GENESIS 1:5

The Formation of the Canons

▲▶

Naked I came from my mother's womb, And naked shall I return there.
The Lord gave, and the Lord has taken away;
Blessed be the name of the Lord.

Job 1.21

The arrival of Alexander the Great in Judea in 332 BCE brought the Biblical territory into the orbit of the Hellenic world. Soon the new Jewish colony in Alexandria became one of the most important centers of Jewish literary production, functioning like an autonomous province. But over time the local Jewish population lost its fluency in Hebrew, necessitating a translation of the Jewish scriptures into Greek. This was accomplished sometime between 300 and 130 BCE. The translation of the Torah was said to have been made by seventy learned Jews called from Jerusalem: each working on his own produced the identical translation. This is the genesis of the name by which the translation is known: The Septuagint. The text of the Old Testament in early Christian Bibles is that of the Septuagint.

At the same time, new books written in Hebrew were appearing in Babylon, Palestine and Alexandria. They include Tobit, Judith, Wisdom, Baruch, Sirach (Ecclesiasticus), and Maccabees I and II. These early texts were used by early Christian communities and incorporated into the Greek text. They are considered Deutero-canonical (second canon). The canon of the Jewish Bible, which was established in Palestine in 97 BCE rejected these books.

To the Old Testament, written primarily in Hebrew with some Aramaic, was added the New Testament, written in Greek, which we will turn to in the following pages. Combined together, they

▲ *Alexander the Great. His Hellenization of Asia influenced the New Testament.*

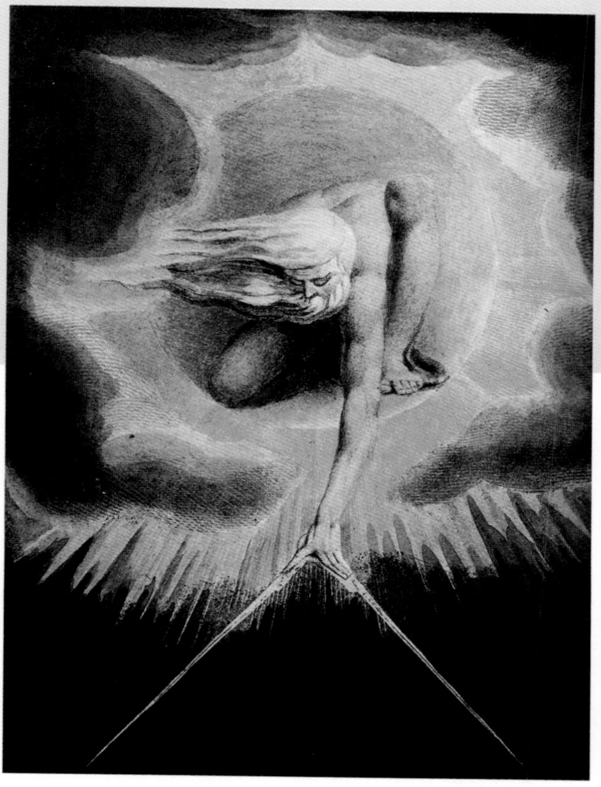

form the Catholic Bible, the official catalog of text considered normative regarding questions of faith and morality, regulating the lives of the faithful. Later on Protestants accepted the Hebrew canon for the Old Testament, considering the Deutero-canonical books to be Apocrypha.

▲ *William Blake,* The Ancient of Days, *1794. Blake's Urizen was for him a symbol of the rational mind, in opposition to imagination and rebellion, but he also represents Jehovah and eternity.*

*Translator's note: The traditional division into twenty-four books is as follows: the five books of Moses; eight books of the Prophets, with the twelve Latter Prophets considered one book; and the eleven books of Writings, with Ezra and Nehemiah considered one book.

▶ Christianity

The Song of Songs

▲ *Piero della Francesca,* Legend of the True Cross *(detail), 1452–1456, Church of San Francisco, Arezzo, Italy. This fresco cycle adorns the Basilica of Saint Francis in Arezzo, Italy. Shown here is the meeting of the Queen of Sheba and Solomon, the purported author of the Song of Songs.*

The deliberations concerning the inclusion of a poem celebrating romantic love in the Scriptural canon engaged the full energies of both Jewish and Christian theologians. The intense sensuality of the Song of Songs seemed ill-suited to a sacred work, but the fact that the work was attributed to King Solomon (and in fact is often called the Song of Solomon) ended up being the decisive factor. Afterward esoteric and allegorical interpretations rendered the heated poetry palatable to a religious audience.

> « Your lips are like a scarlet ribbon; your mouth is lovely. »
>
> Song of Songs 4:3

A Celebration of Physical Love

▲ *Brother Luis de León was condemned by the Inquisition for attempting to translate the Song of Songs.*

The Song of Songs is one of the poetic books of the Old Testament, along with Job, Psalms, Proverbs and Ecclesiastes. Its Hebrew name, Shir Hashirim, is grammatically in the superlative case. The friar Luis de Léon, who was condemned by the Church in 1574 for translating the poem directly from the original Hebrew, wrote: "The name 'Song of Songs' signifies the most eminent and exalted of all songs, just as in common parlance one speaks of a man among men."

As is the case with numerous examples of the erotic literature of antiquity (especially Egyptian epithalamiums), the poems expresses the feelings of lovers without any attempt at moralizing or religious interpretation. The name of God is not mentioned at all, something rare in the Biblical corpus. In the face of this, Jewish exegesis looked upon the poem as an allegory of God's love for Israel, and the cabbalistic author of the Zohar affirmed that it encompassed the entire faith of the Chosen People. Later, Christianity interpreted the lovers as Christ and his Church, Christ and humanity, Christ and the Virgin Mary, or in the mystical poetry of St. John of the Cross, Christ and the human soul.

The Song of Solomon

Scholars attribute the work to a compiler of the fourth century BCE,

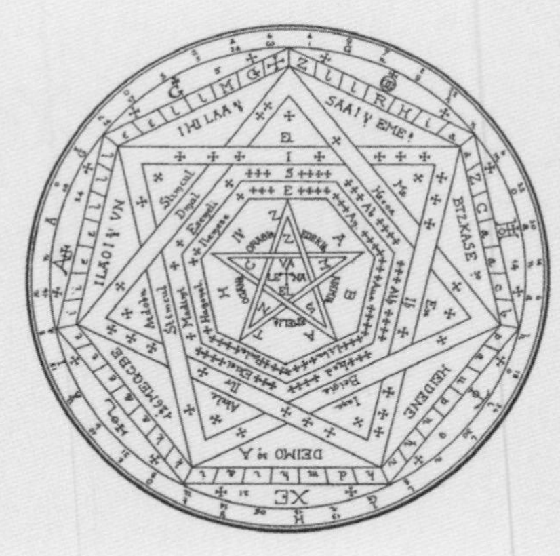

who combined several poems. Some researchers have suggested that the poem was written by a woman, given the weight the poem gives to its female protagonist. Tradition, however, stands opposed to the scholarly consensus, ascribing authorship to King Solomon himself, who lived around 1000 BCE, which the first verse of the book confirms.

Solomon was the second son of David and Bathsheba and inherited the throne from his father. According to the Biblical narrative the kingdom was a vast one, stretching between the borders of Egypt and Mesopotamia. Solomon possessed untold wealth and built the Temple in Jerusalem to house the Ark of the Covenant. He was also famous for his wisdom, which the Bible tells us he owed to Yahweh. Master of the Kabbala and infallible in his judgments, according to legend his reputation came to the attention of the Queen of Sheba, who visited him and bore him a son named Menelik. Some readings link the lovers in the poem with Solomon and his bewitching foreign paramour. Tradition also considers Solomon to be the author of Proverbs and Ecclesiastes.

▲ *Justus van Ghent,* King Solomon, *ca. 1474, Galleria Nazionale delle Marche, Urbino, Italy. Both the Book of Proverbs and the Song of Songs are attributed to Solomon.*

▲▶ *Kabbalistic pentagram. Kabbalists interpret the Song of Songs as an allegory representing the union of God and the intellect.*

▶ *Eugene Oudiné,* Bathsheba, *1859, sculpture on the north façade of the Louvre. Bathsheba was the wife of David and mother of Solomon.*

◀ *The humanist Sebastian Castellion doubted that the Song of Songs was divinely inspired.*

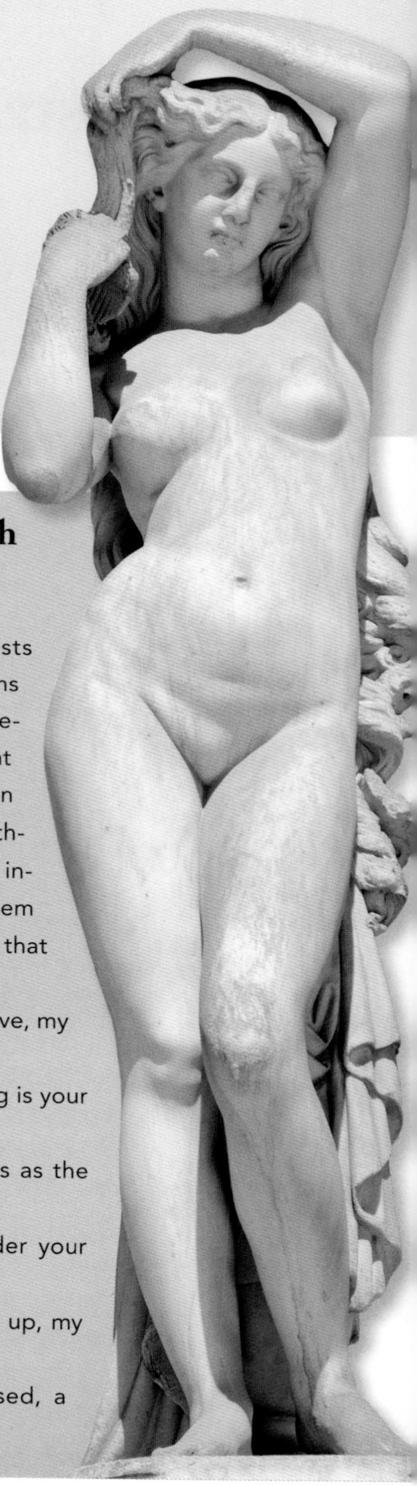

Let Him Kiss Me with the Kisses of His Mouth

The Song of Songs was initially rejected because of its profane character and its numerous erotic images:
"My beloved is to me a sachet of myrrh resting between my breasts.
I am a rose of Sharon, a lily of the valleys"

The lovers avidly seek one another, come together and separate, hoping to possess each other once and for all. Their dialogue is accompanied by a chorus of maidens. The language is sensual rather than sexual.
"Let him kiss me with the kisses of his mouth — for your love is more delightful than wine.
Pleasing is the fragrance of your perfumes; your name is like perfume poured out.
No wonder the young women love you!"

Renaissance humanists had doubts about claims that the poem was divinely inspired, given its ardent sensuality and emphasis on physical attributes. Whether or not it was divinely inspired, the voluptuous poem presents an ideal beauty that can represent divinity:
"How delightful is your love, my sister, my bride!
How much more pleasing is your love than wine,
Your lips drop sweetness as the honeycomb, my bride;
Milk and honey are under your tongue.
You are a garden locked up, my sister, my bride;
You are a spring enclosed, a sealed fountain."

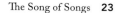

▶ Christianity

New Testament

▲ *Rembrandt,* Head of Christ, *1648, Gemäldegalerie, Berlin. Rembrandt's depiction of Jesus is unusual in that he endows Him with Semitic features.*

In the Old Testament, God's covenant with the Chosen People includes the promise of a liberator who will establish his reign on earth, disperse the enemies of Israel and govern with justice for all time. The New Testament announces that this prophecy is fulfilled in Jesus Christ: "After John was put in prison, Jesus went into Galilee, proclaiming the good news of God. The time has come," he said. "The kingdom of God has come near" (Mark 1:14–15). Jesus is the central figure of the four Gospels, the Messiah revealed to the Christians of the first century.

Crucified for Blasphemy

Jesus of Nazareth was born in Palestine (Judea), a Roman colony, during the reign of Augustus. Almost everything we know about his life comes from the accounts written in the Gospels of Matthew, Mark, Luke and John: his preaching in Galilee, his stay in Jerusalem and his death during the reign of Tiberius, successor to Augustus. The first mention of his name outside of the early Christian literature is in the Annals of Tacitus, a Roman historian of the first century. Other authors noted in passing that Jews worshipped an individual they referred to as Christ. Christianity, a sect of dissenting Jews, grew rapidly in just a few decades.

Jesus did not himself write anything. His earthly passage was recounted by some anonymous disciples who later became identified with the Evangelists. Their works were more devotional than biographical. In their semi-clandestine meetings early Christians would read the sacred texts of the Jewish Bible, but soon found that they had to include the Gospel accounts since Jesus was the fulfillment of the Law and ancient Messianic prophecies. They sought to accurately preserve the words and the memory of the acts of the Savior, transmitted by those who were his contemporaries, to defend his teachings from the passage of time and false doctrines that might arise.

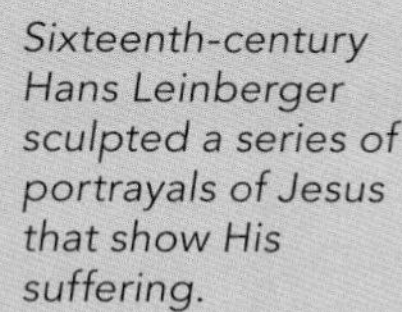

Sixteenth-century Hans Leinberger sculpted a series of portrayals of Jesus that show His suffering.

▲ Fresco from the Church of Santa Maria of Vespiolla presents the four principal apostles.

A Slow Process of Development

The New Testament is not recognized as a sacred text by Judaism. It is part of the Christian Bible. It comprises the four Gospels, the Acts of the Apostles (attributed to Luke), diverse epistles including those of Paul, Peter, James and John, and the Book of Revelation. The oldest of all of these writings are the epistles of Paul, which were set down in writing in the middle of the first century CE, during his voyages to Asia Minor, Macedonia and Greece.

The stories about the life of Jesus were not at first written texts. They derive from oral traditions from different places that were assembled and redacted by scribes who also added additional material from later sources. The elaboration of the Gospel narratives took place over the course of forty years (from about CE 50 to 90). The one exception is the Gospel of John, which was completed at the beginning of the second century. The oldest written document extant is a fragment of the Gospel of John dated to the year CE 125.

▲ Icon of Christ Pantocrator from the Monastery of Saint Catherine on Mount Sinai.

Gospels: The Good News

The Greek word *evangelion* means "good news." It was soon adopted as the name for this literary text as it contained the report of human salvation. The "inventor" of this new genre was probably Mark, whose narration is cast in the present tense, giving it a sense of immediacy and vivacity. Each of the Evangelists offered distinct versions of the life and teachings of Jesus. The first three Gospels, how-

ever, draw from identical or closely related sources holding many verses in common and following the same order of events. For this reason these three Gospels are labeled as synoptic. If the accounts of Matthew, Mark and Luke are set side by side in parallel columns one can read them without noticing wide divergences.

The fourth Gospel, written by the "disciple whom Jesus loved" (John 21:20), attains the height of theological expression beginning with the proclamation: "The Word became flesh and made his dwelling among us." In addition he modified the narrative structure, emphasizing key moments, providing detailed topographic and chronological information, and above all drawing out the symbolic value of Jesus' life and teachings. Students of the Bible have wrestled with the question of how a simple fisherman from Galilee could illuminate such profound matters, and then add the eschatological vision of the apocalypse in the Book of Revelation (the last book in the New Testament).

▲ *Title page from a Lutheran Bible of 1769 depicting the Resurrection.*

▶ Christianity

Revelation

▲ *Matthias Gerung,* The Whore of Babylon, *ca. 1530. Chapter 1 of Revelation describes "the great harlot who sits on many waters, with whom the kings of earth committed fornication."*

The last book of the New Testament abounds in images of glory and cataclysm. Its overall thrust is clear: the forces of evil will attack Christians; there will be human and cosmic calamities; but in the end the triumphant Christ will inaugurate a new world of light and harmony. The details of the account, however, are steeped in symbolism. The author has set us a nearly insoluble puzzle that requires an act of decoding to interpret. Above all, Revelation is a visionary work that is one of the religious and artistic treasures of humanity. Since its creation it has excited the imagination and given rise to many important works of art.

Prophecy, Vision, Recapitulation

The Greek word *apocalipsis* means "revelation," in the sense of showing something hidden. But in this case one does not explain the mystery simply by removing the veil that covers it. The book is considered to be a prophecy and a chronicle of the Last Judgment and its consequences. In the first chapter Christ says to John: "Write, therefore, what you have seen, what is now and what will take place later." This command triggered a dream filled with enigmatic scenes and figures. But one can look at the Apocalypse not as a prediction, but as a recapitulation: an unveiling of the supernatural meaning of past events.

Apocalypses constitute a literary genre within the Biblical corpus. They play a dominant role in Daniel and then culminating in Revelation. There are also the apocryphal revelations of Paul, Peter and Thomas. The question whether the apostle John was the actual author of Revelation cannot be definitively answered, since although it is attributed to John, it does not state that this is John the apostle. It may have been written by someone else named John, one of the apostle's followers or perhaps another inspired early Christian. Whether or not it was written by the disciple "whom Jesus loved," it is clear from its stylistic unity that it was written by a single author.

A Tormented Apostle

Revelation was put into its final form around the turn of the second century during the reign of the Emperor Domitian, who proclaimed himself *dominus ac deus* (lord and god). Those who refused to participate in his cult were marginalized or persecuted. According to tradition, the apostle John, along with Peter and James, had the privilege of being present during Christ's transfiguration on Mount Tabor. At Christ's death, John fled from Roman-controlled Palestine to Ephesus, where he performed numerous miracles and baptized many into the faith. Tertullian recounts that John was subjected to torture: submerged in boiling water, he escaped unscathed.

▲ *Tradition attributes the authorship of Revelation to St. John, although modern scholarship has called that into question.*

John had his vision on the Isle of Patmos where he had been

▲▶ *Detail from a tapestry showing the dragon and the beast from Revelation. The tapestry hangs in the Musée de la Tapisserie, Château d'Angers, Angers, France.*

▼ *Detail showing the dragon giving his power to the beast from illuminated manuscript of the* Commentary on the Apocalypse *of St. Beatus of Liébana.*

exiled by Domitian. The book begins with the majestic appearance of the Son of Man, surrounded by seven golden lampstands, representing the seven churches of Asia Minor. From that point on, the reader encounters marvels and prodigies. The Almighty is adored by four beings covered in eyes front and back, and by twenty-four elders clothed in white. In His hand He bears a scroll with seven seals that can only be opened by the Lamb of God.

The Number of the Beast

As each of the first four seals is broken, one of the four horseman of the Apocalypse appears (Conquest, War, Hunger and Death). Further calamities ensue as the next two seals are opened. The opening of the final seal announces the salvation of 144,000 from the twelve tribes of Israel and a great multitude. The cycle of disasters is repeated, with several variations always coming in sevens (seven seals, seven trumpets and seven bowls), the number in scripture accorded to divine works.

These septenaries precede the announcement of the ruin of Babylon, the great prostitute that represents apostasy, and the battle between her and the Word. She is described as follows: "There I saw a woman sitting on a scarlet beast that was covered with blasphemous names and had seven heads and ten

> *And I, John, saw the holy city, the New Jerusalem.*
>
> Apocalipsis 21:2

horns" (Revelation 17:3). Much has been written about this servant of the devil. She probably represents Imperial Rome but has served as a stand-in for Napoleon, Hitler, Stalin, and other oppressors. Interpreters of prophecy are given another valuable key: "This calls for wisdom. Let the person who has insight calculate the number of the beast, for it is the number of a man. That number is 666" (Revelation 13:18). This motif has been used in many horror movies to represent agents of evil who come to wreak destruction upon the earth.

▲ *Michelangelo,* The Last Judgment *(detail), 1536–1541, Sistine Chapel, the Vatican. This section of the work shows the angels announcing to humanity the hour of reckoning.*

At the end of this catastrophic era, evil is defeated once and for all, and the Last Judgment gives rise to the New Jerusalem, the celestial city, where God reigns eternally over humanity, surrounded by songs of praise. Thus, what begins with fear and alarm turns into a powerful message of hope.

▲▲ *Lucia Signorelli,* Last Judgment, *1499–1504 (detail), Orvieto Cathedral, Orvieto, Italy.*

▶ Old Testament Apocrypha

Book of Enoch

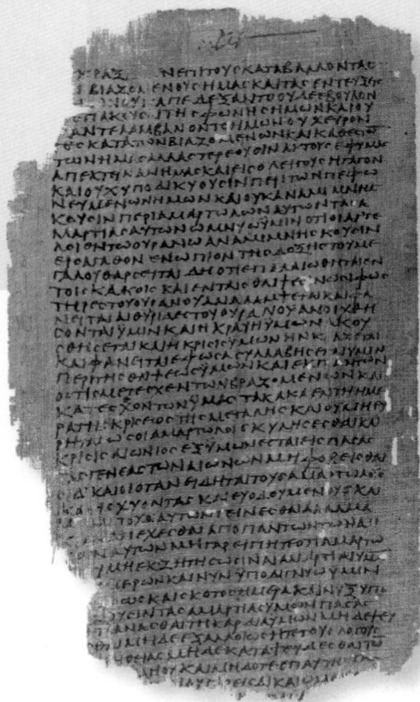

▲ *Fragment of the Book of Enoch. Greek manuscript part of the papyri of Chester Beatty. This manuscript also contains a homily attributed to Melito of Sardis.*

▲▶ *The six archangels depicted in a Russian icon of the nineteenth century. The belief in their role on earth as governors was condemned by the Council of Laodicea (363–364).*

Catholics call "apocryphal" (hidden, arcane) those books written outside the canon of the Old Testament. Protestants call them "pseudoepigraphic" (falsely titled), and Judaism refers to them with the Hebrew term *sefarim ha-hisonim* (external books). According to tradition they were books with secret teachings that should not be divulged; reading them was forbidden. One of the texts so stigmatized is the Book of Enoch. This apocalyptic book was rejected by rabbinical Judaism and all Christian churches except that of Ethiopia.

Secret, Dangerous, Condemned

Authorship of the books of Apocrypha of the Old Testament was attributed to various Biblical personages, including Adam, Abraham, Moses and Solomon. Scholarship today challenges these attributions as well as the antiquity and authority of these texts. In the early days of Christianity, however, they were taken at face value and exercised considerable influence, despite being rejected and even condemned as "dangerous and inimical to the truth." Listed among the Apocrypha are the Book of Jubilees, the Life of Adam and Eve, the Testament of Abraham, the Apocalypse of Abraham, the Testament of Moses, as well as other titles. These works were composed in a variety of genres: didactic elements are combined with autobiography, prayers, narrative and wisdom writings.

Most of these texts, including the Book of Enoch, underwent various vicissitudes. This book was excluded from the canon at the Council of Laodicea in CE 363–364. The Greek version disappeared from the West and was considered lost for over a millennium, until copies written in Ethiopian were discovered in Abyssinia in the eighteenth century. The book had long been part of the liturgy of the Ethiopian Church. In the middle of the twentieth century, Hebrew and Aramaic fragments of the work were discovered at Qumran.

The Fall of the Watchers

▲ *Ancient manuscripts in the Strahov Monastery near Prague. The Book of Enoch was discovered in Abyssinia in 1773 by the Scottish explorer James Bruce. The Ethiopian Church is the only Christian denomination that includes the book in its canon.*

Who was Enoch, the book's protagonist and supposed author? According to the Old Testament, Enoch was the seventh Patriarch, father of Methuselah and great-grandfather of Noah. Genesis tells us: "After he became the father of Methuselah, Enoch walked faithfully with God three hundred years and had other sons and daughters. Altogether, Enoch lived a total of 365 years. Enoch walked faithfully with God; then he was no more, because God took him away" (Genesis 5:22–24). We will look further into this mysterious removal.

> *And the Eternal God will tread from there upon Mount Sinai, and he will appear with his Host.*
>
> Book of Enoch 1:4

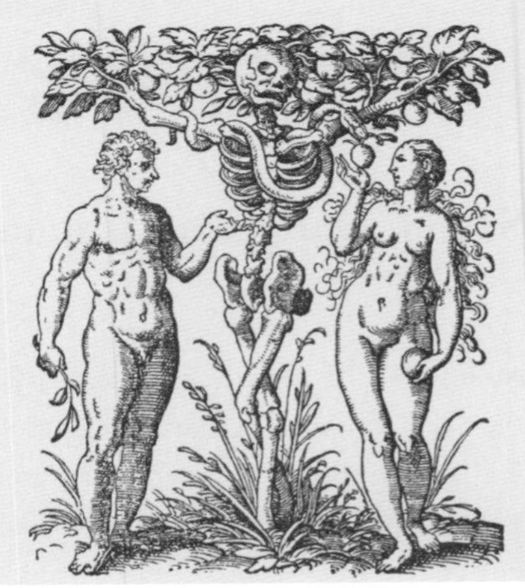

▲ *Marco d'Oggiono,* Altarpiece of the Three Archangels, *ca. 1516, Pinacoteca di Brera, Milan. The painting shows Michael, Gabriel and Raphael sending a fallen angel down to hell.*

The Book of Enoch, the richest of the known apocryphal works, is a compilation that talks about the secrets of heaven, the movements of the stars and the Flood. It contains visions, prophecies and parables. The most astonishing section is The Book of the Watchers, wherein the author explains the origin of evil. The watchers were angels who, under the leadership of Shemhazai and Azazel, were to have been protectors for humanity. Instead they had sexual relations with the daughters of Adam and corrupted them with lust. Their union produced the nephilim, giants who dedicated themselves to oppress suffering people. Furthermore, they rejected the manna provided by Yahweh, and ended up refusing cooked meat. Rather they devoured living animals and finally resorted to cannibalism.

For all of these sinful activities, Yahweh sends the archangels Michael, Uriel, Raphael and Gabriel to imprison the angels and destroy the giants. The fallen angels implore Enoch to intercede for them, but to no avail. The human race, now totally corrupted, is destined to be wiped out in the time of Enoch's great-grandson Noah.

▲ *The angel Metatron staying Abraham's hand in a woodcut from the* Nuremberg Chronicles.

The Angel Metatron

According to Hebrew legend, Enoch was instructed in all of the secrets of heaven and earth during the course of his time on earth. Some important Jewish writers have suggested that he was the inventor of books and writing, and the ancient Greeks identified him with Hermes Trismegistus on account of his great wisdom. It is also said that he taught his contemporaries to build cities, provided them with admirable laws, discovered the signs of the Zodiac, and mapped out the movements of the planets. He is also said to have abstained from intoxicants and eating meat.

For these reasons Yahweh spared him from death, the common lot of man, and brought him directly to heaven where he was transformed into the angel Metatron (meaning "near the throne"). Yahweh placed him next to his throne, put a glittering crown on his head and provided him with seventy-two wings and numerous eyes. An ancient Hebrew manuscript reads: "Enoch's flesh became flames, his tendons fire, his bones embers, his eyes flaming torches, his hair rays of light; and he was enveloped in storm, thunder, whirlwinds and flashes of lightning."

▶ New Testament Apocrypha

Apocryphal Gospels

▶ *The Apocrypha of the New Testament inform us that Mary's parents were named Anna and Joachim and that God told Joachim that Anna would give birth to a daughter infused with the Holy Spirit and that she should be named Mary.*

The Apocrypha of the New Testament were never seen as secret books, like those of the Old Testament. They were simply texts that were not included in the canon because they were seen as having only limited doctrinal value. However, thanks to them we know: that Mary's parents were named Anne and Joachim; the names of the Three Kings; that an ox and an ass were present in the manger; that Mary was perpetually a virgin; and that St. Peter was crucified upside down. Many remarkable details can be found in the pages of these "rejected" works and were incorporated into Christian tradition. Today they form an inextricable part its liturgy and iconography.

◀ A mosaic that depicts the Three Kings as described in one of the Apocryphal Gospels.

"Deviant" Scriptures

What we know about the approximately sixty apocryphal New Testament texts is that they were all composed between the first centuries of the Common Era and the Middle Ages. Only fragments or imperfect translations from their original languages remain. Despite this and their doubtful authenticity, they serve to fill in lacunae in the canonical texts, even though the Church's official position has always been that the teachings they contain are "deviant."

▲ Plaster bowl from the sixth century discovered in Babylon and containing Aramaic texts from the Apocrypha.

Although not all of the Apocryphal New Testament texts are gnostic, many were written at a time that coincided with the apogee of Gnosticism, a primitive form of Christianity that the guardians against heresy arduously pursued. The proliferation of Gospels, lives of the apostles, and apocalypses required the Church hierarchy to establish which and how many were true. This was not definitively resolved until the Council of Trent in the middle of sixteenth century. Among the Apocryphal works that are clearly gnostic, the Gospel of Thomas stands out. It collected 114 quotations from Jesus. A complete copy was discovered in the Nag Hammadi Library.

> *If the savior found her worthy who are you to reject her?*
>
> Gospel of Mary

▲ *Caravaggio,* The Holy Family, *1602–1604, Metropolitan Museum of Art, New York. The painter emphasizes the human qualities of the Biblical figures in a domestic scene.*

▲▶ *This woodcut from the* Nuremberg Chronicles *shows St. Peter being crucified upside down.*

The Family of Jesus and Lives of the Apostles

The exuberant, imaginative quality of these old Apocryphal books accounts for their popularity. They contain many accounts of the early days of the Savior's life and the life of his family, providing details that did not find their way into the canon. In this category we find the Protoevangelium of James. Written in the middle of the second century, it describes Jesus' infancy and contains much curious information about the Virgin Mary. We learn of Jesus' grandparents, Anne and Joachim, the late birth of Mary, her education in the Temple, and her betrothal to Joseph. It also tells the story of Mary's birth in a cave in Bethlehem and affirms her perpetual virginity, noting that Joseph was a widower, so that references to Jesus' brothers refer to Joseph's sons by an earlier marriage.

Along with these stories about the Holy Family, the Apocrypha that recount the deeds of the apostles are real adventure stories, in which the saints play a role much like that of the heroes of Greco-Roman myth. They are subjected to terrible tortures for their faith and perform miraculous deeds. For example, the Acts of Peter recounts the confrontation between the apostle and Simon Magus, probably a gnostic, and Peter's later upside-down crucifixion.

Disquieting Revelations

▲ Henryk Siemiradzki, The Christian Dirce, *1897, National Museum in Warsaw. This myth of Greek origin was appropriated by the Church, which cast it as the story of a Christian woman martyred during the time of Nero. St. Thekla was tortured by the Romans in the arena, but unlike her mythological counterpart, she was saved and continued preaching.*

Nor is romance lacking. The most famous episodes appear in the Acts of Paul. This account seems to have been influenced by contemporary sentimental novels. The young Thekla is so enamored of the Saint Paul that, in an example of exalted chastity, she fights off the advances of a young nobleman. She is then sentenced to die in the arena for striking him. But she is miraculously saved from danger and goes on to preach the Word of God along with St. Paul. She was canonized and was very popular in the Middle Ages as a representative of purity and chastity and for the unlimited love that she showed for her master.

In other places the Apocrypha offer unsettling versions of stories that stand in stark contradiction to those in the canon. The Acts of John, for example, contain heretical docetist material, claiming that Jesus confesses to his disciples on the Mount of Olives that he will not be crucified and that his nature is very different from what they imagine it to be.

No less interesting are the many apocalyptic stories that narrate the journey of Christ through the seven heavens, the details of the Last Judgment and the functions of the various angels in the concluding events of history. For example, the Apocalypse of Paul portrays Paradise and the sufferings of the damned. This work served as primary source material for Dante's *Divine Comedy*, and for centuries provided imagery for numerous works of art.

▲ Scene from the Last Judgment according to the Christian Apocrypha.

The New World Translation of the Holy Scriptures

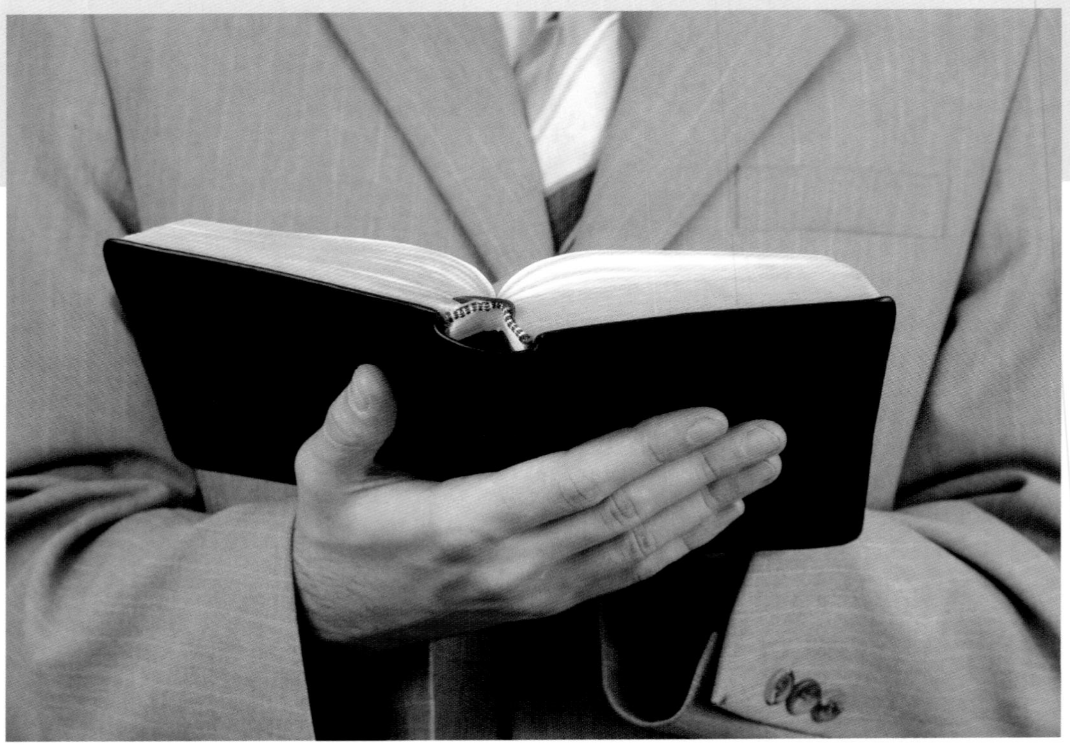

▲ *Jehovah's Witnesses use their own translation of the Bible. It warns of the imminent destruction of the world and the salvation of the elect.*

Since the end of the nineteenth century, Jehovah's Witnesses have been announcing that the end of the world is imminent. According to the sect's founder, Charles Taze Russell, it should have occurred in 1914. In that year the celestial host was to defeat the forces of evil in the battle of Armageddon. Although Russell died in 1916 without this having happened, the group found a way of postponing the event into the indefinite future. The Witnesses continue to persevere. According to their Bible, the New World Translation of the Holy Scriptures, this prediction will soon come to pass.

The word was with God and the word was God.

New World Translation of the Holy Scriptures, John 1:1

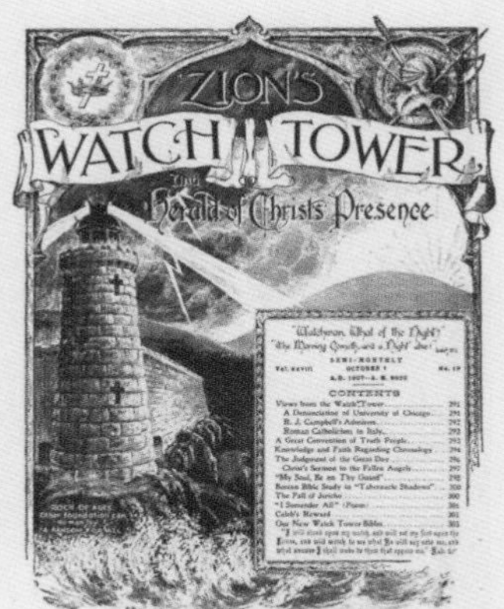

A Militant Version

▲ *Michelangelo,* The Last Judgment, *1536–1541, Sistine Chapel, the Vatican. During the Last Judgment, Satan and his followers will be destroyed and Jehovah's Witnesses will inherit the earth.*

▲▲ The Watchtower *is the principal organ for spreading the Witnesses' message. Today, it can be found translated into 127 different languages.*

The leaders of the movement begun by Russell look upon the translation of the Bible from ancient sources that are used in most Christian denominations as arcane and inexact. For this reason they established a committee of experts to produce a new translation, which was completed in 1961. The New World Translation of the Holy Scriptures presents itself as absolutely faithful, word for word, to the original manuscripts of the Bible. Its appearance, however, was surrounded by controversy. Because the participants of the committee maintained their anonymity, it was impossible to evaluate their knowledge of Greek and Hebrew; questions arose regarding the alteration of verb tenses, suppression of some verses and the alterations in meaning that the translation endorses. That their translation has not been accepted or recognized by other denominations has given further support to those who question or doubt its reliability. The consensus of impartial scholars is that although the text can be faulted for being overly literal and containing some errors, it is not deliberately misleading.

During their labors, the committee wrote the name "Jehovah" 7,210 times, wherever the tetragrammaton (YHVH) appears. As Jewish tradition avoided the pronunciation of YHVH, the word Adonai (Lord) was often used as a substitute. Jehovah is one of the variants of God's name, equivalent to Yahweh. In the Middle Ages the letter J replaced the Y, so God's name became pronounced Jehovah. This name came

▲ C.T. Russell and J.F. Rutherford were the first presidents of the Watch Tower Society.

▲▶ In Nazi concentration camps, a violet triangle was used to identify members of the Jehovah's Witnesses.

to have special significance for the sect.

The 144,000 Elect

Jehovah's Witnesses reject the Catholic Church's doctrine of the Trinity. They hold that Jehovah alone is to be worshipped and that He created Jesus Christ, who in turn created the world. They consider the Holy Spirit not as the third person of the Trinity, but rather as the active force of Jehovah, so it is always written in lower case letters, "holy spirit." They believe that Christ died on a single upright post, not a cross, thus rejecting Christianity's most widely recognized symbol, and maintain that Christ was resurrected in an immaterial body. His physical body remains in an uncorrupted state in an unknown location, whence it will arise at the world's end.

They have successively predicted that the end of the world would arrive in 1914, 1925, and 1975. Present-day leaders of the group maintain that it will come to pass soon but do not specify the year. After Armageddon and the return of Christ, 144,000 of the elect of the sect, both the living and the dead, will go directly to heaven (Revelation 7:1–8). The rest of the Jehovah's Witnesses will remain eternally on earth, which will be transformed into a paradise.

No Time to Lose

Since Jehovah's Witnesses believe that the end times are close at hand, they devote their energies to proselytizing by home visits and publications. In all major, and most smaller, cities of the world, one finds Jehovah's Witnesses going from house to house to alert nonbelievers of the coming tribulations. Their first priority is to warn people, whether secular or religious, of the need to change their lifestyles and detach from worldly pursuits. They stress the urgency of preparing for the imminent conclusion of earthly existence. What is the use of climbing the corporate ladder if everything is about to come to an end? The only activities worth pursuing are studying and devoting all of one's efforts to assisting the community.

The conviction with which Jehovah's Witnesses embody the principle of their faith comes from their literal reading of the Bible. One of their most controversial positions is their rejection of blood transfusions based upon Mosaic injunction: "The life of every creature is in its blood. That is why I have said to the people of Israel, 'You must never eat or drink blood, for the life of any creature is in its blood.' So whoever consumes blood will be cut off from the community." This prohibition is extended to treatment with serums and vaccines.

▶ Mormonism

Book of Mormon

▲ *Monument dedicated to Joseph Smith in the White River Valley near his birthplace in Sharon, Vermont.*

▶ *Statue of Joseph Smith in Salt Lake City, the headquarters of the Mormon faith.*

The origin of the Mormon Church offers a symphony of fantastic elements: the journey across America of a mysterious prophet, the discovery of scripture written on golden plates that had been buried for centuries, and the prophet's use of transparent stones as glasses to decipher them. The founder, transmitter and protagonist of these adventures, Joseph Smith, established a congregation that adopted the name The Church of Jesus Christ of Latter-day Saints (LDS Church). Its holy text is the Book of Mormon. The story of its discovery is incredible even for those accustomed to the improbabilities of sacred history.

And I know that the record which I make is true.

First Book of Nephi 1:3

The Book of Gold

Smith was born at the beginning of the nineteenth century in Sharon, Vermont, to a working-class family. He displayed exceptional oratorical skills at an early age and was only eighteen when he first experienced a vision of the angel Moroni. The angel told him where he had hidden a book in the year 421 of the Common Era, that he himself had written. The book provided an account of his time on earth and the history of the Nephites, descendants of Lehi, who along with others was brought to the Americas by God from Jerusalem before the Babylonian conquest (587 BCE). Smith received another visitation from the angel four years later in 1827, and consequently climbed Mount Cumorah where he discovered the book the angel had announced to him.

It was a heavy tome made of plates of gold joined by thick rings. Its shining pages were covered with strange seemingly indecipherable characters of Egyptian origin. Moroni showed Smith how to read them using the *urim-thummim* (oracular stones referred to in Exodus 28:30). These transparent stones were attached to a breastplate that was joined to the book. Moroni counseled Smith to transcribe and publish the book, but he had to return the original to the angel once this work was completed.

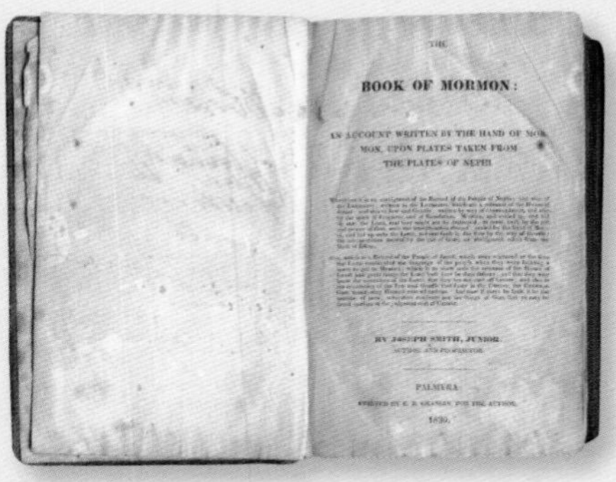

THE

BOOK OF MORMON:

AN ACCOUNT WRITTEN BY THE HAND OF MOR-
MON, UPON PLATES TAKEN FROM
THE PLATES OF NEPHI.

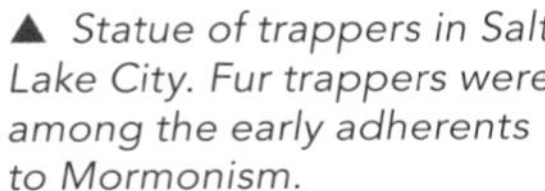

▲ *Statue of trappers in Salt Lake City. Fur trappers were among the early adherents to Mormonism.*

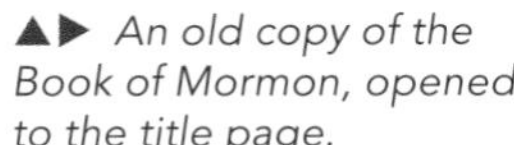

▲▶ *An old copy of the Book of Mormon, opened to the title page.*

The Magic Glasses

The process of translation was supernatural. As Smith looked through the *urim-thummim*, he did not see impenetrable Egyptian script but rather plain English writing. An amanuensis listened to him recite the text and copied it down, but if there were any errors in transmission (Smith was in a trance and spoke in whispers), the characters remained visible until the correction was made, and then they were replaced in the following line. Finally, the angel took back the plates. According to Mormon tradition eleven other people saw the book. Their testimony is included in most modern editions.

The book purports to contain nothing less than the history of America from 600 BCE to CE 421. The book abounds in surprising details. The ancient inhabitants of America were originally from Jerusalem. They traveled across the Atlantic and landed in the New World centuries before the birth of Christ. They called themselves Nephites after the name of their prophet Nephi, the first in the prophetic lineage. Following God's commandment, Nephi and his descendants composed detailed annals of their history. These annals constitute the Book of Mormon. Mormon was the father of Moroni, who had sealed and hidden the Mormon scripture.

Christ in America

The Book of Mormon recounts that Jesus Christ appeared to the pre-Columbian inhabitants of America in the first century, after his resurrection, and remained with them preaching until he had established the foundations of the true church. It also states that Adam and Eve lived in Davies, Missouri, after the Fall, and that at the Last Judgment, Mormons will be allowed to dwell for a brief time in the New Jerusalem, which is also located in Missouri.

Critics skeptical of Mormon claims contend that the text cannot be authentic. It contains phrases from Shakespeare and, even more troubling, direct quotes from the King James Bible (published in 1611). Further it speaks of horses and mules, which were introduced into the Western Hemisphere by the Spanish. They also note that Mormonism bears many resemblances to Islam. In part because of these anachronisms, the book's publication elicited fierce opposition even as it signaled the birth of the new religion. Smith was imprisoned in 1844, and then assassinated when an anti-Mormon mob stormed the jail. After this, his followers moved west, settled in Utah, and founded Salt Lake City, today the center of the Mormon religion, which claims fifteen million adherents worldwide.

▲ *Mormon temple in Snowflake, Arizona, crowned with the angel Moroni.*

▲◀ *Members of the Mormon Battalion photographed in 1896. The Battalion distinguished itself in the Mexican-American War.*

Doctrine and Covenants

▲ *Statue of Joseph Smith in the visitor's center at Times Square.*

▶ *Mormon teaching was spread after Smith's death through the book Doctrines and Covenants.*

According to Joseph Smith and his successors in the Mormon Church, the message of Christ was not completed upon the death of the last apostle. The teaching is ongoing. Each Mormon is potentially a prophet and can modify or correct previous teaching if inspired by God. It is understood that this weighty responsibility is reserved for the leaders of the congregation. The book that recognizes such rectifications is entitled Doctrine and Covenants. Along with the Book of Mormon it is a canonical text of the sect.

◀ *Mormon Temple in Mesa, Arizona.*

Doctrine Is Subject to Change

The 138 sections of the work are mostly revelations given to the founder of the sect and those who succeeded him as Church leaders. But they also include official declarations. One, in 1890, ended the practice of polygamy. Another, in 1978, abolished racial bars to the priesthood. These were confirmed by divine messages to Mormon leaders. In addition the book lays out the administrative structure of the Church in detail. All of the teachings are considered to have been communicated by God to prepare the faithful for the Second Coming of Christ.

The originality of Doctrines and Covenants in contrast to the Book of Mormon is that it does not claim to be a translation of an ancient work. Its origin is modern, a result of God's direct communication with chosen leaders of the Church. Through their mediation, Mormon teaching can continue to be reinterpreted and rectified. The work was first published in 1835 and has been revised since to include the testimony of later Mormon prophets. No major theme has been left out, from the concept of God and the origin of the world, to the nature of the afterlife and the bases of salvation.

▲ *The angel Moroni can be found at the top of many Mormon temples.*

▶ *Salt Lake City, Utah is the world capital of Mormonism.*

Many Gods

Mormonism is polytheistic. In addition to the Trinity of Father, Son and Holy Ghost, there are many other Gods. In each universe, there is a supreme deity endowed with a corporal presence: "The Father has a body of flesh and bones as tangible as man's," according to Doctrine and Covenants. In our galaxy, God the Father reigns. He was once a holy man who descended to Paradise on earth in Missouri to give Adam a series of instructions that he later disobeyed. God's spiritual children, born of the union with a goddess, include Jesus Christ, Satan and all human beings. Just as God was once a man, so we also can achieve the exaltation of divinity.

Accordingly, it is understood that Mormons do not consider God the creator of eternal matter, but only its administrator. When sending the good angels to earth, His purpose was to encourage humanity to unite with the Divine. Some of the elect (such as Abraham, Moses, Joseph Smith and Nephi) were charged with special missions. In the final days the souls of the just, baptized in the Mormon Church, will go directly to Paradise.

▲ *Cartoon showing Brigham Young, Smith's successor, and Ulysses S. Grant discussing the issue of polygamy.*

> *Prepare ye, prepare ye for that which is to come, for the Lord is nigh.*
>
> DOCTRINES AND COVENANTS

▲ Mormon Temple in San Diego is the third temple built in California.

To Become Gods

After the Battle of Armageddon, a sign visible to all the inhabitants of the earth will appear in the heavens. This prodigy marks the beginning of the last days (whence the name Church of the Latter-day Saints), a millennium ruled by Mormons. During this period an opportunity will be afforded to non-Mormons to convert to the true religion. The truly wicked will be sent to the fires of Hell, and all others will be consigned to eternal glory of a second rank. Those who accept the true religion of Mormonism will attain the status of Gods.

The Mormon scriptures explain how this highest state is to be attained. Mormons need to go through a series of rites. They need to be baptized through immersion and continue through the different stages of the priesthood during their adolescence and youth. Mormon couples may go through a "sealing ceremony" that leads to eternal marriage. This "celestial marriage" must be finalized by the Holy Spirit, which can occur here on earth or after death. It is ratified by God and will last through all of eternity.

▼ Temple Square in Salt Lake City.

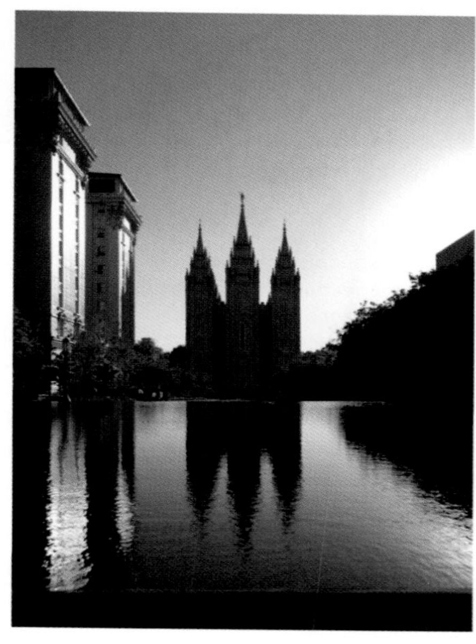

The Conflict of the Ages

▲ *The expectation of the imminent Second Coming and observance of the Sabbath are among the fundamental tenets of the Seventh-day Adventists.*

In 1843, a poor Baptist farmer named William Miller began to devote himself to the full-time study of the Bible. Reading the Book of Revelation he calculated that the Second Coming of Christ would take place in 1844. His prophecy raised such expectations that, when it was not fulfilled, Miller was totally discredited. The group of Adventists that he had founded mostly disappeared, but one devoted young woman, Ellen White, followed in his footsteps and was inspired to write a number of works, the first entitled *The Great Controversy* (published in 1858).

A Lesser Light

Ellen White (1827–1915) was born in Maine to a Methodist family. She had the gift of clairvoyance and received thousands of visions over the course of her life. Despite chronic illness she never stopped writing, preaching and organizing her followers. Her literary production comprised eighty books, about five thousand articles and sixty thousand pages of sermons and tracts. However, she made it clear that her works were not canonical; only the Holy Bible could claim that status. She wrote: "We must not think, 'Well, we have all the truth, we understand the main pillars of our faith, and we may rest on this knowledge.' The truth is an advancing truth, and we must walk in the increasing light." Her works contain the doctrinal pillars of the Seventh-day Adventist Church.

The name of the sect points to two of its most important beliefs: the hope and expectation of the Second Coming ("adventist" derives from the Latin *adventus*, meaning "arrival") and the celebration of the Sabbath, the seventh day of the week, on which God rested after His work of Creation. According to Adventist doctrine, after the death of the body, the soul remains asleep or unconscious until the Last Judgment. The believers will rise embodied to dwell in eternity.

▲ *James White with his wife, Ellen, whose visions were the foundation of the sect.*

▲▲ *A Millerist waiting for the Parousia (Library of Congress).*

> *Many are to believe on Christ through the communication of truth by His servants.*
>
> ELLEN G. WHITE

▼ Hans Memling, St. John Altarpiece, ca. 1479, Memling Museum, Bruges, Belgium. This panel from a triptych shows St. John transcribing Revelation on the Island of Patmos.

A Time of Trouble

Of the many visions that White received the most significant took place on March 14, 1858. Over many hours she felt herself surrounded by light and witnessed the final battle between the armies of Christ and Satan. It was a panoramic vision encompassing the past, present, and future and included the Adventists walking a narrow path to Jerusalem.

Adventist tradition states that two days later, the Evil One tried to take her life so that she could not reveal the mysteries vouchsafed to her in this vision. But God sustained her, and she described her eschatology in her book, *The Great Controversy* (later included in her five-volume work, *The Conflict of the Ages*).

The Great Controversy deals with the cosmic battle recounted in the Book of Revelation (ascribed to John, son of Zebedee, and brother of James, both of them among Jesus' twelve original disciples). It affirms that although the exact date of the Christ's return is uncertain, preparations are already underway. They note that Miller's prophecy of the Second Coming initiated a new phase in Christ's intercessionary mission, and begins a period of tribulation, "a time of trouble," in which people need to join with the forces of good to purify the earth from

Health, Diet and Breakfast Cereal

While awaiting the return of the Messiah, the Adventists follow strict diets so that their bodies remain pure. They recommend the vegetarian diet of Adam and Eve, and at a minimum insist upon compliance with the dietary laws of the Old Testament. They do not eat pork, shellfish or other "impure" animals listed in Leviticus, supplementing their intake with milk and eggs. Unlike Jehovah's Witnesses they permit blood transfusions, but not food containing blood (following Leviticus 17:10). They also abstain from alcohol, tobacco and drugs (except when administered for medical purposes).

The promotion of a healthy lifestyle is one of the sect's distinguishing characteristics. The missionary work of the group includes medical schools, hospitals, clinics, leprosariums and emergency medical facilities throughout the world. (We also owe our enjoyment of breakfast cereal to an early member of the church, John Harvey Kellogg.) Studies show that as a result of these practices, Adventists live on average between four and ten years longer than the general population of which they are a part.

apostasy and the evil that had corrupted it.

Adventists consider themselves to be the "remnant" spoken of in Revelation 12:17, a pure nucleus of believers dedicated to maintaining the faith and keeping its commandments in the face of all attack. In the end time, they will blissfully reign in heaven for a thousand years, and then, once others are given the opportunity to redeem themselves, they will dwell on earth totally purified, Satan and the evil angels having been annihilated.

The Holy Piby: Sacred Book of Rastafarianism

▲ *Rastafarians look upon Haile Selassie as the living god. At his death they believed that he ascended Mount Sion. His symbol was the Lion of Judah, which was part of a ring that he always carried with him.*

More than a religion, Rastafarianism is a view of the world based on tolerance, generosity and an optimistic vision of the future, as the following verses from its sacred text, the Holy Piby, indicate: "We believe in the utilization of the power and blessings of God for the good of mankind . . . when earthly toil is over we shall be rewarded a place of rest in the kingdom of Heaven, there to sing with the saints of Ethiopia." The Rastafarians, or rastas, have developed their own unique style and appearance. They revere marijuana as a vehicle for achieving mystical experience and let their hair grow in long dreadlocks, symbolic of the lion's mane.

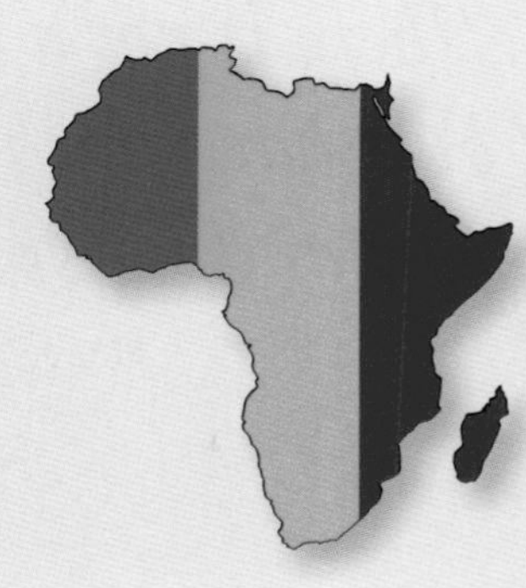

King of Kings

▲ *Africa as one country under the Ethiopian flag, as Bob Marley tells us in his song "Africa United."*

▲◀ *Haile Selassie, reigned as Emperor of Ethiopia from 1935 to 1974. Rastafarians consider him to be the last king of Solomon's dynasty.*

Rastafarianism was born in Jamaica in the 1920s, under the influence of the black political leader Marcus Garvey. He promoted the Pan-Africanist movement that advocated the return to Africa to shake off the yoke of white colonialism and recover the roots of black culture and civilization. His prophesied of "a new Ethiopia, a new Africa, stretching her hands of influence throughout the world, teaching man the way of life and peace, The Way to God."

His prophecy seemed to have been confirmed when Ras Tafari was crowned emperor of Ethiopia in 1930, taking the name Haile Selassie (Power of the Holy Trinity). He became the head of one of the first officially Christian nations in history: Abyssinia. He claimed descent from King Solomon and the Queen of Sheba, and was given an impressive range of titles: King of Kings, Chosen of God, Conquering Lion of Judah. His followers added the title "Jah" (abbreviation of Yahweh) and looked upon him as the living Messiah sent to the black race to lead it to the true promised land.

Haile Selassie was a devout Christian and did not accept any claim to divine status. He did, however, welcome Rastafarianism in his country, and his visit to Jamaica in 1966 was met with the greatest enthusiasm. He was deposed in 1974 in a military coup and died in the following year. But Rastafarianism continued to gain adherents propelled by the works of Bob Marley and reggae.

▲ *Ethiopian Orthodox church in Lalibela. The Ethiopian Church preserves the faith of one of the oldest Christian countries in the world.*

> *There is not a heaven nor a hell but that which ye make of yourselves and for yourselves.*
>
> HOLY PIBY, CHAPTER 1:14

Bible for the Black Race

Rastas accept the King James Version of the Bible as Holy Scripture but call into question a number of passages that they consider to have been rewritten for the benefit of the white race. The Holy Piby affirms that Africans are the children of Israel.

The book's title is a Creole translation of "Holy Bible." It was written by Robert Athlyi Rogers, a militant Pan-Africanist from Antigua. The book designates Ethiopians (by which it refers to Africans in general) as God's chosen people. Rogers claimed that the book was a translation from Amharic, the ancient Semitic language of Ethiopia. It proclaims self-determination for African peoples, and refers to Haile Selassie as the Messiah and Marcus Garvey as his prophet.

◀ *Marcus Garvey was the founder of the Universal Negro Improvement Association and African Communities League.*

▲▲ *Bob Marley, Jamaican musician and composer, helped spread the Rastafarian movement throughout the world.*

Marijuana As Sacrament

The Holy Piby announces the destruction of "white Babylon" and the union of black Israelites in Africa, the true Zion. For this reason it has been called the "Bible of the Black Race." It was quickly adopted by Rastafarianism as a foundational religious text. But its message is not one of vengeance or destruction, but rather of peace and brotherhood.

In addition to doctrinal questions, the book enjoins many rules of conduct, diet and hygiene. Rastas do not eat meat, drink alcohol, or wear expensive clothes. They subscribe to the vows of the Nazirites (Numbers 8:5), cutting neither their beards nor their hair, and are known for their long dreadlocks. They consider this as representing the lion's power.

Rastafarian adepts regularly consume marijuana, but not for kicks or as an escape. They consider it to be a sacramental herb that opens an inner channel, allowing them to approach Jah and true wisdom. They find support for this in certain Biblical verses: "You will eat the plants of the field" (Genesis 3:18); "He makes grass grow for the cattle, and plants for people to cultivate — bringing forth food from the earth" (Psalms 104:14); "Better a small serving of vegetables with love than a fattened calf with hatred" (Proverbs 15:17).

▲ *Rastafarians endorse the use of marijuana for spiritual purposes.*

▲◀ *The house of a Rastafrian draped in the colors of the Ethiopian flag.*

▶ **Swedenborgianism**

The Heavenly Doctrine

▲ *Entrance to Hell from the façade of the Orvieto Cathedral, Orvieto, Italy.*

The Swedish thinker Emanuel Swedenborg was a renowned scientist and inventor before he became a mystic who conversed with angels "just as one person speaks with another." In his home in Stockholm, which was filled with mirrors, he would frequently enter into trance states and experience intense visions. Although he did not found a sect, his descriptions of the spiritual world exercised a major influence on occult philosophy and provided the foundation of the New Swedenborgian Church. Some Masonic Lodges practice an initiatory rite named after him.

Physics and Metaphysics

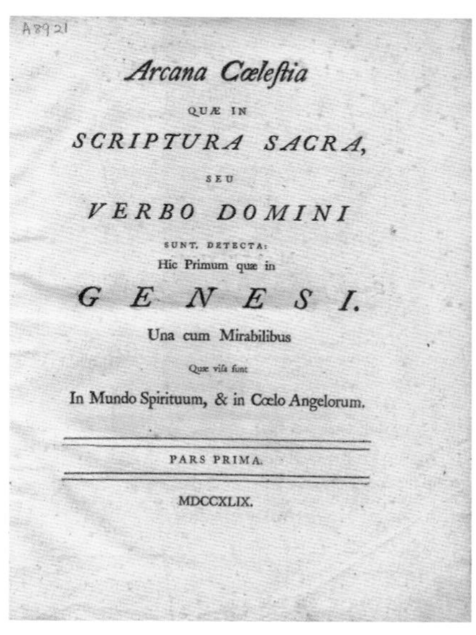

Arcana Cœleftia

QUÆ IN

SCRIPTURA SACRA,

SEU

VERBO DOMINI

SUNT. DETECTA:

Hic Primum quæ in

GENESI.

Una cum Mirabilibus

Quæ visa sunt

In Mundo Spirituum, & in Cœlo Angelorum.

PARS PRIMA.

MDCCXLIX.

▲ *Title page from Swedenborg's first major theological work,* Arcana Coelestia. *The book, written in Latin and eventually in eight volumes, examined the spiritual meaning of the first two books of the Bible, Genesis and Exodus.*

Swedenborg was the son of a Lutheran minister who eventually became a bishop. He was born in Stockholm in 1688 (d. 1772). He was a scientist, theologian and philosopher. He received a strict religious education but showed an interest in the sciences from his youth. His discoveries in the fields of physics, mathematics and medicine were significant. He created plans for a flying machine and a submarine, came up with a new method for calculating longitude based upon the phases of the moon, did important research in minerals and metallurgy, explained the formation of the solar system, and articulated modern theories of the atom, the vibrations of light and the kinetic basis of heat. No scientific field seemed beyond his grasp.

By the age of forty he had established an international reputation. His counsel was sought by the King of Sweden. But then he underwent a life change. He started wondering, what good was knowledge of the physical world if the world of the spirit remained unknown? Determined to discover the organ of the body where the soul resides, he studied the function of endocrine glands, brain and cerebellum, but this only managed to win him accolades as a great anatomist. Since physiology was not sufficient, he turned his attention to theology.

« *I have seen angels cast thousands of evil spirits into hell.* »

The Heavenly Doctrine

▲ *In 1745, Emanuel Swedenborg received a vision in which he was summoned to reveal the true meaning of the Holy Scriptures.*

▲▶ *Swedenborg Chapel in Cambridge, Mass., near Harvard University.*

Conversations with Angels

Swedenborg experienced a spiritual crisis in 1745. The Lord appeared to him and commanded him to unravel the secret meaning of the Bible. He spent years working to fulfill this divine command. The fruits of his labor culminated in the eight volumes of Arcana Coelestia ("Heavenly Mysteries"), which contains his exhaustive analysis of Genesis and Exodus from historical, psychological and spiritual perspectives. After that, he continued to meet with angels, who visited his house lined with mirrors, which he said enabled him to see them more clearly.

Many doubted that Swedenborg was in his right mind. He wrote to a friend, "Repeated encounters with spirits is a road that can lead to madness." But his prestige was great, and he tried to conceal as far as possible his role as prophet, continuing to publish scientific works. He led an absolutely respectable life; he was a vegetarian and a gardener. He corresponded with some of the leading philosophers of his day, including Kant and Voltaire. When an aristocratic lady asked him where her late husband had hidden certain important documents, he did not hesitate to tell her to look in the drawer of an old bureau; apparently his angels had told him where she should look.

The Choice of Heaven or Hell

In 1758, Swedenborg published his most famous work, *De Caelo et Ejus Mirabilibus et de Inferno, ex Auditis et Visis* (commonly known as

"Heaven and Hell"), the result of his continuing dialogue with angelic beings. Many curious observations are to be found in its pages. For example, life after death is similar in many ways to life on earth. Angels live active lives, breathing, eating, reading and engaged in service to others. The inhabitants of hell look like ordinary people. Only celestial beings can see their real corrupted appearance.

▲ *Hieronymous Bosch,* Garden of Earthly Delights, *ca. 1500, Prado Musueum, Madrid. Bosch's famous triptych depicted heaven and hell in fabulous imagery. Swedenborg insisted that only those who chose hell were sent to hell.*

Perhaps Swedenborg's most original contribution is his view of the afterlife. He conceives of heaven and hell as dependent upon the disposition of the individual soul, not as reward or punishment. People end up in heaven or hell through their own choice. After the death of the physical body, the soul resides in an intermediate spiritual world to undergo a period of purification and is ultimately free to choose its own destiny. No one is barred from entering heaven or permanently condemned to hell.

Swedenborg predicted the day and hour of his own death (March 29, 1772) three years earlier. It is said that he greeted the prospect with equanimity.

The Nag Hammadi Library

▲ *Bridge at Nag Hammadi, Egypt. The eponymous trove of manuscripts was found in this vicinity.*

The strange circumstances surrounding the discovery of the Nag Hammadi Library could be taken from the plot of a mystery story or from the *Thousand and One Arabian Nights*. The Egyptian peasant who discovered the thirteen papyrus codices that radically changed our understanding of early Christianity was accused some weeks later of avenging the death of his father in a horrible fashion: after tracking down the victim, he dismembered him with the help of his brothers and then, following an ancient custom, tore out his heart and devoured it. (Other sources offer variations on this story.) No less extraordinary were the incidents surrounding the publication of the codices and the hypotheses about their origin.

> *Jesus said, "I have cast fire upon the world, and see, I am guarding it until it blazes."*
>
> Gospel of Thomas

Saved from the Fire

The peasant's name was Muhammad Ali, and one day in December of 1945, he was spreading fertilizer on his crops near the town of Nag Hammadi in Upper Egypt. While digging he came upon a clay jar about one meter high that he opened with great caution, fearing that it contained an evil genie, but hoping that he might find a treasure within it. Inside were thirteen papyrus codices written in Coptic with numerous Gnostic texts, the controversial belief system that had so disturbed the early Christian Church. Returning home he threw some of them into the oven to serve as fuel. Questioned later, his mother admitted that he had burned some pages, but that they had provided a good fire.

▲ *Two pages from one of the Nag Hammadi manuscripts in the Coptic Museum in Cairo.*

When investigation began into the murder that Muhammad Ali was accused of, he and his brother decided it best to get rid of the manuscripts in order not to draw unwanted attention to themselves. They handed them over to a less than scrupulous clergyman, who sent most of them to a merchant in Cairo. Almost immediately dealers in antiquities and collectors sought to get their hands on the trove. The Egyptian authorities were alerted. They confiscated ten of the codices, which were given to the Coptic Museum in Old Cairo. One of them was smuggled out of Egypt and was offered for sale in the United States. Scholars raised a hue and cry, beginning a fierce academic battle with quarrels, accusations and denunciations flying back and forth that delayed publication of the find. Finally UNESCO (United Nations Educational, Scientific, and Cultural Organization) had the library put onto microfilm, completing the work in 1979.

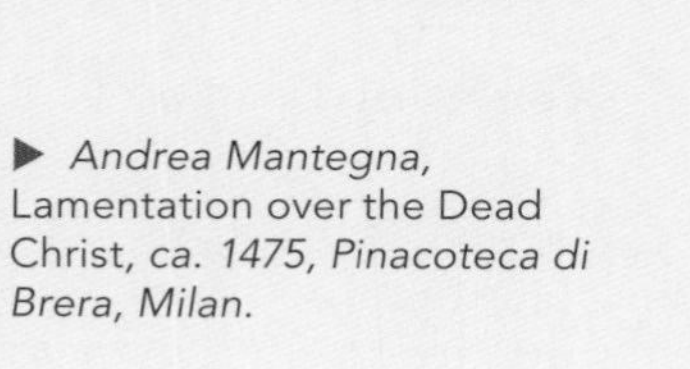

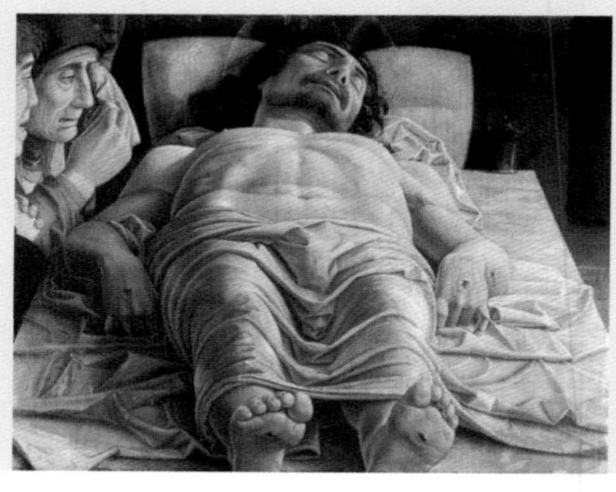

▶ *Andrea Mantegna,* Lamentation over the Dead Christ, *ca. 1475, Pinacoteca di Brera, Milan.*

▲ *Icon from the Monastery of St. Catherine at the foot of Mount Sinai.*

Sensuality and Mysticism

The Nag Hammadi Library is a faithful witness to the convulsions that gripped early Christianity. The papyri date to the fourth century of the Common Era, but some of them are copies of older texts. In those days Gnostics were accused of heresy by orthodox theologians such as Iraneus of Lyons. His work *Adversus Haereses* (Against Heresies) was an attempt to refute "Gnostic superstition." Gnostics were persecuted not only by the Church but by the emperors as well. Once Christianity became the official religion of the Roman Empire, possession of Gnostic texts became a criminal offense. We probably owe their preservation to a monk from the monastery of Saint Pacomius in Upper Egypt, who knew they were under threat and buried them in a jar so that they would not be destroyed.

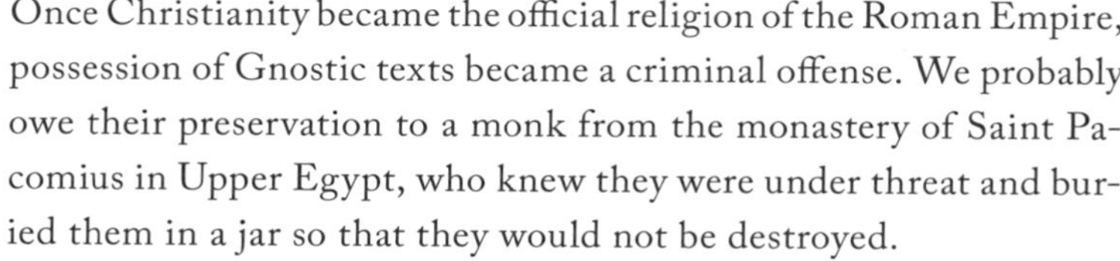

It is not surprising that the Gnostic Gospels scandalized the early Church, since in addition to their controversial doctrinal positions, which were confusing and not easily understood, they offered many sayings and episodes from the life of Jesus and the apostles that contradicted the canonical accounts. The Gospel of Thomas, for example, quotes many cryptic sayings of Jesus: "If you bring forth what is within you it will save you; if you do not bring it forth it will destroy you." In the Gospel of Philip the relationship between Jesus and Mary Magdalene is at the very least suggestive. It speaks of

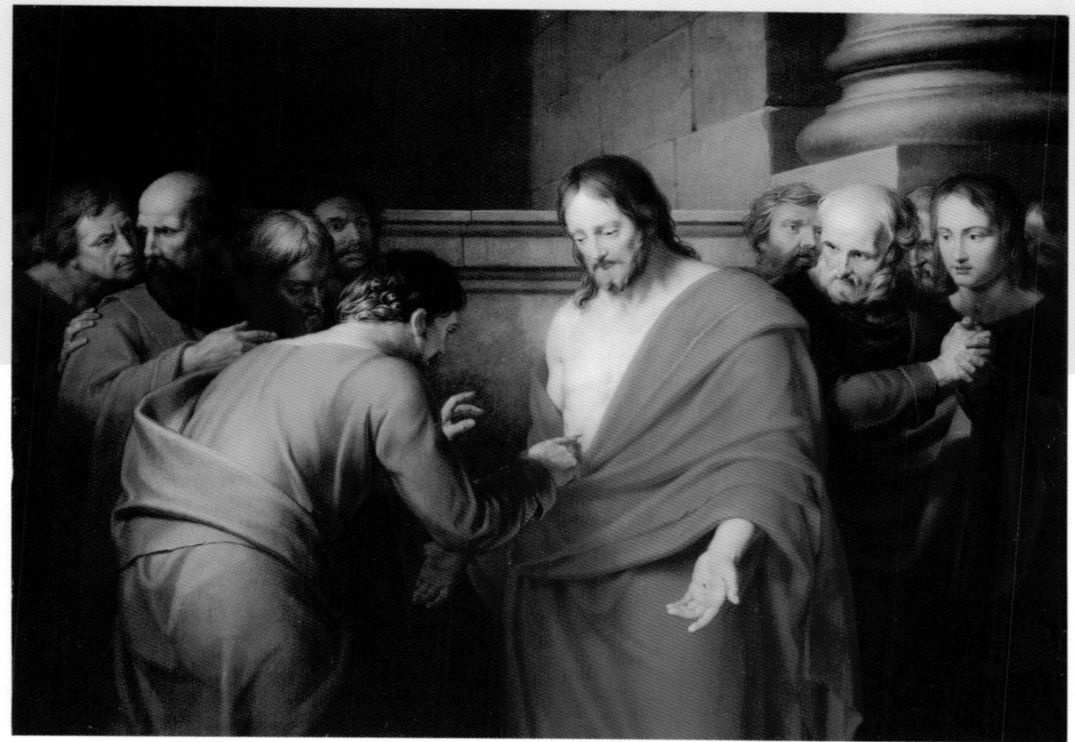

▲ *Benjamin West,* The Incredulity of St. Thomas, *ca. 1790, Leeds Art Gallery, United Kingdom. One of the most important works in the Nag Hammadi Library is the Gospel of Thomas.*

tender kisses that made the other disciples jealous. Other texts are marked by sensuality and mysticism, such as the Gospel of Truth, or by their hermetic content, as in the Apocryphon of John and Gospel of the Egyptians, which speak of "the great invisible Spirit," the supreme truth according to the Gnostics, completely separate from the false and tyrannical demiurge of the Old Testament that claimed to create and rule the universe. All of these books are part of the Nag Hammadi Library, thirteen papyrus codices bound in leather and buried in a clay jar. The entire library consists of fifty-two Gnostic tracts along with a partial translation of Plato's *Republic*. They were preserved as if by a miracle from the ravages of time, fire and religious dogma.

Ginza

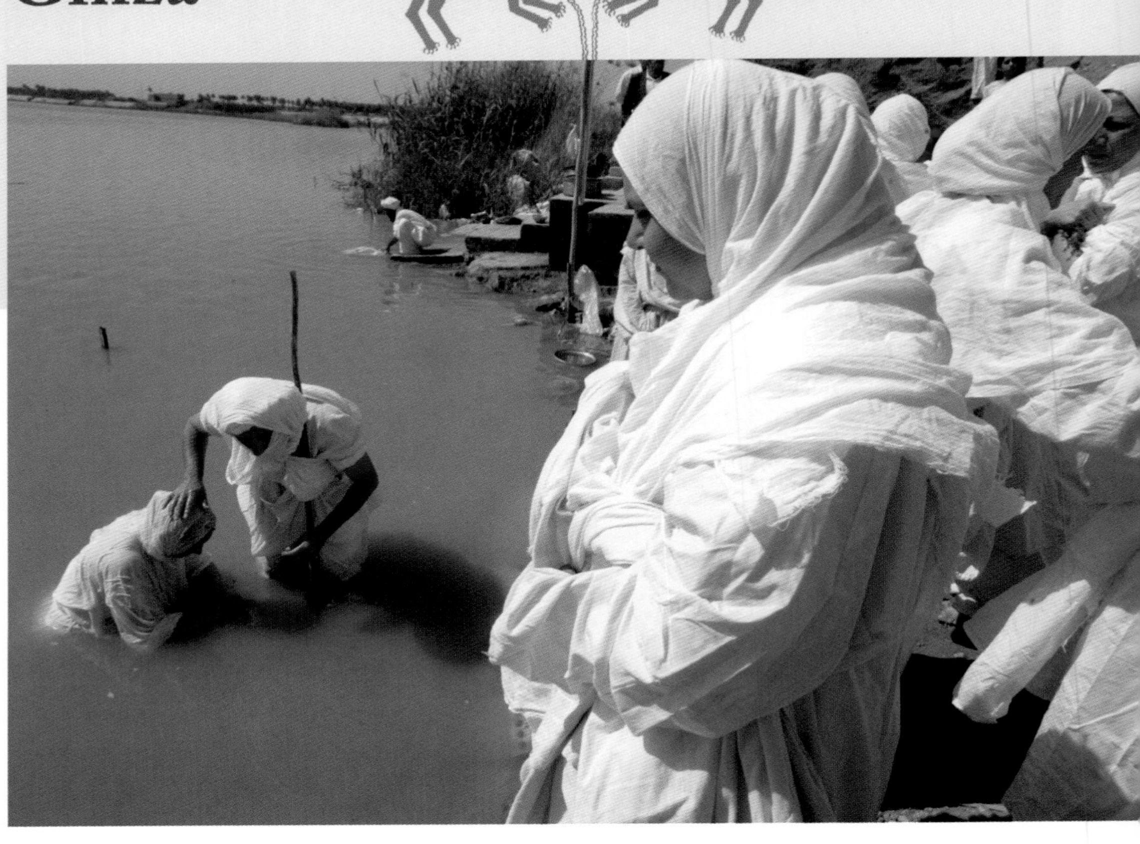

▲ *A Mandaean priest baptizes an acolyte in the Tigris River during the five-day Benja festival celebrated by the Mandaeans in Iraq.*

Mandaeism is a Gnostic sect that still thrives. It is a kind of living fossil. For historians of religion, studying its anomalous belief system is comparable to the work of a paleontologist. In the same way as the dinosaurs became extinct, so did the primitive groups of Christians allied with what we now call Gnosticism disappear from the face of the earth in Late Antiquity. The Mandaeans are the only group that still survives. They possess a large body of sacred writings. Most important is the Ginza, which recounts the origin of the world according to the Mandaean faith.

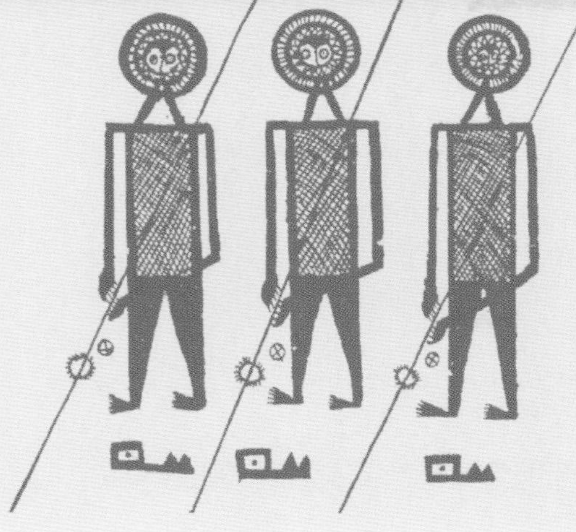

The Mandaean Diaspora

The Mandaeans were originally a Mesopotamian people who spoke Aramaic. Their Arab neighbors called them Baptists. They are also known as Sabaeans, but their name is derived from *manda* (Aramaic for "knowledge"). According to their traditions they lived in Palestine in the first century and practiced their religion with no connection to early Christianity. They were guided by a priestly caste (referred to as Nasoreans), the recipients of secret knowledge revealed to them by mysterious celestial envoys.

Expelled from Jerusalem by the Jewish authorities for their Gnostic beliefs, they settled in Haran in Syria, and then at the end of the third century in Mesopotamia. They founded religious communities in what are today Iraq and Iran.

▲ *For the Mandaeans, John the Baptist was the true messiah. They look upon Moses, Jesus and Muhammad all as false prophets.*

▼ *Many Mandaeans sought refuge in Jordan. Pictured here is the ancient city of Petra.*

At the end of the twentieth century, the Gulf War accelerated their disappearance. By 2007, only about five thousand believers still resided in Iraq. It is believed that about fifty thousand Mandaeans survive today, scattered through Jordan, the United States and Australia.

◀ *Elijah and Enoch. The latter was one of the mediators sent to liberate Mandaeans from the power of evil.*

A Dualistic Universse

Over the centuries numerous Mandaean texts have come to light, such as the Ginza, which deals with origins, the Book of John, based upon the life of John the Baptist, the Qolasta (the Mandaean prayer book), and the Harran Gawaita, an incomplete scroll that recounts the legendary vicissitudes of the sect.

The Ginza offers various dualistic accounts of the origin of the universe that display similar themes. According to Mandaeism, the higher realm of light is radically separate from the lower realm of darkness. At the highest level reigns a Supreme Being who is called by different names: Lord of Light, Lord of Life, the Great Ruler. At the beginning of time other beings issued forth, including Abatur, whose job is to judge the souls of mortals, and Yushamin, whose role is somewhat obscure. It seems that he tried to create his own universe and was severely castigated for this by the Lord of Light.

The embodiment of the principle of darkness is Ptahil, the creating demiurge who took over after Yushamin's fall. He sought to convince the other celestial beings that humanity was created under his direction. But the true enemy of the Lord of Light is Ruha, the feminine principle of darkness, whose incestuous relations with Ur, the serpent of the abyss, engendered the signs of the zodiac and the planets.

▼ *Baptism by complete immersion is the most important rite for the adherents to this sect.*

« He perverted the words of light, changing them into darkness. »

Harran Gawaita, Words of John Spoken about Jesus

John the Baptist, the True Messiah

To free the Mandaeans from the grip of evil, the world of light has dispatched diverse prophets, including Abel, Enoch, Noah, and John the Baptist, figures drawn from the Bible, who acted as mediators.

In fact, Mandaeism considers John the Baptist, rather than Jesus, the true Messiah. Jesus, Moses, Abraham, and Muhammad are all considered false prophets. In line with their veneration of John, Mandaeans' most important rite is baptism, which involves total immersion in flowing water. This would take place in the Tigris or the Euphrates, symbolic substitutes for the Jordan. They also bathe every day to remove worldly impurities. It is written in the Ginza: "Only those baptized in living water will be able to enter the realm of light." Along with this ritual, which has remained unaltered for centuries, the Mandaeans perform other rites: Sabbath observance, almsgiving, abstention from red meat. However, they believe that chastity is a sin. One must have descendants to be admitted into heaven.

▲ *Andrea del Sarto, John the Baptist, ca. 1523, Pitti Palace, Florence. For the Mandaeans, Jesus was a traitor, crucified for turning against John the Baptist.*

▲▲ *Abel (Hibil) in an illustration by William Blake. Mandaeans consider Abel to have been a prophet.*

▶ Gnosticism

Pistis Sophia

▶ *Fra Angelico,* The Transfiguration, *1442, Fresco in the Convent of San Marco, Florence.*

▼ *The manuscript written in Coptic was kept secret for a hundred years. It was finally translated in 1851.*

After his crucifixion, Jesus descended into Hell to impose a new order upon the Archons of destiny, powerful adversaries who seek to enslave humanity. Then he reunited with his disciples, remaining with them for eleven years to reinforce his teachings. Pistis Sophia details this period after the resurrection, which is not mentioned in any other Christian gospel, whether canonical or apocryphal. Its rediscovery and publication in the nineteenth century initiated the modern study of Gnosticism, more than a century before the library of Nag Hammadi was unearthed. It prompted a tremendous level of interest, especially in esoteric circles.

> *I will explain all of the mysteries and withhold nothing from you ...*
>
> PISTIS SOPHIA

▲ *Sophia, celestial wisdom, appears in this Russian icon from the early nineteenth century. Mary is enthroned and flanked by seven figures, among them Moses, Aaron and Solomon.*

The Grotesque Fruit of Sophia

Pistis Sophia, which can be translated as "Faithful Wisdom," is an allegorical Coptic text. It is a manuscript of 348 pages that was copied in the sixth or seventh century. Discovered in Luxor, Egypt, it remained in private hands until its acquisition by the British Museum. Over the centuries it remained practically unknown, until it was translated into Latin and Greek in 1851. In 1896, an English translation was published. It was soon identified as a Gnostic text tentatively attributed to Valentinus, an Egyptian heretic of the second century who is credited with founding the principal Gnostic sect before being expelled from the fold of Christianity.

According to Valentinus and his disciples, the Kingdom of Light was formed by an ineffable Supreme Being, who engendered fifteen pairs of Aeons (entities emanating from divinity) that attained or created the *pleroma* (the plentitude of existence). The divine harmony was shattered when one of the Aeons, located farthest from its origin, fell into the worldly space, exposing herself to its perils. According to Gnostic doctrine this being was Sophia, celestial wisdom (or the soul). Instead of remaining coupled with her Aeon brother-spouse, she sought to emulate the original creator and engender her own progeny. The fruit of her pride was a grotesque demiurge, a mon-

▶ *A.A. Ivanov,* Appearance of Jesus Christ to Mary Magdalene, *1835. The Gospel of Mary Magdalene is one of the Gnostic gospels.*

strosity, who retained her spiritual character but was capable of passion and evil. Gnostic doctrine identifies this proud and vain hybrid with the God of the Old Testament, who sought to mimic the pleroma by surrounding himself with sycophants and creating the material world.

The Gnostic Myth of the Broken Pair

The Valentinian tradition explains this process with the allegory of the broken couple. To become separate from the androgynous being formed by the feminine soul and her masculine consort, the soul is hurled from the pleroma and rushes into the void, where she is exposed to earthly perils, forced into slavery by the Archons (servants of the demiurge) and imprisoned in the physical body. The only possibility of salvation open to her is the descent of a savior from the Kingdom of Light. This divine being is the Aeon Christ, incarnated in the human form of Jesus of Nazareth. He transmits to Sophia the true knowledge (*gnosis*) of her origin and transcendent destiny.

This doctrine is meticulously explained in Pistis Sophia. In its pages the apostles and holy women question Jesus, who responds with Gnostic discourses upon themes of cosmogony, the theory of emanation, the hierarchy of the spiritual world and the origin of evil. These ideas are radically different from those put forth in canonical Christian texts. The Gnostic description of the spiritual powers that guide the universe, its belief in reincarnation and the frequent use of magical invocations are just a few of many differences.

Sophia's Descent into the World

Pisitis Sophia charts the progressive stages that Sophia goes through as she is beckoned by the Divine Light to free herself from the shackles of earthly existence. Sophia first describes her tormentors: "And when I looked unto the height, I saw all the rulers of the æons, how in their numbers they looked down on me and rejoiced over me, though I had done them no ill; but they hated me without a cause. And when the emanations of Self-willed saw the rulers of the æons rejoicing over me, they knew that the rulers of the æons would not come to my aid; and those emanations which sore pressed me with violence, took courage, and the light which I had not taken from them, they have taken from me." But later she addresses her savior in emotional terms: "But I looked up unto the height toward thee and had faith in thee. Now, therefore, O Light of lights, I am sore pressed in the darkness of chaos. If now thou wilt come to save me — great is thy mercy — then hear me in truth and save me. Save me out of the matter of this darkness, that I may not be submerged therein, that I may be saved from the emanations of god Self-willed which press me sore, and from their evil doings. Let not this darkness submerge me, and let not this lion-faced power entirely devour the whole of my power, and let not this chaos shroud my power. Hear me, O Light, for thy grace is precious, and look down upon me according to the great mercy of thy Light. Turn not thy face from me, for I am exceedingly tormented. Haste thee, hearken unto me and save my power."

Judaism

וילך שפי ויקר אלהים אל בלעם ויאמר אליו את
שבעת המזבחת ערכתי ואעל פר ואיל במזבח
וישם יהוה דבר בפי בלעם ויאמר שוב אל בלק
וכה תדבר וישב אליו והנה נצב על עלתו הוא
וכל שרי מואב וישא משלו ויאמר מן ארם ינחני
בלק מלך מואב מהררי קדם לכה ארה לי יעקב
ולכה זעמה ישראל מה אקב לא קבה אל ומה
אזעם לא זעם יהוה כי מראש צרים אראנו
ומגבעות אשורנו הן עם לבדד ישכן ובגוים
לא יתחשב מי מנה עפר יעקב ומספר את רבע
ישראל תמת נפשי מות ישרים ותהי אחריתי כמהו
ויאמר בלק אל בלעם מה עשית לי לקב איבי
לקחתיך והנה ברכת ברך ויען ויאמר הלא את
אשר ישים יהוה בפי אתו אשמר לדבר ויאמר
אליו בלק לך נא אתי אל מקום אחר אשר תראנו
משם אפס קצהו תראה וכלו לא תראה וקבנו
לי משם ויקחהו שדה צפים אל ראש הפסגה
ויבן שבעה מזבחת ויעל פר ואיל במזבח ויאמר
אל בלק התיצב כה על עלתך ואנכי אקרה
כה ויקר יהוה אל בלעם וישם דבר בפיו ויאמר
שוב אל בלק וכה תדבר ויבא אליו והנו נצב
על עלתו ושרי מואב אתו ויאמר לו בלק מה
דבר יהוה וישא משלו ויאמר קום בלק ושמע
האזינה עדי בנו צפר לא איש אל ויכזב ובן
אדם ויתנחם ההוא אמר ולא יעשה ודבר ולא
יקימנה הנה ברך לקחתי וברך ולא אשיבנה
לא הביט און ביעקב ולא ראה עמל בישראל
יהוה אלהיו עמו ותרועת מלך בו אל מוציאם
ממצרים כתועפת ראם לו כי לא נחש ביעקב
ולא קסם בישראל כעת יאמר ליעקב ולישראל
מה פעל אל הן עם כלביא יקום וכארי יתנשא
לא ישכב עד יאכל טרף ודם חללים ישתה
ויאמר בלק אל בלעם גם קב לא תקבנו גם ברך
לא תברכנו ויען בלעם ויאמר אל בלק הלא
דברתי אליך לאמר כל אשר ידבר יהוה אתו
אעשה ויאמר בלק אל בלעם לכה נא אקחך
אל מקום אחר אולי יישר בעיני האלהים וקבתו
לי משם ויקח בלק את בלעם ראש הפעור הנשקף
על פני הישימן ויאמר בלעם אל בלק בנה לי
בזה שבעה מזבחת והכן לי בזה שבעה פרים
ושבעה אילים ויעש בלק כאשר אמר בלעם
ויעל פר ואיל במזבח וירא בלעם כי טוב בעיני
יהוה לברך את ישראל ולא הלך כפעם בפעם
לקראת נחשים וישת אל המדבר פניו וישא
בלעם את עיניו וירא את ישראל שכן לשבטיו
ותהי עליו רוח אלהים וישא משלו ויאמר נאם
בלעם בנו בער ונאם הגבר שתם העין נאם שמע
אמרי אל אשר מחזה שדי יחזה נפל וגלוי עינים

מה טבו אהליך יעקב משכנתיך ישראל כנחלים נטיו
כגנת עלי נהר כאהלים נטע יהוה כארזים עלי מים
יזל מים מדליו וזרעו במים רבים וירם מאגג מלכו
ותנשא מלכתו אל מוציאו ממצרים כתועפת ראם לו
יאכל גוים צריו ועצמתיהם יגרם וחציו ימחץ כרע שכב
כארי וכלביא מי יקימנו מברכיך ברוך וארריך ארור
ויחר אף בלק אל בלעם ויספק את כפיו ויאמר בלק
אל בלעם לקב איבי קראתיך והנה ברכת ברך זה
שלש פעמים ועתה ברח לך אל מקומך אמרתי כבד
אכבדך והנה מנעך יהוה מכבוד ויאמר בלעם אל
בלק הלא גם אל מלאכיך אשר שלחת אלי דברתי
לאמר אם יתן לי בלק מלא ביתו כסף וזהב לא אוכל
לעבר את פי יהוה לעשות טובה או רעה מלבי אשר
ידבר יהוה אתו אדבר ועתה הנני הולך לעמי לכה
איעצך אשר יעשה העם הזה לעמך באחרית הימים
וישא משלו ויאמר נאם בלעם בנו בער ונאם הגבר
שתם העין נאם שמע אמרי אל וידע דעת עליון
מחזה שדי יחזה נפל וגלוי עינים אראנו ולא עתה
אשורנו ולא קרוב דרך כוכב מיעקב וקם שבט
מישראל ומחץ פאתי מואב וקרקר כל בני שת והיה
אדום ירשה והיה ירשה שעיר איביו וישראל עשה
חיל וירד מיעקב והאביד שריד מעיר וירא את
עמלק וישא משלו ויאמר ראשית גוים עמלק
ואחריתו עדי אבד וירא את הקיני וישא משלו
ויאמר איתן מושבך ושים בסלע קנך כי אם יהיה
לבער קין עד מה אשור תשבך וישא משלו ויאמר
אוי מי יחיה משמו אל וצים מיד כתים וענו אשור
וענו עבר וגם הוא עדי אבד ויקם בלעם וילך וישב
למקמו וגם בלק הלך לדרכו
וישב ישראל בשטים ויחל העם לזנות אל בנות
מואב ותקראן לעם לזבחי אלהיהן ויאכל העם
וישתחוו לאלהיהן ויצמד ישראל לבעל פעור
ויחר אף יהוה בישראל ויאמר יהוה אל משה קח
את כל ראשי העם והוקע אותם ליהוה נגד השמש
וישב חרון אף יהוה מישראל ויאמר משה אל שפטי
ישראל הרגו איש אנשיו הנצמדים לבעל פעור
והנה איש מבני ישראל בא ויקרב אל אחיו את
המדינית לעיני משה ולעיני כל עדת בני ישראל והמה
בכים פתח אהל מועד וירא פינחס בן אלעזר בן
אהרן הכהן ויקם מתוך העדה ויקח רמח בידו ויבא
אחר איש ישראל אל הקבה וידקר את שניהם את
איש ישראל ואת האשה אל קבתה ותעצר המגפה
מעל בני ישראל ויהיו המתים במגפה ארבעה
ועשרים אלף
וידבר יהוה אל משה לאמר פינחס בן אלעזר
בן אהרן הכהן השיב את חמתי מעל בני ישראל
בקנאו את קנאתי בתוכם ולא כליתי את בני ישר
בקנאתי לכן אמר הנני נתן לו את בריתי של

Torah

◀ *Maurycy Gottlieb,* Jews Praying in the Synagogue on Yom Kippur, *1878, Tel Aviv Museum of Art.*

One thousand years before Muhammad called Israelites "the People of God," the Jews had discovered that God's voice could be heard through the written word. This divine speech was set down in ancient scrolls after the time of Moses (ca. thirteenth century BCE) in the Hebrew Bible, referred to in Christianity as the Old Testament. The first five books, known from Greek as the Pentateuch, are traditionally ascribed to Moses. They contain Yahweh's revelation to the Jewish people and constitute the Torah, the foundation of the Jewish religion.

◀ *Torah scroll.*

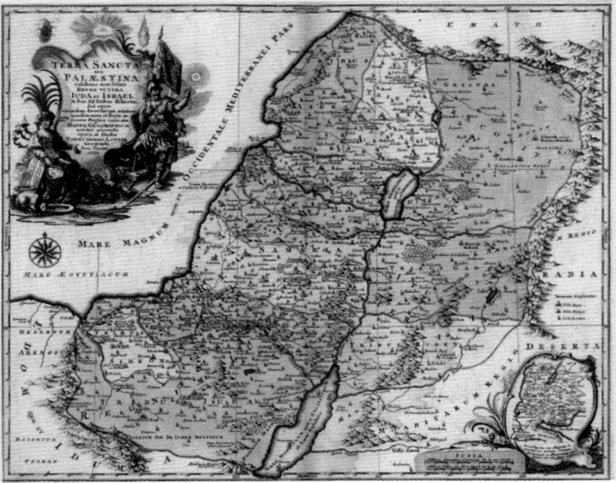

▶ *Old map of the Holy Land showing the territories of the twelve tribes of Israel.*

▲ *Rembrandt,* The Sacrifice of Isaac, *1635, Hermitage, St. Petersburg. Abraham was the first patriarch. God promised Israel to Abraham and his descendants.*

The Plan of Creation

The Hebrew Bible is called the Tanakh, an acronym formed from the three constituent parts of the Hebrew Bible: Torah, Nevi'im (Prophets) and Ketuvim (Writings). The first of these, the Torah, consists of the five Books of Moses: Genesis, Exodus, Leviticus, Numbers and Deuteronomy. The literal meaning of torah is "teaching" or "instruction." But according to Jewish tradition it is far more than that. It is said to have existed prior to the creation of the universe, the manifestation of God's primordial wisdom that contains the project of creation later set down in writing by Moses. For the Jews, Torah comes from heaven, and even though it was only the Jews who accepted it without reservation, it is equally valid for all humanity.

The book of Genesis recounts the story of creation and the origins of the human race from Adam and Eve through the patriarchs, the progenitors of the Jewish people. The first patriarch was Abraham, who God promises will be the father of a great nation that will inhabit "a land flowing with milk and honey." Abraham had left his home in Mesopotamia to travel to the "promised land" of Canaan, where he would further the completion of the divine plan. So Genesis is not only a religious document; it is a kind of foundational text of the Jewish nation.

▼ *Adrien Guignet,* Joseph Interpreting Pharaoh's Dream, *1845, Musée des Beaux-Arts, Rouen. The pharaoh raised Joseph from prison to become his chief minister.*

The Tanakh

The Tanakh consists of twenty-four books, divided into three parts: the Torah, the Prophets, and the Writings.

The first part, the Torah, consists of the five Books of Moses: Genesis, Exodus, Leviticus, Numbers, and Deuteronomy.The second part, the Prophets (or Neviim), is further divided into two groups: the Former Prophets and the Latter Prophets. The Former Prophets includes Joshua, Judges, First and Second Samuel, and First and Second Kings. The Latter Prophets consists of Isaiah, Jeremiah, Ezekiel and the Twelve Minor Prophets (Hosea, Joel, Amos, Obadiah, Jonah, Micah, Nahum, Habakkuk, Zephaniah, Haggai, Zechariah and Malachi). Tradition counts the Latter Prophets as one book.The third part, the Writings (Ketuvim), is formed of eleven books that are divided into three groups: Wisdom Literature, the Five Scrolls and the historical books. To the first group belong Psalms, Proverbs, and Job. In the second group are the Song of Songs, Ruth, Lamentations, Ecclesiastes, and Esther. These books are read during various Jewish festivals. The Song of Songs is read during Passover, which celebrates the liberation of the Jewish people from slavery; Ruth is read on Shavuot, commemorating Moses' receiving the Torah on Mount Sinai; Lamentations is read on Tisha B'Av, the saddest day in the Jewish Calendar, in remembrance of the destruction of the Temple in Jerusalem; Ecclesiastes is read on Sukkot, a holiday that is celebrated according to a command in the Book of Numbers that the Jews wandering in the desert should camp out in booths (temporary shelters); and finally, the Book of Esther, which, read on Purim, explains the origin of the holiday in which Esther saves the Jewish people from destruction at the hands of Hamaan, the King of Persia's wicked counselor.

The historical books comprise a looser grouping: Daniel, Ezra, Nehemiah, and First and Second Chronicles. According to Jewish tradition, some of these books are counted together as one to arrive at the total of twenty-four.

> ***Then God formed man from the dust of the earth.***
>
> GENESIS 2:7

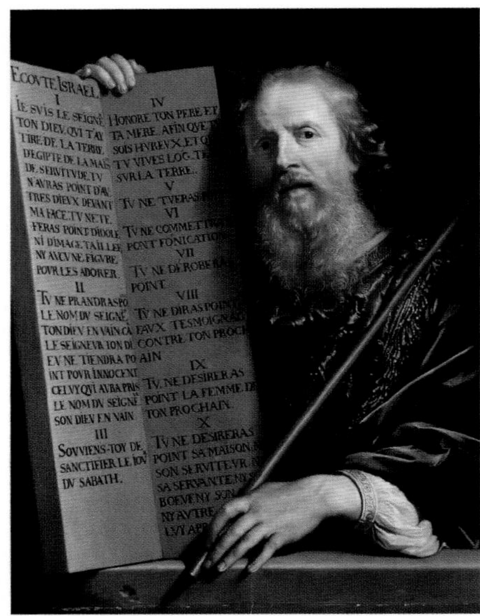

▲ *Philippe de Champaigne,* Moses and the Ten Commandments, *1648, Hermitage, St. Petersburg.*

▲▶ *Paolo Veronese,* The Finding of Moses, *ca. 1580, Prado, Madrid.*

A Complete Teaching

The enslavement of the Jewish people in Egypt and their departure for Palestine are described in Exodus. Moses leads them across the desert. They cross the Sea of Reeds on dry ground, but the sea closes upon and drowns the pursuing Egyptian army. Here the weather patterns of the region do not rule out an occurrence of this kind, though the Bible looks upon it as a miracle wrought by God.

While the Jews are camped around Mount Sinai, God delivers to Moses two tablets that contain the Ten Commandments; they are deposited in the famous Ark of the Covenant along with the rest of the Torah. As it became necessary over time to adapt the instructions to changing circumstances, the rabbis proposed that, in addition to the "written" Torah, God also conveyed to Moses a much vaster "oral" Torah. This body of knowledge contained all of the instructions necessary to live according to the Law. Thus any successful interpretation of Torah was included in this original message.

▶ *In this illustration by Gustav Doré, David raises the head of the slain Goliath.*

Detailed Instructions

The essence of Torah can be summed up in one phrase: "Whatever is hurtful to you, do not do to any other person." Beyond that, however, Leviticus, Numbers and Deuteronomy contain detailed laws that form the basis of Jewish life. For example, there are precise dietary laws regarding permitted and non-permitted foods. Pork, as is commonly known, is forbidden as impure, and shellfish is as well. There are careful instructions regarding slaughtering animals (to minimize the animal's suffering), and the salting of meat to remove the blood. Rabbinical authorities interpreted the Biblical injunction that one should not cook a kid in its mother's milk to prohibit eating dairy and meat products together. Not only should one not mix them, but the kosher household must have two sets of silverware and cooking utensils.

In addition to the Torah, which is the direct word of God, the rest of the Bible was written before 150 BCE by people inspired by God. The Prophets and the Writings contain important books such as Isaiah, which prophesizes about the coming conquest of Jerusalem by Babylon and the subsequent exile, and Psalms, a collection of liturgical poems, many of which are attributed to the charismatic King David, the great hero of the Jewish people and progenitor of the coming Messiah.

◀ *Reading from the Torah.*

Talmud

▶ *Cover of an old copy of the Talmud.*

הדרן עלך כל ישראל יש וסי׳
סליקא לה מסכת סנהדרין
ודין סימנהון: דיני ממונות:
כהן גדול: זה בורר: אחד דיני
היו בודקין: נגמר הדין: ארבע
מיתות: בן סורר: הנשרפין
הנחנקין: חלק: חזק

▲ Codex Reuchlinianus, *was given by Frederick III to Johannes Reuchlin, a German philosopher, humanist, and student of the Kabbalah. It contains eighty extracts from the Targum Yerushalmi, an Aramaic version of the prophetic books of the Bible.*

The Jews have been called "the people of the Book," an allusion to their respect for and interminable discussions about their sacred literature. The continuing work of interpretation in search of understanding and fidelity to God's commandments is one of the primary characteristics of Judaism. Over the course of centuries, scholars, rabbis and various spiritual leaders produced an immense corpus of commentaries that was codified in the Talmud, the most important book in Judaism after the Tanakh. At the end of the day, study and debate over religious questions is not only a duty but a passion for Jews.

▶ *Jewish symbols: seven-armed candelabra (menorah), prayer shawl (tallis), skullcap (yarmulke), and Torah.*

Commentaries on Torah

According to the account in Deuteronomy, Yahweh delivered two tablets to Moses on Mount Sinai, that he engraved with his own finger, which contained all the words he had spoken to his "chosen people." According to Rabbinic tradition, this included not only the Torah, but the Talmud and other sacred literature as well. They asserted that all of this was part of the divine revelation, which encompassed both the "written" and "oral" Torah. This continues to be elaborated. The circle is never closed.

Upon the return from exile in Babylon, the priest Ezra (according to Nehemiah, chapter 8) read diverse texts from the Bible to the faithful congregated before the Temple in Jerusalem. This set the precedent for the periodic reading of the Torah and its interpretation by religious leaders. While synagogues deal with application of the teaching in daily life, scholars seek to explicate other essential questions. This interpretative process is called *midrash* (discovery or seeking). It seeks to articulate the oral Torah foreseen by Yahweh at the beginning of time.

קרבן נתנאל

קארל פרידריך

קארלסרוא

cum Licentia superiorum

נגילה ונשמחה בו

▲ *Title page of the* Korban Netan'el *(dated* 1775*) by the Talmudic scholar Nethan'el Weil.*

> *The addition of one letter disqualifies a Torah parchment.*
>
> TALMUD

▲ *Orthodox Jew praying at the Wailing Wall in Jerusalem.*

▲▲ *Recitation of the blessing over wine.*

Commentaries on Commentaries

A number of steps led to the completion of the Talmud. The first post-Biblical collection of Jewish writing is called the *Mishnah* (copy). It deals with legal questions under six headings: agriculture, marriage, civil and criminal law, offerings and sacrifices, ritual purity, and holidays. All the commentaries are difficult to use since they are not logically structured, but follow the thematic sequence of the Torah. In CE 279, various learned men in Jerusalem put together the *Gemara* (complement), a compendium with new explanations based on the *Mishnah* , that was supposed to be easier to use. The *Mishnah* and the *Gemara* together constitute the Talmud ("teaching").

One hundred years after the redaction of the Jerusalem Talmud, a new conclave of the rabbinic authorities of Babylon brought together a more exhaustive edition of the Gemara and combined it with the Mishnah to produce the Babylonian Talmud. Babylon was at that time the center of Jewish scholarship and learning. This Talmud has become the canonical version for Judaism. It offers interpretations from authors from different times and places and serves as a manual for the practice of observant Judaism.

◀ *Procession carrying Torah scrolls around the Wailing Wall on the Jewish festival of Simchat Torah.*

613 Commandments

The authors of the Talmud sought to reconcile the contradictory interpretations offered in the Mishnah as well as to provide answers to questions that were not originally addressed. In addition to faithfulness to the literal meaning, they sometimes used allegory to explicate the more obscure legal and mystical passages. In this way many extravagant narratives came to be included in its pages. They can be fantastic and sometimes incoherent, and seemingly little in keeping with a religious text. For this reason, the Talmud was the object of scorn in Medieval Christian Europe. The first written attack was attributed to the Byzantine emperor Justinian: he ordered the book to be publically burned. This was the start of an endless cycle of prohibitions, persecutions and controversies.

Judaism distinguishes between two genres of Rabbinic literature: *halakah* (normative), which forms the basis of Jewish legal decisions, and *aggadah* (narrative), used to illustrate a point. The *aggadah* includes parables, legends, and various literary curiosities, some humorous. At times these genres are intermarried. One well-known example concerns the Talmudic calculation of the number of commandments in the Torah. The authors arrive at a total of 613. They consider 248 of these affirmative (in keeping with the number of constituent elements of the human body, according to Talmudic anatomy) and 365 negative (corresponding to the number of days in the solar year).

▶ **Judaism**

Bahir

▶ *Stephan Michelspacher,* Mirror of Art and Nature, *a Kabbalistic work from 1654.*

The origins of Kabbalah, the mystical tradition of Judaism, are lost in the mists of time. Over the centuries esoteric interpretations of the Torah produced fantastic theories, transmitted orally and maintained in secret. They were eventually set down in writing in books such as *Sefer ha-Bahir* (Book of Brightness), that appeared at the end of the Middle Ages. While some see Kabbalah as an authentic branch of revelation that has its beginnings with Adam, others consider it to be simply superstition that was nourished by the obscurantism of medieval Europe.

> ***«Why does the Torah begin with the letter beth? To allude to benediction.»***
>
> BAHIR

מעריב ליל יום כפור

ומתחיל הש"ץ כל נדרי ברתת בחרדה ובכוונה :

כל נדרי

ואסרי · וחרמי · וקונמי · וכנויי · וקנוסי · ושבועות : דנדרנא · ודאשתבענא · ודאחרימנא · ודאסרנא על נפשתנא · מיום כפורים זה עד יום כפורים הבא עלינו לטובה · כלהון אחרטנא בהון · כלהון יהון שרן · שביקין · שביתין · בטלין ומבטלין · לא שרירין ולא קימין · נדרנא לא נדרי · ושבועתנא לא שבועות : ג"פ

▲ *Declaration read before entering the synagogue on Kol Nidre, the evening service of Yom Kippur.*

The Cosmos as a Living Organism

Looked upon as the first Kabbalistic treatise, *Sefer ha-Bahir* is one of the most amazing works of Hebrew literature. For a long time the *Bahir* was attributed to Rabbi Nehunya ben HaKanah, an authority on the oral Torah, who lived in the first century CE. Modern scholars, however, believe that it was written by Isaac the Blind, a French Kabbalist who lived at the end of the twelfth century in France. The interpretations that it offers are disjointed, and the majority of rabbis whose works it cites seem not to have been real-life figures. However, it is written in an extremely pure Hebrew, and the myths and parables it contains provoked a revolution in the world of Jewish thought.

The tract is quite brief, only about thirty pages. It consists of 141 paragraphs, most of which take the form of a dialogue between a master and his disciples over obscure passages from the Torah and over another still older Hebrew text, the *Sefer Yetzirah* (Book of Creation), the oldest mystical text of Judaism, that articulates an interpretation of Torah based upon numbers and establishes a relationship between the human organism and the cosmos.

The *Bahir* follows this line of thought providing an occult interpretation of the letters of the Hebrew alphabet, including the vowels added to the Torah by medieval Jewish scholars called Masoretes. (Written scrolls of the Torah contain only consonants; vowels were added sometime before CE 1000.) It declares that vowels "reside within the consonants as the soul resides in the body." It also offers a detailed explanation of the doctrine of reincarnation, a theme

espoused in other Kabbalistic texts as well. The author asks: "Why do some sinners enjoy happiness and righteous men suffer disgrace? The just may have been wicked in their former lives, and the wicked righteous."

▲ *Athanasius Kirchner drew this diagram showing the names of God. Jews consider God's name sacred and avoid pronouncing it; instead they use the substitute* Adonai.

The *Sefirot*

The *Bahir* provides the first discussion of the doctrine of the *sefirot* (sing. *sefira*), later fully developed in the Zohar. This term designates the ten potencies or emanations of God's creative power. Over time this idea comes to be of primary importance in Kabbalistic thought. The structure of the *sefirot* is represented as a tree with roots. It states that God created the universe by himself without the help of angels: "I alone planted this tree so that everyone may delight in it." This mythical tree, which is the tree of the world and all of the souls in it, has all "divine power placed in it."

In a somewhat opaque fashion, which is characteristic of Kabbalistic thinking, the books explain the elements of the Tree of the Sefirot, whose trunk and branches represent divinity. There are ten *sefirot*. Listed from highest to lowest they are Keter (Crown), Chokhmah (Wisdom), Binah (Understanding), Chesed (Kindness), Gevurah (Severity), Tiferet (Beauty), Netzach (Eternity), Hod (Splendor), Yesod (Foundation), and Malkuth (Kingship). All of them are interconnected. The highest (Keter) extends to the limits of transcendence and the infinity of God's deepest interiority, which is inaccessible to human understanding. It is the "root of roots" that nourishes

◀ This woodcut from around 1800 shows Jews in the courtyard of the synagogue on the Sabbath.

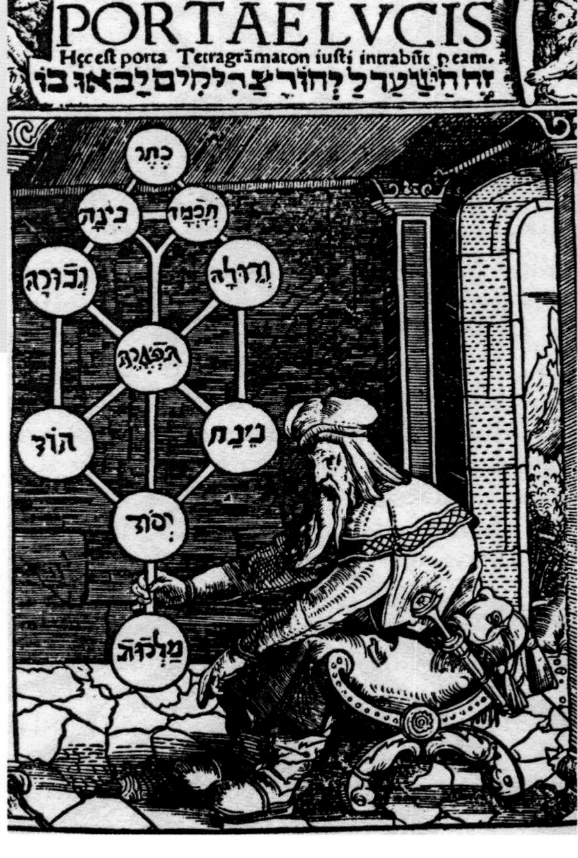

the entire tree. The lowest (Malkuth) is the point of intersection between God and humanity, that is, with Israel — not only the historic community, but also as personification of human spirituality. Its fertility allows humans to reproduce and spread on earth.

The *sefirot* determine the course of events on the material plane, but they are at the same time subject to the influence of God's "chosen people." If Jews obey the Law, this can have a positive effect, but if they depart from the true path and sin, the effect can be just the opposite. The central *sefira,* Chesed, symbolizes the Torah as it existed as God's first awesome and frightening utterance that only Moses could hear without being consumed by its power.

▲ *The ten* sefirot *in a medieval engraving.*

Zohar

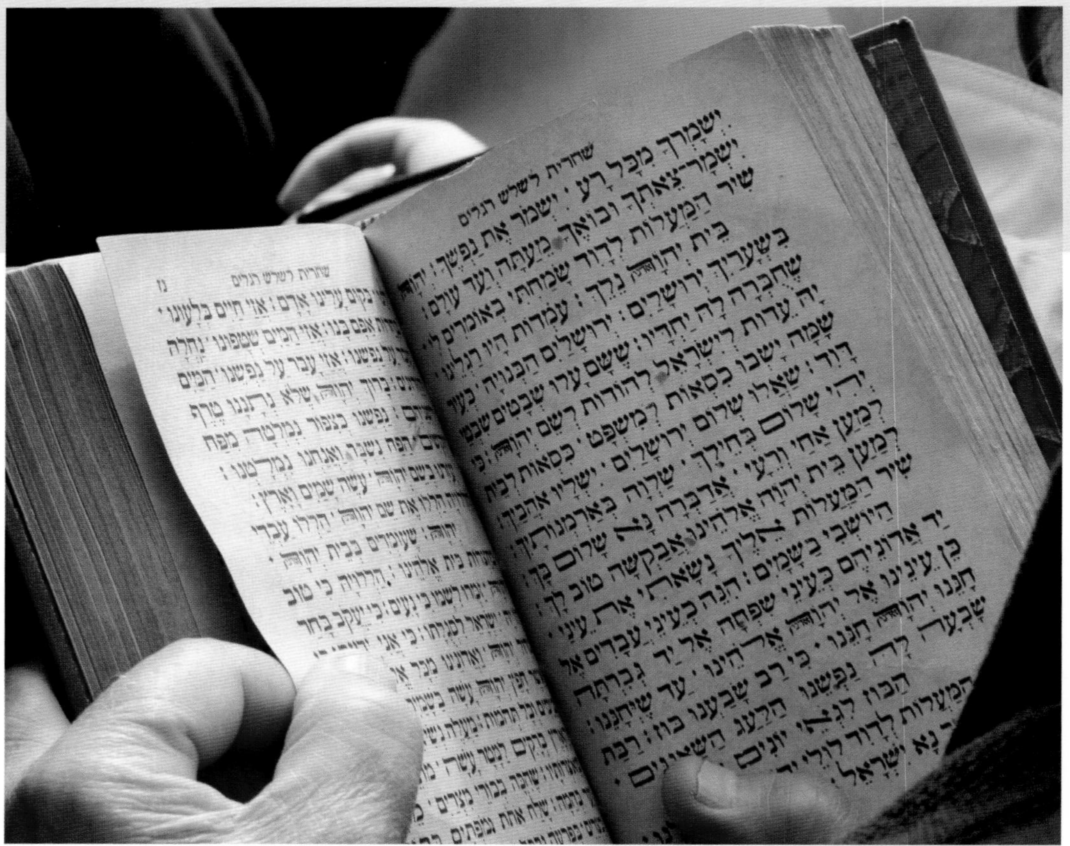

▲ *The two primary texts for Kabbalists are the Zohar and the Sefer Yesira. The Zohar (shown above) can be translated as "Book of Splendor."*

The Hebrew word kabbalah means "tradition." Many esoteric currents have enriched this depository of occult ideas over the centuries, but among these the most important contributions were made by Moses of León and Joseph Gikatilla, medieval Spanish Jewish creators of what is regarded as the classic system of Kabbalah. The former is credited with authorship of the Sefer ha-Zohar (Book of Splendor), a text of disquieting beauty that is considered sacred in many Jewish circles. For Kabbalists it is second only to the Torah itself.

▶ *The Star of David is one of the most widely recognized symbols of Judaism. It has often been used as an identifying mark to single out Jews.*

Bridegroom of the Torah

Although the Zohar was originally attributed to Shimon bar Yochai, a second-century rabbi, it is now known that its author was Moses of León, who died in that city in 1305. In his youth he devoted himself to the works of Maimonides and then dove into the study of Kabbalah. All of his writings were published pseudonymously. In all likelihood the Zohar is an elaboration of much older material, infused by the author's own mystical vision. Like most Kabbalistic works, the Zohar is composed of commentaries on the Bible. It focuses on the Torah, Psalms, Proverbs and the Song of Songs.

In that time, Kabbalists had to engage deeply in the study of Torah before venturing into occult studies. This follows a saying of Maimonides: "No one is worthy of entering Paradise who has not first had enough bread and meat." The Zohar describes the process using a famous parable inspired by troubadour poetry. The Torah is the elusive beloved who begins to reveal her secrets only after a long courtship by the lover who wants to know her and become her "bridegroom." The Kabbalist's objective is to arrive at a genuine understanding of the seemingly impenetrable ideas and mysterious imagery that abound in the Hebrew Bible.

▲ *The Wailing Wall in Jerusalem is all that remains of the Second Temple.*

▲ *The Zohar considers each letter of the Torah to be filled with significance.*

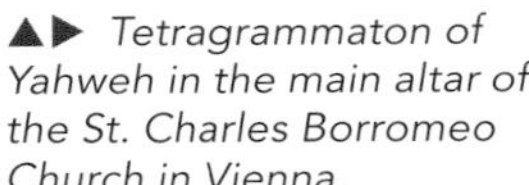

▲▶ *Tetragrammaton of Yahweh in the main altar of the St. Charles Borromeo Church in Vienna.*

The Language of God

"Every word radiates light," says the Zohar, referring to the infinite meaningfulness of the divine word. For Yahweh letters and numbers are not only means of communication; each embodies a range of significances that the Kabbalist seeks to translate into human language. To accomplish this the Zohar explores the symbolism of the letters in the Torah scroll. It asserts that they were set down by Yahweh in an order that was conditioned by Adam's sin of disobedience, but they will be combined in a different way when the Messiah comes to deliver the Jewish people.

It is said that the 340,000 consonants in the Torah are one articulation of the name of God, and at the same time form all of God's names. According to the Zohar, the Torah taken in its entirety forms the unique sublime Name. Furthermore, the words of the Torah were not set down in the correct sequence. If they had been, anyone who reads it could raise the dead and perform other miracles. Only God knows the precise order, although Kabbalists try to discover it.

> *Just as the rose has thirteen petals, so is the Congregation of Israel surrounded by the thirteen attributes of Mercy.*
>
> Zohar

The Golem

▲ *The golem is the subject of a 1920 film by the German expressionist Paul Wegener,* The Golem: How He Came Into the World.

Knowledge of the correct order of the words of Torah allows one to create life. This idea is the source of the legend of the golem (unformed matter), a monster endowed with supernatural powers who acts on the orders of his master. The process begins with modeling a man out of mud. He is brought to life by placing in his mouth a paper on which is written the Tetragrammaton. The golem does not have the power of speech, but he can follow orders and perfectly perform the duties of a servant, although he should never be allowed out on his own. This could lead to problems, as narrated in Gustav Meyrink's novel, *The Golem*, when the inhabitants of the house begin to be afraid of him. The solution was simple. When the automaton was formed, the Hebrew word *emet* (truth) was written on his forehead. All that was needed was to erase the first letter of the word to arrive at *met* (death), and the creature crumbled into pieces.

In some versions of the story the end was not so happy. The great Rabbi of Prague, Judah ben Bezalel, created a golem, and he grew so big that the rabbi could not erase the letter from his forehead. The golem went on a murderous rage. The rabbi ordered the golem to take off his shoes and was able to erase the first letter on his forehead when he bent down. The monster fell to pieces, crushing the one who had created him.

The Dead Sea Scrolls

▲ *The Isaiah Scroll belonging to the Dead Sea Scrolls discovered in Qumran.*

In the spring of 1947, a Bedouin shepherd named Mohammed ed-Dhib was looking for a lost goat along the slopes of the Qumran Valley. He came across a cave lined with large clay vessels. They contained a series of remarkably well-preserved parchment scrolls wrapped in cloth. Subsequent investigations confirmed the discovery of a priceless treasure: hundreds of Biblical manuscripts over one thousand years older than any previously known. The Qumran texts are the best source we have for providing access to the enigmas of Second Temple Judaism and early Christianity.

The Qumran Find

Following the first discovery, investigators explored other caves in the desert sides of the Qumran Valley, a wadi situated near the northeastern shore of the Dead Sea. Scrolls were found in eleven caves. The archaeological excavations, which took place between 1947 and 1956, uncovered abundant materials: coins, ceramics, and first and foremost the famous scrolls, some deposited in clay jars, others simply placed in openings in the cave walls.

In total some 100,000 documents of diverse lengths, from complete books to fragments a few inches long, were brought to light. These have been identified as forming parts of 870 different manuscripts, of which 220 are texts of the Old Testament. They are written on parchment or hides in Hebrew and Aramaic. In addition, Cave 7 contained fragments of the New Testament written in Greek on papyrus.

There is a scholarly consensus that this extensive library bears witness to the existence of a monastic type community that settled in this isolated and inaccessible spot. Although many hypotheses have been suggested, there is no agreement about who those people were.

▲▲ Ruins of Qumran. The site is thought to have been a settlement of Essenes, the probable authors of the Dead Sea Scrolls.

▲ *The scrolls were preserved in jars such as this one.*

The Essene Hypothesis

Historians from the first century CE such as Philo of Alexandria, Pliny the Elder, and Flavius Josephus mention that there was in the vicinity of the Dead Sea a community of ascetics, the Essenes, who sought to distance themselves from cities they saw as corrupted by sin. They were celibate and vegetarian and lived austere lives, strictly following the laws set down in the Torah. They did not engage in business or the military, occupying themselves in peaceful pursuits such as agriculture and beekeeping. They held goods in common, including land, homes, food, and even clothing. They looked upon themselves as "pure" in contrast to the establishment Jews of the time, whom they considered apostates or even pagan.

As the manuscripts were discovered in the location referred to by the first century historians, some scholars believe that the community must have been of Essenes. According to this thesis the sectarians hid the manuscripts from the advancing Roman army after the fall of Jerusalem. Some authors believe that John the Baptist and even Jesus were members of the group, though no convincing evidence has been produced to support these claims.

◀ *Caves in the mountains around Qumran.*

The Isaiah Scroll

It is not possible to establish a direct connection between the documents found at Qumran and primitive Christianity, but we know that the Essenes, like the early Christians, considered themselves to be the nucleus of the "true Israel." They proclaimed their separation from the corruption of the established Judaism of the time, some leaving the synagogue, others stretching doctrine beyond its accepted limits. The eschatological visions of both groups also had much in common. The scroll entitled War of the Sons of Light and the Sons of Darkness is filled with fantastic details and describes how the army of the Twelve Tribes of Israel, under the command of the Messiah, battled against renegade Jews and idolaters. The war goes through seven stages, following the divine plan, until the final victory of the celestial host.

One of the most fascinating of the extra-Biblical manuscripts found at Qumran is The Manual of Discipline, which details the norms of the community and the requirements for inclusion in the sect, as well as the battle between the forces of light and darkness for the human soul. Perhaps the most astonishing discovery was the Great Isaiah Scroll. This is the oldest complete extant manuscript of a book from the Bible. This text, redacted in the second century BCE, is written in fifty-four columns, forming a scroll over twenty feet long.

Islam

thee : in reality
Plan is to punish them
ese things in this life,[1316]
their souls may perish
ery) denial of God.

by God
indeed
y are not
are afraid
r true colours).

57. If th
A place
Or caves, or a
Of concealment
Turn straightway
With an obstinate r ... ould

nd among them are me
ho slander thee in the ma
the distribution of) the alms
y are given part thereof,
re pleased, but if not,
they are indignant !

had been content
od and His Apostle
nd had said,
o us is God !
ostle will soon
unty :
our hopes !"—
en the right
course).[1319]

إِنَّمَا يُرِيدُ ٱللَّهُ لِيُعَذِّبَهُم بِهَا فِي ٱلْحَيَوٰةِ
ٱلدُّنْيَا وَتَزْهَقَ أَنفُسُهُمْ وَهُمْ كَٰفِرُونَ
٥٦ وَيَحْلِفُونَ بِٱللَّهِ إِنَّهُمْ لَمِنكُمْ
وَمَا هُم مِّنكُمْ وَلَٰكِنَّهُمْ قَوْمٌ
يَفْرَقُونَ
٥٧ لَوْ يَجِدُونَ مَلْجَـًٔا أَوْ مَغَٰرَٰتٍ
أَوْ مُدَّخَلًا لَّوَلَّوْا إِلَيْهِ وَهُمْ
يَجْمَحُونَ
٥٨ وَمِنْهُم مَّن يَلْمِزُكَ فِي ٱلصَّدَقَٰتِ فَإِنْ
أُعْطُوا مِنْهَا رَضُوا وَإِن لَّمْ يُعْطَوْا
مِنْهَآ إِذَا هُمْ يَسْخَطُونَ
٥٩ وَلَوْ أَنَّهُمْ رَضُوا مَآ ءَاتَىٰ
وَرَسُولُهُۥ وَقَالُوا حَسْبُنَا
سَيُؤْتِينَا ٱللَّهُ مِن فَضْلِهِۦ
وَرَسُولُهُۥٓ إِنَّآ إِلَى

o run like a runawa

en in God's nam
rse but one.
per cent. of me
on this subject.

e fair game for ra
ch standards is alw
r his strictness to prin
rinciples or those who
e given to all, whether
cellent advice to say : de

nd obstinately.
needy, and for
ry charity

ou

The Qur'an

The Qur'an is not only the sacred book of the Muslim faith, but also a code of conduct for believers and the source of their laws. It dominates Islamic philosophy and is the ultimate reference work for the Arabic language: its dictionary, grammar, and literature. It infuses Arabic architecture and art, and indeed all audiovisual media. Its influence is omnipresent throughout the Muslim world. Its unchallenged preeminence derives from the firm belief that it is the authentic word of God and the only path to leading a good life, as the book itself says.

▲ *A group of the faithful praying in the old mosque in New Dehli.*

◀ *Page from a bilingual edition of the Qur'an. Muslims believe that it is God's own words.*

◀ *A scene showing Muhammad in a seventeenth-century Indian manuscript.*

▶ *A plate carrying the inscription* Allah hu Akbar *(God is great).*

▲ *A seventeenth-century ceramic tile depicting the Great Mosque of Mecca, from the ancient city of Nicaea (now Iznik) in Turkey.*

Meditation and Revelation

For the first forty years of his life Muhammad practiced the traditional religion of the Arabian Peninsula, a tolerant polytheistic faith that facilitated commercial ties with neighboring peoples. However, on one of his trips he met people who believed in one God, and the contrast between their faith and his own unsettled him. He retired to Mount Hira on the outskirts of Mecca to meditate on these questions. One day in either CE 610 or 612, a powerful presence communicated with him; it turned out be the angel Jibril (Gabriel). From that moment on for the next twenty years, the angel revealed to Muhammad the Qur'an, directly from heaven.

Accordingly, Muslims believe that Allah is the author of the book and that Muhammad transmitted it in its entirety. According to tradition, the Prophet was responsible for the first edition; either he transcribed what was transmitted from Gabriel or he dictated many passages to scribes, but it is more likely that his followers memorized his words and transcribed the complete text after his death. Many of the figures in the Qur'an are also found in the Bible.

The Seal of the Prophets

For adherents to the Muslim faith the Qur'an is the final and perfect edition of a text that actually resides with Allah, just as Muhammad is the culmination of a long list of prophets drawn from the Bible. The following are mentioned in the Qur'an: Adam, Noah, Enoch, Abraham, Ishmael, Isaac, Lot, Jacob, Joseph, Moses, Aaron, David, Solomon, Elijah, Elisha, Job, Joshua, Jonah, Zechariah, John the Baptist and Jesus. Four of these are considered not only *nabi* ("prophets") but *rasul* ("chosen ones") as well, bearers of a new revelation to humanity. They are Ibrahim (Abraham), Musa (Moses), Isa (Jesus) and finally, the Prophet Muhammad.

Muhammad supersedes his predecessors just as the Qur'an supersedes earlier books of revelation: the Torah of Moses, the Psalms of David and the New Testament. Islam says that Moses and Jesus were messengers of "heavenly religions," but that their teachings were misinterpreted by their followers. Muhammad is the greatest prophet. His message restores and fully realizes the monotheism of Abraham. He is the "Seal of the Prophets," the last in the line of messengers sent by God.

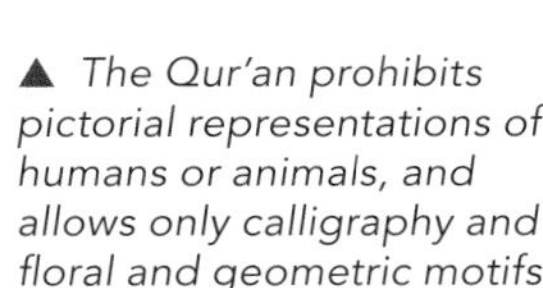

▲ *The Qur'an prohibits pictorial representations of humans or animals, and allows only calligraphy and floral and geometric motifs.*

▼ *Prayer beads are used in Christianity and Islam.*

▲ Mihrab *(niche)* decorated with phrases from the Qur'an.

Paradise in Islam

The Qur'an that is used today is the complete and definitive edition, published during the reign of the third Caliph, Uthman (CE 644–656). Written in "clear Arabic," it contains 144 *suras* ("chapters") divided into brief *ayahs* ("verses"). With the exception of the first sura called Al-Fatiha (The Opening), the *suras* are ordered in decreasing length, from the longest (286 *ayahs*) to the last chapter, which is only four *ayahs*. The dominant themes are the unity of God, the end of the world, the resurrection, and the Day of Judgment. But it also deals with social issues such as the family, the role of women, marriage and law.

According to the Qur'an, Allah has decreed that some time in the future the Antichrist will appear and will be utterly defeated by Jesus. Then the bodies and souls of the dead will be reunited. The dead will issue forth from their tombs, and the world will come to an end. Not only humans but also *djinns* ("genies") will assemble for the final

> *In the name of Allah, the Merciful and Compassionate.*
>
> Qur'an

judgment. The deeds and faithfulness of each will be examined. The souls of the just will be sent to Paradise (Al-Jannah), which is described as a marvelous garden where each will find his heart's desire. In regards to women, the Qur'an enjoins that they be treated "according to reason," but they are imperfect beings, inferior to men and subject to their dominion. There is, however, an extensive discussion about whether husbands should beat their wives and if so, when and to what extent.

In many respects the teachings of the book are not that distant from those of the Old Testament. The foundation is an all-powerful God who reveals His will to men, instructs them in the proper form of worship that they owe Him, and sets the rules for correct individual and social behavior. All of the facets of ritual, belief, morality and the law are infused with His unwavering presence.

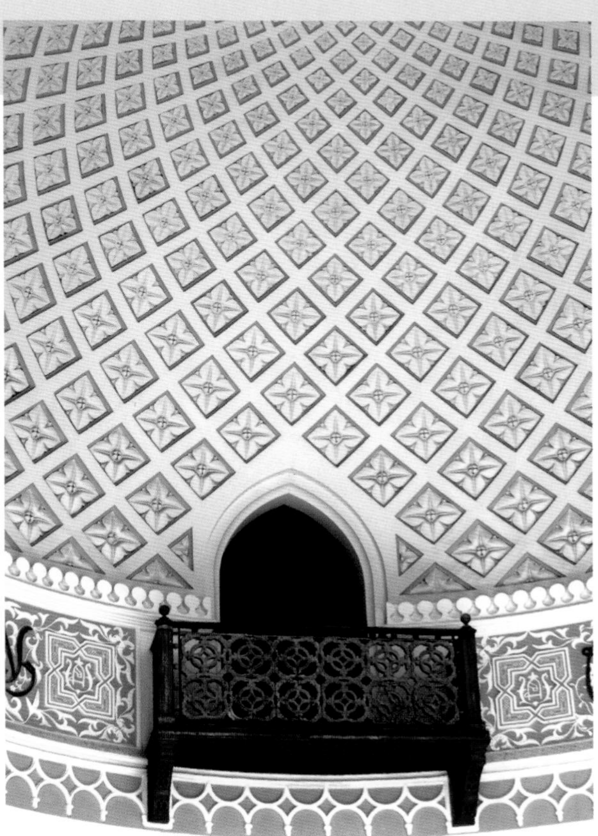

▲ *Balcony and dome in the Vorontsov Palace in the Ukraine.*

Hadith

▲ *The characters that make up the script in which the Qur'an is written are of great beauty. Owing to the prohibition against representing the human figure, the art of calligraphy flourished in Muslim countries.*

▶ *The minaret of Kalyan is the highest point in Bukhara in Uzbekistan.*

Islam is a religion of the book, the Qur'an. But it is complemented by a vigorous tradition, the *sunnah* ("usual practice"). Just as the Qur'an transmits Allah's traditions, the exemplary life of Muhammad provides a new *sunnah*, which should be imitated by the community. This source of religious inspiration is codified in the hadith ("accounts" or "reports"), which comprises the words and deeds of the Prophet. Together, the Qur'an and the hadith constitute the foundation of Islamic law, the sharia.

« *Actions are judged by motives, so each man will receive what he intended.* »

HADITH OF THE PROPHET

Apocryphal Hadith

Muhammad's followers always paid strict attention to his words and actions in accordance with the Qur'an, which states, "Keep before you the beautiful example of the one sent by Allah." His words and his silences, his actions and inactions, all were scrupulously recorded and transmitted to posterity. Over time there grew up abundant oral narratives that were not always accurate but depended upon the testimony of individuals and the needs of the moment. Sometimes they included accounts not only of Muhammad but also of his companions and their followers. Muslim historians admit that political and ideological forces engendered many apocryphal reports that include false testimony ascribed to Muhammad.

It quickly became apparent that there was a need for authentication, since legislators were guided by all of the hadith as well as the Qur'an, and the wheat had to be separated from the chaff. The task was not an easy one. The authenticity of each hadith depended on its *silsila* ("chain of transmission"), and its correct text (*matn*) had to be established. The selection process excluded a large number. Those that were accepted were divided into three categories: sound, good (suffering from a minor deficiency) and weak. In the eighth and ninth centuries, eight compilations came to be regarded as reliable.

The classification of the hadith did not end here. Some are considered *prophetic*, since the chain of transmission goes back to the Prophet himself. Some are considered *sacred*, since they enunciate a thought that the Prophet claimed was divinely inspired. For Muslim theologians this distinction is fundamental. The contents of the Qur'an are

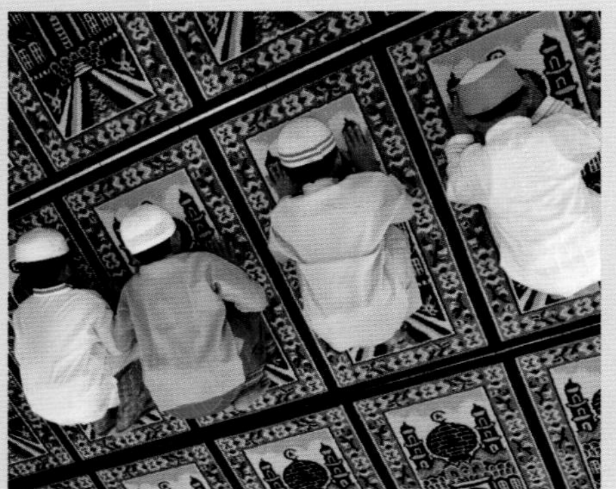

> *You will not enter Paradise until you love one another and spread peace.*
>
> Hadith of the Prophet

attributed directly to Allah. The *prophetic* hadith pertain strictly to Muhammad. The *sacred* hadith are a product of a collaboration. They proceed from God in a form determined by the Prophet.

Sunnis and Shiites

The hadith have played an important role in the internal divisions that have plagued Islam throughout most of its history. The majority of Muslims believe in the hadith and their status as regulator and guide to the morals and behavior of the community (*umma*). If Islamic law does not address a particular topic or situation of political or social life, it is the duty of the community to reach a decision. Some schools endow the *sunna* with the authority to annul or modify a text from the Qur'an. These individuals, the Sunnis (followers of the *sunna* of the Prophet), consider the community of Muslims to be infallible, as it states in the Qur'an: "My community will never unanimously lapse into error."

▲ *The Kaaba surrounded by pilgrims during the* hajj.

▲▲ *Muslim boys praying in a mosque during Ramadan.*

This orthodox vision resists innovation and affirms the cohesiveness of the community of believers. It is opposed by Shia Islam, the other major branch of the religion. The Shiites (*shiat Ali*, "followers of Ali") began to coalesce after the death of Muhammad, when the Umayyad dynasty was established instead of Ali, the cousin and son-in-law of the Prophet. Ali's followers believed that the true leader ought to come from Muhammad's

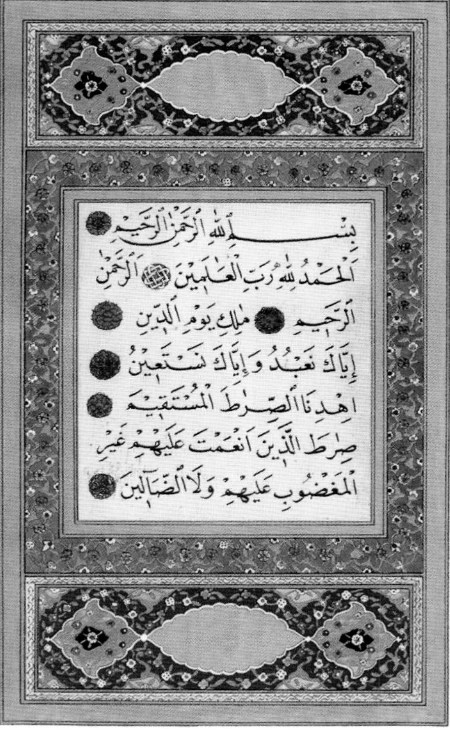

line. As a result of this division, Shia Islam developed its own legislative system based upon the Qur'an, but they downplayed the hadith, especially the class labeled "prophetic." For much of the religion's history the Shiites faced a more powerful orthodox majority. With the Iranian revolution of 1979, they adopted a more radical stance. Shiites place primary importance on the figure of the imams, the infallible leaders of the community and repositories of the authentic and esoteric meaning of the Qur'an. Eliciting the outrage of the Sunnis, they assert that the imams are superior to the prophets, just as Ali was superior to Muhammad. Historic grudges nourished by opposing doctrines and political grievances have converted the two major forces in Islam into implacable enemies. The Shiites revere Mecca, but aside from that they have different places of pilgrimage.

▲ *First sura of the Qur'an in a manuscript by the Turkish calligrapher, Aziz Efendi (1871–1934).*

▲◀ *"There is no victory except with the Imam Ali, and no sword except Dhu al-Fiqar" is inscribed on this panel. The Dhu al-Fiqar is the double-edged sword of Muhammad.*

Bayán

▲ *The sanctuary of the Báb in Jerusalem contains the remains of the founder of Bábism. It is the second most sacred site in the religion after the sanctuary of Bahá'u'lláh in Acre.*

Some Muslims hope for the appearance before the end of the world of a messiah, whom they refer to as the Mahdi (the good guide), who will bring triumph for the true religion and defeat the satanic forces. Many Sunnis believe that the messiah will be Jesus, who shows himself to be a Muslim. For Shiites it is the twelfth imam, known as the "hidden one." He is identified with an imam who disappeared in 878, who, according to his followers, is in a period of occultation until the final days. In the middle of the nineteenth century, a religious leader arose claiming to be a messenger of God, triggering one of the bloodiest conflicts in the Islamic world.

▶ *Sanctuary of Shaikh Tabarsi in Mazandaran, Iran. Here the forces of the shah confronted the followers of the Báb in 1848.*

The Longed-for Messiah

The Qur'an does not speak of a divine messenger, but many traditions cite the words of Muhammad recorded in a hadith: "Allah will bring the Mahdi out of hiding before the Last Judgment, and he will spread justice and equality over the earth and end tyranny and oppression." In certain difficult times, many self-proclaimed *mahdis* arose in the Islamic world, promising to fulfill this eschatological vision. One of them was Siyyid 'Ali-Muhammad, born in Shiraz (in Iran) in 1819 ,and the founder of Bábism.

▼ *House of the Báb in Shiraz. The original structure was destroyed, and in its place a mosque and a highway were built. The site of the Báb's revelation is marked by a utility pole.*

After abandoning a business career, which he had been involved in since his youth, he turned to meditation and began to gather followers around him. He took the name of the Báb (the Gate) for himself, a term that appears frequently in Islamic tradition and carries a deep spiritual significance. At first he said that he was the first in a series of prophets sent by God and later claimed to be the longed-for messiah. At first, Bábism was seen as a relatively harmless branch of Shia Islam, but that changed when the Báb began to denounce corrupt officials.

Rupture with Islam

In 1848, the Báb announced to his disciples that he was breaking with the religion of his ancestors and founding

«This religion is in the eyes of God the essence of Muhammad's faith.»

BAYÁN, CHAPTER 48

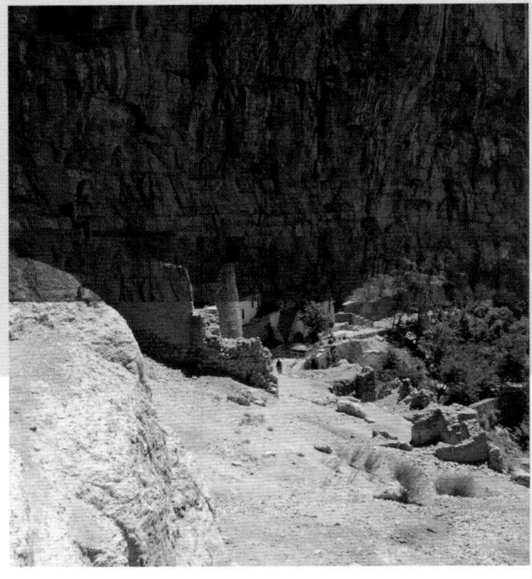

▲▶ *Fortress of Mah-Ku where the Báb was held prisoner for nine months.*

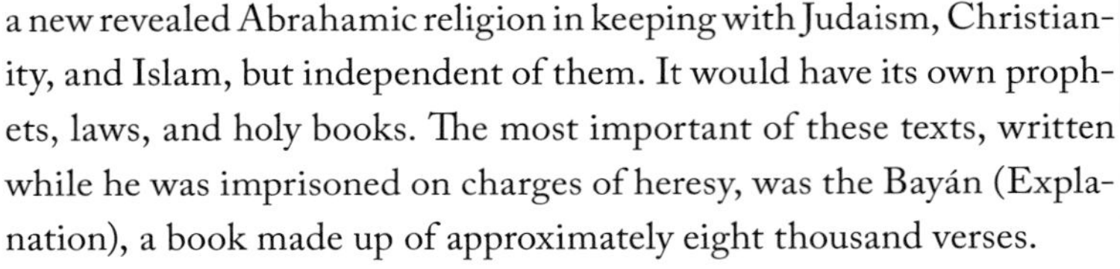

a new revealed Abrahamic religion in keeping with Judaism, Christianity, and Islam, but independent of them. It would have its own prophets, laws, and holy books. The most important of these texts, written while he was imprisoned on charges of heresy, was the Bayán (Explanation), a book made up of approximately eight thousand verses.

To start with, the Bayán discusses the most important ideas treated by other religions: heaven, hell, death, resurrection and the Last Judgment. The book gives these a spiritualized interpretation. For example, heaven and hell are not physical places but rather states of the soul that can be experienced during one's time on earth. Additionally the book sets down new religious laws, dismissing Qur'anic precepts regarding prayer, fasting, marriage, divorce and the rights of inheritance. It does, however, retain belief in the Muhammad's prophetic mission. It also challenges the Gospels but accepts the divine origin of Christianity. In the same way, Bábism rejects the Qur'an but accepts the sacred character of Islam.

▲ *The five-pointed star was used by the Báb and by Bahá'u'lláh. It is called* haykal, *the Arabic word for "temple."*

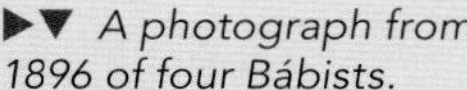

▶ Vakil Mosque in Shiraz where the Báb appeared before the people in 1846.

▶▼ A photograph from 1896 of four Bábists.

The 20,000 Martyrs

The Báb wrote in his sacred book: "Until the arrival of the day of resurrection, the Bayán will serve as the infallible Judge." Many of its rules seem benign and tolerant. It teaches that one ought not take up arms except in case of necessity and that judges should avoid corporal punishment. It forbids cruelty to animals and holds that children should not be seriously beaten. But other aspects of the teaching are quite harsh, especially regarding the relationships of Bábists with other religions. Its devotees were prohibited from living in the five central provinces of Iran; holy sites of other religions were to be destroyed and their books were to be burnt. Possessions of non-Bábists were subject to confiscation, and the faithful were forbidden to marry them or even sit next to them.

It quickly became clear that Bábism was not simply an effort to reform Islam from within but rather an independent religion that was spreading quickly through Iran and appealing to all segments of the population. The Shiite clerics, who were closely allied with the governing authorities, reacted to this questioning of their belief with ferocious persecutions. The Báb was shot by a firing squad in Tabriz on July 9, 1850, and it is estimated that 20,000 of his followers suffered martyrdom, especially after a failed revolt against the Persian ruler Shah Nasr al-Din in 1852. The survivors took refuge in Iraq. One of them, Bahá'u'lláh, established himself as the Báb's spiritual heir and created a new movement with a pacifist creed, Bahá'í.

Kitab al-Aqdas

▲ *Bahá'í symbol in which the phrase "Glory of Glories" is inscribed in the interior of a nine-pointed star.*

Bahá'í is a tolerant, universal, and pacifistic religion. Its primary sacred book is Kitab al-Aqdas ("The Most Holy Book"), which teaches that all humanity and all faiths are one. As examples of this oneness, Bahá'ís maintain places of worship (called *maskrik al-adkar,* "place for the remembrance of God") open to the faithful of all religions. There everyone can follow his or her own ideas. The Bahá'í religion is informal, dispensing with initiatory rites, sacraments and priests or imams to direct devotions.

Birth of the Bahá'í Faith

Bahá'u'lláh (sometimes written as Baha Allah), born in Tehran on November 12, 1817, was the founder of Bahá'í. He was one of the earliest disciples of the Báb, and like many Bábists had to flee Persia for Iraq. He settled in Baghdad in 1852. His standing among the group of Bábist exiles increased to the point that he was declared the prophet whose advent had been foretold by the master. Most Bábists rallied to his cause, although there were some dissidents who opposed the new leadership. Bahá'u'lláh moved to Istanbul, then finally to Acre in Palestine where he died in 1892. His last resting place has become a shrine for his followers.

▲ *'Abdu'l-Bahá, son of Bahá'u'lláh, the founder of Bahá'í. His name can be translated as "servant of the glory of God." He was born in 1844 and traveled with his father, who named him his successor.*

No one could have predicted that the Bahá'í, who were persecuted in all Muslim countries, would persist as an alternative to Islam, but the successors of Bahá'u'lláh strove to perpetuate his message and succeeded in founding important groups in England and the United States. Today, followers of Bahá'í are also found in Israel. Although the religion forbids political militancy or membership in secret societies, Muslim governments consider it to be a kind of fifth column in the pay of the Western powers.

▲ *Bahá'í's Universal House of Justice in Haifa.*

Replacing Bábism

In the eyes of his followers Bahá'u'lláh was a prophet sent by God to expand upon the message of his predecessors. But whereas other monotheistic religions regard themselves as the conclusion of the cycle of prophets, Bahá'ís believe that every thousand years or so a new prophet appears to craft a message appropriate to changing historical circumstances. This millennial focus presupposes a certain provisional quality. But according to the Bahá'ís, the religion established by Bahá'u'lláh is superior to that of Zoroaster, Buddha, Jesus and Muhammad, the other divine messengers.

Bahá'u'lláh wrote the basic text for the Bahái faith, Kitab al-Aqdas, in 1873. The book accepts some of the laws set down in the Bayán but modifies or rejects many others. Bahái's grant the Bayán the status of a sacred text but do not feel bound to its decrees. Additionally, the Kitab al-Aqdas is not only a book of laws. It is above all an ethical teaching that enjoins a new focus on individual spirituality and the role the individual plays in society. Bahá'ís look upon it as the foundation of collective social norms that is the Magna Carta of global civilization to come.

▼ *The Orientalist Edward Granville Browne was a translator of 'Abdu'l-Bahá.*

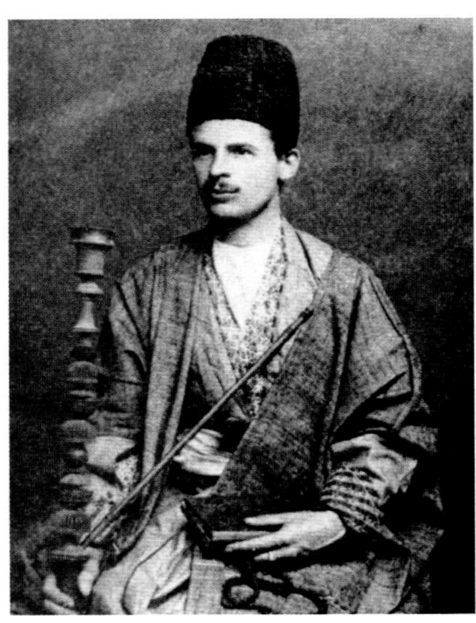

«The earth is one country and all of humanity its citizens.»

Baha Allah

◄ Symbolic Ringstone designed by 'Abdu'l-Bahá, formed by two haykal with his name in the center.

▲ The Sanctuary of Bahá'u'lláh in Acre is the repository of his ashes.

Working toward Universal Peace

The Bahá'í faith affirms the unity of the human race and the necessity for the individual to seek the truth in a personal and independent fashion. It asserts that all religions share the same foundations; that is to say, it presents a philosophy or style of life that strives for harmony and understanding between all human beings. Since its first priority is social justice, Bahá'í has created an administrative system to advance that goal: the Universal House of Justice, which has its offices in Haifa, Israel. It fights against racism and nationalism and affirms equality of the sexes, observing that man and woman represent the "wings of humanity, and only if both wings are moved by a common force can a bird take flight and reach the sky." There are, however, inconsistencies in the application of this principle: women are ineligible to be chosen as members of the Universal House of Justice.

In his writings, Bahá'u'lláh said that one of the main problems facing humanity is that people tend to accept what they are taught without questioning it, often fanatically embracing these unquestioned ideas. For that reason he urged his readers to discover their own principles and values, seeing conventional wisdom as brainwashing, and utterly rejecting the concept of "holy war," or whatever form of aggression religious doctrine promotes. He expanded upon the principle of nonviolence articulated by the Báb. Bahá'ís are to eschew violence even if circumstances seem to warrant it, even in cases of self-defense. "It is better to die than to kill; to be hurt than to hurt one's neighbors."

▲ Shoghi Effendi became head of the Bahá'í faith after the death of 'Abdu'l-Bahá. He organized and strengthened the community, which found itself in a precarious position.

Hinduism, Ayyavazhism, Sikhism and Jainism

▶ Hinduism

Vedas

The Vedas (or the Veda, a Sanskrit word meaning "knowledge") are the oldest monuments of the religious literature of Hinduism. Its authors were seers (*rishi*) who listened to the sounds of the truth resonating within themselves and transmitted it without alterations, acting as an echo chamber. For this reason the Vedas are described as *shruti* (what is heard). They were revealed directly from Brahma. This is contrasted with later texts considered to be *shmriti* (what is remembered) and thus of human origin. The Brahmin caste jealously preserved these sacred books as their exclusive patrimony, until European scholars published the first editions in the nineteenth century.

▲ *A statue of Rama and Hanuman in Rishikesh.*

▲◀ *Brahma, Hindu god of creation.*

◀◀ *Shiva Nataraja, Lord of the Dance.*

◀ Page of the Rigveda from a nineteenth century manuscript written in Sanskrit.

▶ Indra riding the elephant Airavata in a relief from Angkor in Cambodia.

▲ Varuna, the Hindu sea god, rides a crocodile. In the primitive Vedic religion he was one of the principal gods.

Vedic Polytheism

The four collections that form the Vedas are the Rigveda, the Yajurveda, the Samaveda and the Atharvaveda. Set down in writing in Sanskrit around the year 1000 BCE, they constitute the unique testimony of ancient Hinduism, which emerged when India was invaded by Aryan peoples from the Asian steppes. This migration introduced new divinities to the Indian subcontinent and sacred songs that became the basis of the Vedas.

From this early polytheism, which predates the appearance of Shiva and Vishnu, arose the Rigveda (shining knowledge), the oldest of the Vedas. It is dedicated to many different deities. Some personify natural phenomena such as the stars, the earth, and the wind, among others. Thus, Varuna, lord of heaven and the waters, appears as the chief god, ranked higher than Indra, the god of war, Vayu, the wind god, and Surya, god of the sun. But the Vedas also personify those powers tamed by civilization, especially fire, which is em-

▲ *Agni, god of fire. Along with Indra and Surya, he formed the trinity of leading gods in the oldest forms of Hinduism. Later, this trinity would be replaced by Brahma, Vishnu, and Shiva.*

bodied by Agni, an important mediator between humanity and the gods because of his important role in sacrifices.

Intoxicating Soma

Another god of secondary importance, the frequent subject of Vedic hymns, is Soma, the personification of a drug obtained from the juice of a plant (which is still unidentified). A beverage distilled from it was used in sacrificial rites. It endowed participants with strength, enthusiasm and a sense of immortality, thus earning it the title of "Lord Soma" and eventually deification. Indra was envisioned as its main consumer and thus as a close friend of the god Soma. Indra, depicted as riding on an elephant, is one of the principal figures in the reliefs of Hindu temples, such as the great temple complex at Angkor in Cambodia. His role as god of war led to his later being elevated to the first of the gods.

Despite its polytheistic cast, the Rigveda also names some gods of a more abstract character, paving the way for the concept of a sole creator. One can adduce in this regard Prajapati (seen as the "father of living beings," who presides over procreation and is the protector of life) and Hiranyagarbha ("the golden egg," source of creation in Hindu cosmogony). These are rudimentary expressions of the univer-

salist spirit that over time would morph into the formless god of the Upanishads, Brahma. The Vedic hymn entitled "The Song of Creation" refers to this idea:

"There was not non-existent nor existent; there was no realm of air, no sky beyond it.

What covered in, and where? And what gave shelter? Was water there, unfathomed depth of water?

Death was not then, nor was there ought immortal: no sign was there, the day's and night's divider.

That one thing, breathless, breathed by its own nature: apart from it was nothing whatsoever.

Darkness there was: at first concealed in darkness, this All was undiscriminated chaos.

All that existed then was void and formless: by the great power of warmth was born that Unity."

▲ *Shiva the Destroyer.*

▲▲ *It is said that Hinduism recognizes 33 million gods and goddesses. One of goddesses is depicted here*

« Sing forth a hymn sublime and solemn . . . »

RIGVEDA

Castes and Creeds

The Vedic pantheon clearly reflects the caste divisions of Aryan society. The spiritual elite, the Brahmins, identified themselves with Varuna; royalty and the warriors with Indra; and the mercantile class, farmers and cattle breeders with Surya or Vayu. Only these three higher classes could take part in Vedic rites, while the aboriginal population, forced into submission by the invading Aryans, were reduced into servitude. They compose the sudra caste. Unsurprisingly, their beliefs were less fully articulated.

Only the Atharvaveda ("Veda of Magical Formulae"), which was added to the three other Vedas at a later date, reflected popular beliefs rather than those of the Brahmin circles. It is a heterogeneous collection of spells, curses and enchantments that were employed to remedy illness, perform exorcisms and combat demons and other enemies. But it also contains spells to ensure prosperity, secure love and achieve success in one's daily activities. The other *samhitas* (Vedic texts) that make up Vedic literature are the Yajurveda (Veda of prayer), which the priests intoned in a low voice while celebrating the rituals of the liturgy, and the Samaveda (Veda of melody), a manual of hymns intoned during sacrifices in honor of the god Soma.

▲ *Mask of a Hindu deity.*

▲◀ *During the festival Chhath Puja, devotees bathe in the Ganges and make offerings to the sun god.*

Upanishads

▲ *Shiva is flanked by Parvati, his consort, and Ganesha, the elephant–headed god.*

The teachings imparted by gurus to their disciples from ancient times form the basis of the Upanishads, the earliest philosophical and mystical writings of Hinduism. These sacred texts reflect upon fundamental themes that have preoccupied people of all times and places, such as the nature of the soul and its relationship to a supreme being. The conclusion they reach is pantheistic: everything is encompassed by the universal spirit (Brahman), and the transmigration of the individual soul (Atman) through various physical bodies will eventually lead to union with it. The conscious awareness of this oneness will liberate the soul from the cycle of death and reincarnation.

> *Ascetics are detached from all of the world's enticements.*
>
> MAITRAYANA UPANISHAD

▲ Kartikeya, the six-headed god of war, is mounted on a peacock.

Vedanta

The etymology of the word "Upanishad" has been the subject of dispute. The literal meaning is "sitting at the feet of," that is, being engaged in the act of learning. Some consider it to mean "secret doctrine," others "knowledge of ultimate truth." In any case it refers to a teaching that was originally transmitted orally from a master to his disciples. The Upanishads known today comprise over one hundred texts of varying lengths, some in prose, others in verse. The earliest compositions date from the eighth century BCE. The three oldest Upanishads are considered the culmination of the Vedas and the foundation of a philosophical system called Vedanta, which addresses the relationship between Brahman and Atman. Because of its unsystematic exposition and hermetic language, the Upanishads are suggestive rather than definitive and have given rise to many different philosophical ideas in India and more recently in the West.

Brahman and Atman

The Upanishads posit the existence of an absolute principle that lies beyond the apparent multiplicity of the universe. This spiritual principle is situated at the heart of all phenomena, preexistent and unconditioned by the imperfection and corruption of the physical world. At the same

◀ *Statue of Durga, whose victory over the demon Mahishasura is narrated in the Devi Mahatmaya.*

▶ *The mantra om is sacred to Hindus and Buddhists.*

time each individual is the bearer of an immortal soul, the Atman, which constitutes its personality. There is a mysterious affinity between Brahman and Atman. In fact, the Upanishads declare them to be ultimately one and the same. The proof of this equivalence is represented by fire (personified by the god Agni), in which that which is burning becomes the fire itself.

The Prince in His Fortress

The two essences are impalpable and immortal. Whereas discussions of Brahman entail a universal scale, the Atman is described as a "prince in a fortress or a city with nine gates" (the male body's nine orifices). This individual soul, which is seen as essentially pure awareness, can remain clothed in its materiality or, through the practice of yoga, cast off the opacity hiding its light. Only the highest spirits, however, can achieve this perfected state in meditation.

One can look at Brahman as the macrocosm and Atman as the microcosm. Ultimately they are interchangeable; they differ only in how one accesses them. To arrive at the first, one looks outward, observing the powers of nature. Awareness of the second requires turning inward in self-contemplation. Both paths arrive at the same destination: "the only reality is Brahman" and "the only reality is Atman."

▲ *Kumbh Mela festival in the city of Haridwar.*

◀ *Devout Hindus seek to die by the Ganges and spread their ashes on the water. Often the deceased is cremated on the banks of the river.*

Life and Death

The Upanishads developed a way of approaching the ultimate philosophical and religious question: What is the meaning of death? If Atman and Brahman are identical, how is it possible that the individual disappears at death? The answer is simple. Death is not the end, nor does it entail being translated into a dimension from which it is impossible to return. The Atman passes through numerous existences (reincarnates) in the same way that a caterpillar experiences metamorphosis.

The mechanism determining reincarnation is karma, the spiritual law of cause and effect. Good deeds lead to good karma and a favorable rebirth. Bad deeds result in the opposite. This dynamic explains the reason for suffering and pain. They are the consequences of people's actions in previous incarnations. But it also conveys a hopeful message of the possibility of amelioration in the future and the eventual union with ultimate reality (Brahman) by following paths of knowledge, devotion or action (Jnana, Bhakti, or Karma Yoga).

Brahmanas

▲ Sun Temple at Konarak features a gigantic solar wheel. The Brahmins were entrusted with caring for the temple.

▲▶ Many festivals are held in Bihar on the shores of the Ganges.

▶ A Brahmin on horseback attending the festival.

The Brahmin caste, which guarded the Vedas as its own private treasure, added extensive commentaries to them. The collection of these commentaries is called the Brahmanas, which can be translated either as "Books about Brahman" or "Books by Brahmins." They contain detailed instructions regarding the performance of ritual sacrifices, which if they are done correctly will compel the gods to grant requests. Thus they are clear evidence of the dominant role of the Brahmins over other social groups, since through jealously guarded transmission they alone possessed the secret magical power to influence divine beings.

The Power of the Brahmins

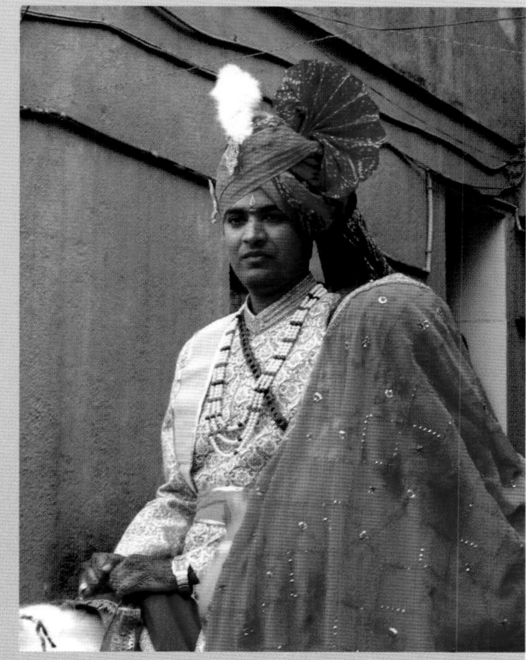

The Brahmanas were added to the Vedic texts sometime around the eighth century BCE. They were used by diverse schools of Hindu priests. Along with the Vedas and the Upanishads, they constitute the revealed part of Hindu sacred literature (*shruti*) that the ancient masters heard directly from the god Brahman. Their directions regarding the performance of rituals, prayers and sacrifices, and explanations of the symbolic significance of liturgical acts are considered authoritative.

The monopoly over religious functions on the part of the Brahmins consolidated their power in Hindu society. One of the hymns in the Rigveda affirms that the four castes originated at the creation of the world, when the primordial man, Purusha, was sacrificed. The Brahmins proceeded from his mouth, the Kshatriya (the warrior and governing class) from his arms, the Vaishyas (agriculturists, merchants and artisans) from his legs, and the Sudras (servants) from his feet. This anthropomorphized origin expresses the function of each caste. The priestly caste of the Brahmins were exclusively entitled to chant the sacred Vedic hymns, which was of paramount importance.

▲ Saddhus *renounce the material world and devote themselves to spiritual pursuits.*

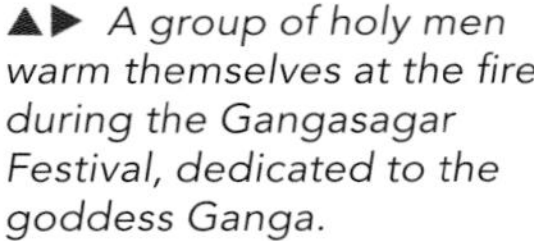

▲▶ *A group of holy men warm themselves at the fire during the Gangasagar Festival, dedicated to the goddess Ganga.*

▲ *A young boy dressed up as Shiva sitting by the roadside.*

The Four Stages of Life

The stages of the life of the Brahmin are clearly explained in the Aranyakas (Forest Books), later additions to the Brahmanas. These highly spiritualized commentaries deal with esoteric matters and were guides for those practicing meditation. (Their name refers to the practice of retreating into the forest for meditative practice.) The four stages in the life of the Brahmin are marked by rites of passage that guide the aspirant from one phase into the next.

The first stage is that of the student. The young Brahmin lives with a master to gain knowledge of the Vedas, learning, for example, how to perform sacrifices. The second stage is as a householder. He starts a family, raises children, hopefully sons, since they will have the responsibility of seeing to his funeral rites. During this period he devotes himself to studying the Dharmasutra, which instructs him on his duties as a Brahmin. The third stage is that of retirement (*vanaprastha*). After seeing to the education of his children, the Brahmin stops working and retires to the forest to live an ascetic life. The Aranyakas pertain especially to the final stage, the most spiritual, centered on meditation, on truth, the nature of gods, nature and humanity. At this point the Brahmin is ready to take up the work of teaching others.

> *The authentic glory is to speak the truth.*
>
> BRAHMANA, THE VOW OF ABSTINENCE

▲ *All of the temples at Khajuraho feature erotic reliefs. For Tantric Hinduism, sexuality is a path to the divine.*

The Story of the Aspara and the King

The final section of the Brahmanas forms the oldest part of the Upanishads. In it the doctrine of the identification of the universal spirit and the individual soul is expounded. But it is not entirely devoted to philosophical speculations and ritual formulae. Also included are mythological elements and fascinating legends such as the story of Pururavas and Urvasi, which is found in the Shatapatha Brahmana (Brahmana of One Hundred Parts).

This delightful narrative begins with Urvasi, an *apsara* (divine nymph), falling in love with King Pururavas. She agrees to marry him under the condition that she not see his naked body when they are in bed together. But the *gandharvas*, musical spirits of the air, are jealously possessive of Urvasi. They cause a bright ray of light to shine in the marriage chamber. Urvasi looks upon the naked body of her husband and promptly disappears. For many years the king searches for her, but without success. He finally finds her, changed into a swan, frolicking in a pond covered in lotus flowers. He begs her to come back to him, but that can only happen if he is transformed into a *gandharva*. Urvasi counsels him to request this boon from the *gandharvas* themselves. They teach Pururavas how to conduct a special fire ritual, at the end of which the transformation takes place. This being done, Urvasi and Pururavas can stay together for the rest of their days. For this reason Hindu law names the bridegroom *gandharva* when the marriage is contracted directly between the couple without the intervention of their parents and a formal ceremony.

▲ *Painting adorning a palace in the Indian city of Jaisalmer.*

Puranas

▲ *Ganesha is a beneficent god, credited with removing obstacles and advancing knowledge.*

▲▶ *Gajendra, king of the elephants, offers Vishnu a lotus flower entreating his aid, as he is attacked by a mythical sea beast, the* makara.

Hinduism is a multifaceted religion in which innumerable beliefs intertwine, mix together, are superimposed, unified, and differentiated in a thousand different, often extravagant, ways. In this luxuriant world the Puranas constituted a common treasure house of legends and traditions, elaborated over a long period of time by diverse sects with the intention of transmitting the truths of the Vedas into a language that common people, especially women and Sudras, could relate to.

A Chaotic Encylcopedia

▲ *A Hindu temple in Singapore with a statue of Vishnu and his many avatars.*

In India the groups occupying the lowest rung of the social ladder were not permitted to have direct access to revealed texts (*shruti*), such as the Vedas, which were thought to have been written by seers in direct contact with the divine. However, they were allowed to study recorded literature (*shmriti*), which was transmitted orally for generations before being written down. The Puranas (ancient accounts) are one of the categories of *shmriti* that spread the elevated knowledge of the Vedas to the popular imagination.

Compiled around the fourth century CE by the principal Hindu sects, such as Vaishnavism and Shivaism, they are a monument of religious sentiment and Hindu knowledge. Their contents are extremely heterogeneous: stories of the gods, genealogies of heroes, moral tracts, guides for the proper activities of each caste, instructions for the creation and display of images of the gods, as well as an inexhaustible fund of everyday information. This wild profusion by its very nature lacks an organic structure; it is a chaotic encyclopedia of all matters human and divine. As with the Mahabharata (discussed below), its authorship is ascribed to the mythical seer Vyasa, a word that, following different authorities, is not a proper name but rather simply means "the compiler."

▲ *Shiva in a temple in Annapurna in Nepal.*

« *Brahman, is the supreme formless spirit.* »

Vishnu Purana

▲ *The three faces of Brahma.*

Genealogy of the Trimurti

The Puranic canon is formed of eighteen principle texts (Maha-Purana) and numerous secondary ones (Upa-Purana). They are all written in poetry with occasional prose passages and range in length from 5,600 to 81,000 verses. Although each Purana has a different subject, most are centered on one of the members of the Hindu trinity (*trimurti*), which consists of Brahma, Vishnu and Shiva, or their various incarnations.

The Puranas provide evidence that these three divinities over time replaced the earlier Vedic gods at the apex of the Hindu pantheon. Brahma, born from a lotus flower sprouting from the navel of Vishnu, is the creator and organizer of the universe, which appears and disappears in a cyclical manner. However, his principal function is to reconcile the forces represented by the other two members of the *trimurti*: the protective energy of Vishnu and the destructive impulse of Shiva.

Vishnu is responsible for maintaining the cohesion of the world. He is incarnated in many avatars, ten of which are most notable: the fish Matsya; the tortoise Kurma; the boar Varaha; half-man, half-lion Narasimha; the dwarf Vamana; Parashurama, the axe-wielding warrior; Rama, hero of the Ramayana and husband of Sita; Krishna, best known of Vishnu's avatars; the Buddha; and Kalki, who will appear in days to come riding a white horse, and will destroy evil once and for all.

▼ *Hindu divinity from a Singapore temple.*

Shiva and His Dangerous Female Emanations

▲ *Representation of the goddess Kali.*

Vishnu protects us, but Shiva is the source of life and death. According to some traditions Shiva is an unapproachable god, who intervenes on earth only in his feminine aspect (Shakti). Each member of the *trimurti* has his feminine consort. For Brahma there is Sarasvati, patroness of science and the arts. Vishnu's consort is Lakshmi, who governs agriculture. But only Shiva's consort, called Mahadevi, plays an important role in human affairs. Mahadevi is known in three different aspects: the benign Parvati, the terrifying Durga, and Kali the black, huntress of demons.

Adherents to Shivaism consider the Puranas to be their primary sacred texts, worshipping Shiva despite his dark feminine projections. In fact, one of the main currents of Shivaism is Shaktiism, which accepts humanity's violent nature and offers Kali bloody animal sacrifices. This aspect of the goddess wears a collar of human skulls, wields a giant sword, and frequents crematoria and funeral pyres.

Vedic Sutras

▶ *An avatar of Vishnu, possibly Krishna.*

▲ *Dakshinamurti, Shiva as divine guru. He tramples underfoot an* apasmara *(demon) representing ignorance. Musée Guimet, Paris.*

A principal genre of Vedic literature is the sutra. The sutra consists of a series of short phrases or aphorisms expressing Vedic wisdom in a condensed form. The Sanskrit word can be translated as "string" or "thread" or "chain." This suggests the mnemonic function of the sutras. They act as the constituent threads that sew together the garment of doctrine. Various schools composed sutras and then added commentary to them to make them more understandable. This was an original contribution of the Hindu spirit; from it is derived much of Chinese Buddhist literature.

> *The Brahmin perfoms sacrifices according to the laws.*
>
> VASISTHA, DHARMASUTRA

Sutra for Life and Death

The sutra first arose around the time the Buddha was preaching. It is possible that they were created to refute opinions that the Brahmin orthodoxy considered heretical. The pupil memorized the sutras at the feet of his master, who would provide an oral explanation. These explicative commentaries were later written down. The need to condense such extensive material, to remember the phraseology, and hold onto essential teaching gave rise to the texts. Their obscure and lapidary character made extensive commentaries necessary. Without them, the sutras are indecipherable for all intents and purposes. The work of setting these commentaries down in writing made the ideas they contain accessible to a wide audience.

Numerous branches of knowledge expounded upon in the sutras are brought together in the Vedangasutras, compilations that form part of the Vedic corpus but are the product of memory or transmission, that is, *shmriti* texts. There are six main sutras, dealing respectively with phonetics, meter, grammar, etymology, astronomy and the performance of ritual. Other important sutras include the Dharma Sutra, a handbook of the rules governing the everyday life of the Brahmin, and the Grhya Sutra, which deals with rites of passage from birth to death and beyond.

▲ *Ganesha, god of wisdom and arts and letters. Ganesha was the son of Shiva and Parvati.*

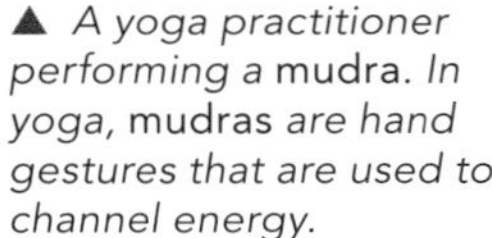

▲ *A yoga practitioner performing a* mudra. *In yoga,* mudras *are hand gestures that are used to channel energy.*

Atomist Theory

The style of the sutras was adopted for many other non-Vedic texts, arising out of different philosophical schools. Vedanta, for example, is treated in the Vedanta Sutra (also called the Brahma Sutra), a collection of fifty-five aphorisms that are unintelligible without the accompanying explanation. The author is thought to be Badarayana, and the renowned Hindu philosophers Shankara (eighth century CE) and Ramanuja (twelfth century CE) wrote commentaries on it.

Another noteworthy sect is the Vaisheshika or Atomist school. Its standard text is the Vaisheshika Sutra. This is a scientific work that was transformed by the Brahmins into a theological system. It proposes that everything in the universe arises from miniscule atoms (*anu*) that are indestructible and differentiated one from another. In combination they form the nine substances that make up the world: earth, water, fire, air, ether, time, space, the soul and consciousness. These phenomena manifest themselves with sixteen attributes: color, sound, touch, quantity, dimension, separation, conjunction, disunion, priority, posteriority, awareness, pleasure, pain, desire, repulsion and will. This empiricist vision shows that the Hindu mindset is not strictly limited to religious interpretations.

Aphorisms about Yoga and the Art of Love

There are two collections of sutra that are particularly well known: the Yoga Sutra and the Kama Sutra. The first treats yoga as a complete philosophical system that includes physical and mental disciplines to reach moksha, that is, liberation from the cycle of reincarnation. Its 195 aphorisms are attributed to the real or mythical philosopher Patanjali. They address the essence and nature of concentration and how to attain supernatural powers, as well as the steps leading to kaivalya, freedom from bondage and absolute consciousness.

The Kama Sutra reflects the importance of sexuality in Hindu culture. This tendency is under the aegis of Shiva and his feminine manifestations. In fact the *lingam* (phallus) is Shiva's primary symbol, and it is often found at the center of temples dedicated to him, sometimes accompanied by its feminine counterpart, the *yoni*. This treatise, attributed to Malianaga Vatsyayana, could be described as triumph in the domain of pleasure (*kama*), which is considered to be one of the fundamental elements of existence.

The aphorisms that make up this "art of love" deal with sexual pleasure, advice about women, marriage, courtesans, the rudiments of gynecology, erotic techniques, and aphrodisiacs. It remains a bestseller to this day and provides us with a wealth of detail about the private lives and customs of ancient India.

Mahabharata

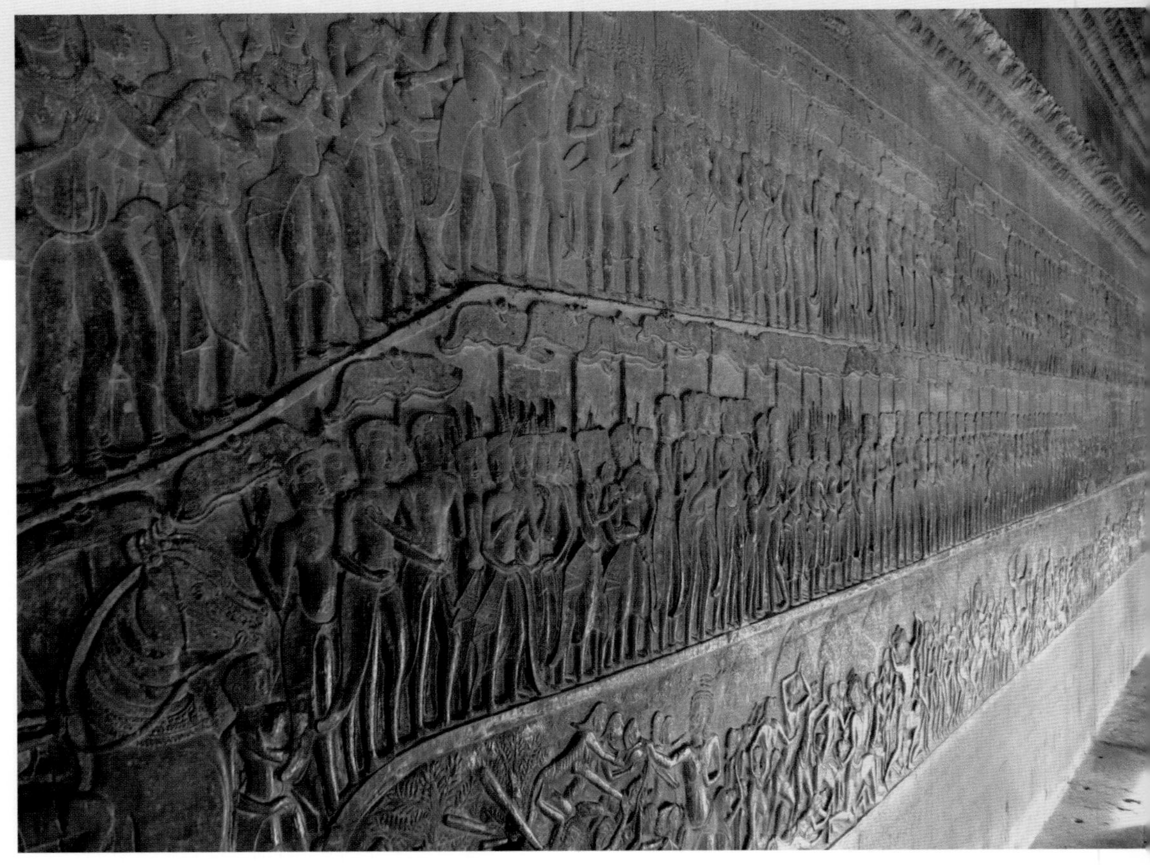

▲ *The Mahabharata narrated in pictorial form on the walls of one of the temples in Angkor. The reliefs showing India's great epic poem are one of the main attractions of the Cambodian temple.*

The longest epic poem ever written is a kind of gigantic encyclopedia that contains all of the traditional religious knowledge of India. The Mahabharata (The Great Poem of the Bharata Dynasty) was written in Sanskrit over the course of eight centuries and consists of eighteen books. It consists not only of the frenetic adventures of certain legendary figures, but it also explains the Hindu teaching of the four goals of life: pleasure (*kama*), accomplishment (*artha*), moral duty (dharma) and, finally, illumination or liberation from the cycle of reincarnation (*moksha*).

◀ *The fabulous Cambodian city of Angkor Wat.*

The Five Pandava Brothers

The nucleus of the poem is the story of the successors of the mythic eponymous hero of India ("Bharat" in Hindi and Sanskrit). At the beginning of the poem, the ancient Bharata family is riven into two rival factions: the Kauravas and the Pandavas, descendants of two brothers Kuru and Pandu. After the death of Pandu the throne passed to his younger cousin, the Kaurava prince, Dhritarashtra, who had one hundred sons and one daughter. In his court lived the five sons of Pandu: the wise Yudhishthira, the brave Arjuna, the herculean Bhima and the twins Nakula and Sahadeva. The brothers were unfairly hated by the king's one hundred sons.

▲ *Fragment of a bas-relief entitled* The Penitence of Arjuna *found in the town of Mahabalipuram in India.*

One day a neighboring king, Draupada, convokes the princes of the surrounding countries to a tournament to compete for the hand of his daughter, Draupadi. The competition entails shooting a target with a mighty steel bow. The five Pandava brothers win, as only Arjuna succeeds in bending the bow. Back home their mother learns that her sons have won and insists that the brothers share the award, not knowing that it is a question of a bride. To obey their mother's wishes all five brothers agree to marry Draupadi. This instance of polyandry, the only example found in Hindu literature, goes against the traditions and laws of India. The explanation seems to be that Pandu had come from Tibet, where it is considered normal for a woman to have more than one husband.

▲ *Relief showing Arjuna from a temple on the Dieng Plateau on the Island of Java. At this site, which is 6,000 feet above sea level, each of the eight small Hindu temples that still remain (there may have been hundreds at one time) is dedicated to Shiva.*

> *It is remarkable to be surrounded by the dying and not think of death.*
>
> MAHABHARATA

Exile and War

The kingdom separates into two lineages, with Indraprastha (now Delhi) as the capital, triggering the hatred of the one hundred Kauravas, who prepare a trap for the Pandavas. The oldest of the brothers, Yudhishthira, is cheated at dice by his uncle Shakuni, a man of evil character, and loses not only his fortune but his liberty as well. The brothers go into exile, retreating into the woods with their wife Draupadi. There they live as hermits for twelve years.

The account of their wanderings during this time make up the third book of the Mahabharata. This is one of the most famous sections since it deals with the love between Rama and Sita (also treated in India's other great epic poem, the Ramayana), as well as the origin of the Ganges and the great flood.

When the Pandavas return to reclaim their kingdom, the Kauravas refuse to turn it over to them. This begins a terrible war that lasts for eighteen years. Assassinations follow, blood flows, and the dead pile up, with the combatants falling one after another. On the eve of the decisive battle Arjuna inquires of his chariot driver (who is in reality the god Krishna) if he should bear arms against his relatives. This leads to the long moral discourse that constitutes the Bhagavad Gita. Only the five brothers survive the ensuing battle. Their lives end on their journey to the Himalayas.

▶▲ *Part of the bas-relief of the Mahabharata from Angkor, showing the Battle of Kurukshetra. The battle forms the backdrop for the Bhagavad Gita.*

A Work of Colossal Proportions

The narration of all of these fabulous deeds along with secondary episodes take up only a fifth of the Mahabharata. Most of the poem consists of didactic fables, parables, and legal, philosophical, and mystical treatises. For example, when the aged Bhishma, the most sober-headed of the Kauravas, is at the point of death, having been pierced by countless arrows, he enunciates his spiritual testament. This autonomous discourse on law and morality accounts for twenty thousand couplets. All told the eighteen books of the poem total 106,000 couplets, seven times the length of the Iliad and Odyssey combined.

Although the traditional attribution of authorship is to one of the poem's characters, the sage Vyasa, there is no doubt that the work was a collaborative effort spanning many generations. Given the time it took to complete this vast literary effort (from the fourth century BCE to the fourth century CE), it is probably the case that the material gradually accreted over time upon an initial plan that continued to be followed. These were turbulent times in India, when the country was roiled by various invasions. The aim of the compilation seems to have been the preservation of traditional religious values in a society whose existence was under threat.

Bhagavad Gita

▶ *Wood carving showing Krishna and Radha.*

▲ *Arjuna seeks the advice of his charioteer Krishna, who explains the concept of dharma to him.*

The Bhagavad Gita (meaning Song of the Lord, often referred to simply as the Gita) is the apogee of Hindu ethical and spiritual teachings. It occupies a place in Hinduism comparable to that of the Gospels in Christianity. Read, studied, memorized, this mystical-philosophical poem presents the admirable teachings of the god Krishna, who offers good counsel in the face of the sufferings of life and a salutary preparation for death.

▲ Krishna and and his consort Radha. For Vaishnavism, Radha symbolizes the love that the human soul has for God.

The Role of Karma

The Gita was probably composed at the beginning of the Common Era. It is part of the sixth book of the Mahabharata. It consists of seven hundred verses, divided into eighteen cantos, that narrate a dialogue between Krishna and Arjuna, one of the five Pandava brothers who are at war with their cousins the Kauravas. Right before the final battle Arjuna hesitates, reluctant to participate in a fratricidal war, and considers laying down his arms rather than shedding the blood of friends and relatives. His reflections are overheard by his charioteer, who turns out to be none other than the god Krishna. Krishna counsels the warrior to wipe out of his mind any doubts concerning the coming battle. He is a warrior, and his duty is to fight. And anyway, he can only kill the bodies of his enemies; their souls are invulnerable and eternal.

In his discourse Krishna touches upon several core Hindu doctrines. The wise man is required to carry out the actions that have been assigned to him (karma) and fulfill his moral obligations (dharma) according to the caste to which he belongs. At the same time he ought to cultivate equanimity, remaining unattached to the outcomes of his actions, through physical and mental self-discipline (yoga) and religious devotion (bhakti). This attitude will lead him to liberation from the cycle of reincarnation (*moksha*) and union with the absolute Brahman, the goal toward which all human aspiration ought to be directed.

◀ *Young Krishna's beauty and eloquence wins over the gopis (female cowherds).*

◀◀ *In this medallion Arjuna and Hanuman are mounted on a war chariot.*

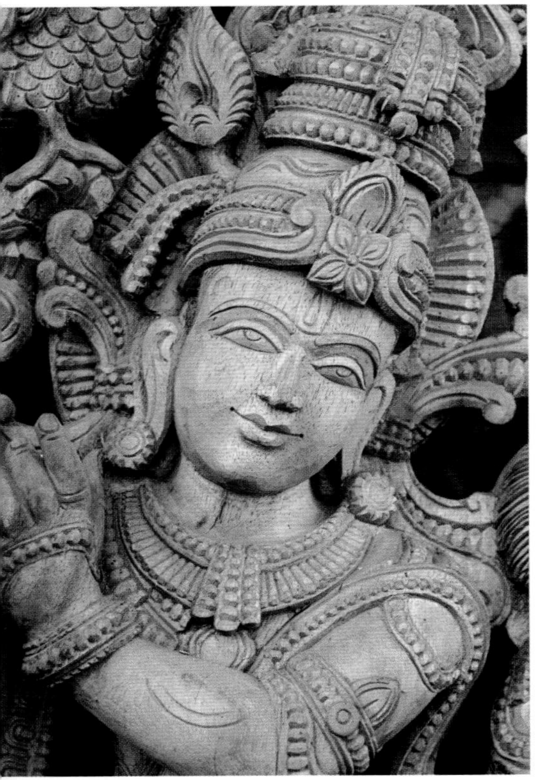

▲ *Sculpture of Krishna.*

The Blue Boy

After expounding this teaching, Krishna, "the blessed one," reveals himself to Arjuna as the Supreme Lord. During the narrative of the Mahabharata, Krishna is portrayed as the head of a clan who contributes to the victory of the Pandavas. At the end of the Bhagavad Gita, he manifests his authentic divine appearance. It is important to remember that Krishna is the eighth avatar of Vishnu, who incarnates when the world is in danger. But Krishna is also worshipped in his own right as an autonomous god.

Among Krishna's best-known feats is slaying the demon king Kansa. Many other legends reveal his virtues as ruler, warrior and lover, as well as his great wisdom. He is often portrayed as a young boy of blue color, like the sea and sky, spreading happiness among his followers as he plays the flute, a skill he learned in infancy when raised by shepherds. He is also known for the passionate devotion borne him by the shepherdesses living in the sacred forest of Vrindvan. His favorite is Radha. Her indestructible love for him is reflected in the devotion of the followers of his cult.

« Better is one's own duty though performed faultily than another's duty well-performed. »

BHAGAVAD GITA

The Mantra of the Loving Krishna

Krishna is worshipped in sumptuous temples found all throughout India, but there are some groups that are devoted to him with special intensity. One of these is the Hare Krishna movement, founded in 1966, which is dedicated to propagating a form of devotion based upon the Bhagavad Gita, the Bhagavata Purana and other traditions. Its origins go back to a sect created by a sixteenth-century mystic and reformer, Visvambhara Misra Caitanya, whose doctrine of spiritual joy centered around Krishna, a personal god who seeks and encourages love, and his consort Radha, who acts as his shakti, that is, his feminine aspect.

This holy man devised a form of prayer that consists of the repetition of the formula: Hare Krishna, Hare Krishna, Krishna Krishna, Hare Hare. Hare Rama, Hare Rama, Rama Rama, Hare Hare. Chanting this mantra is said to awaken in those who recite it Krishna consciousness, a joyous state of union with the "god who is the source of all pleasure." Today, followers of the cult, appearing dressed in orange robes and, for the men, with shaved heads, can be seen in the streets of any major city in the world, dancing and continuously chanting their mantra, playing drums and cymbals, offering incense and smiles, liberated from the everyday cares of the world in their intense devotion to Krishna.

Ramayana

▲ *The Ramayana consists of 24,000 verses divided into seven volumes. It tells the story of Rama, one of the avatars of Vishnu.*

If the Mahabharata is the first epic poem of India, the Ramayana rivals it in popularity and is considered stylistically superior. It recounts the deeds of Rama, beginning with some verses in which the god Brahma assures Valmiki, the author of the poem, that his work will last "as long as the mountains remain standing and the rivers continue to flow." The promise is kept, since the Ramayana continues to inspire readers two millennia after its composition. It is recited in public at religious festivals to conserve the memory of Rama, the ideal warrior, and his love for his wife Sita, a paragon of virtue and fidelity.

The Legendary Valmiki

Unlike the accumulation of legends, discourses, and tractates that make up the Mahabharata, the Ramayana offers an exquisite unity. It is organized into seven parts that total 24,000 verses. The five central parts display a poetic coherence that seems to confirm the theory of single authorship. They offer refined rhetorical figures, and the narration is full of human emotion, chivalric sentiment and appreciation for the natural world. It is probable that this was the original version of the poem, composed in the first century BCE, and the first and last parts were added at a later date.

Was Valmiki, the supposed author of the Ramayana, an actual person? It seems likely, although legendary material has found its way into his biography. He is said to have been a Brahmin who spent most of his life sequestered from the world, after having been a bandit in his youth. Ascetics taught him the art of meditation. He was so dedicated to his practice that he spent days on end not moving, while his body was covered with ants. Indeed, valmiki means "ant." Some groups venerate him as a saint. He is thought to be the inventor of the *sloka*, a type of poetic verse found both in the Mahabharata and the Ramayana and widely used in Hindu poetry.

▲ *The Ramayana is believed to have been written by Valmiki, a legendary sage who lived in the pre-Christian era.*

The Abduction and Liberation of Sita

The poem centers on Rama, son of King Ayodhya. From his youth Rama distinguished himself with his extraordinary courage. Married to Sita and beloved by his people, he is forced into exile, since the king's second wife insists that the throne pass to his half-brother Bharata. For fourteen years the hero lives in the forest with Sita and his brother Lakshmana. While in exile they are beset by demons, whom Rama slays. But the demon king, Ravana, abducts Sita and makes her his prisoner on the island of Lanka (Sri Lanka today). Ravana is a horrible monster with ten heads and twenty arms. He boasts that no one can kill him.

> *The one who speaks truth obtains the highest position in this world.*
>
> RAMAYANA

▲ Rama and his wife Sita sculpted in clay.

▲▲ This rare tapestry shows the marriage of Rama and Sita.

To rescue his love, Rama seeks help from the monkey god Hanuman, son of the wind. Hanuman mobilizes a monkey army led by Sugriva. Hanuman has his army join together to form a bridge between the continent and the island so that Rama is able to cross the sea. He kills Ravana in a duel and frees Sita. But then she must undergo an ordeal by fire, which demonstrates that she has remained pure despite the demon's enticements. After this, Rama ascends triumphantly to the throne of Ayodhya, where he reigns for many years and then passes the crown on to his twin sons Kusa and Lava.

From Hero to God

It is believed that the Ramayana was originally conceived as an epic poem whose protagonist was a mortal man, albeit adored for his exceeding virtues. This national hero who weeps at the death of his father but remains unmoved in the face of exile, repeatedly demonstrates his integrity, valor and deep feeling — remarkable but nonetheless very human qualities. However, with the addition of Books I and VII, Rama is recast as an incarnation of Vishnu, created to eliminate the demon Ravana. Accordingly in the last book, Rama does not die. He is reincorporated into the divine nature of the Supreme Being.

In this way Rama acquired the status of divinity. At first he was

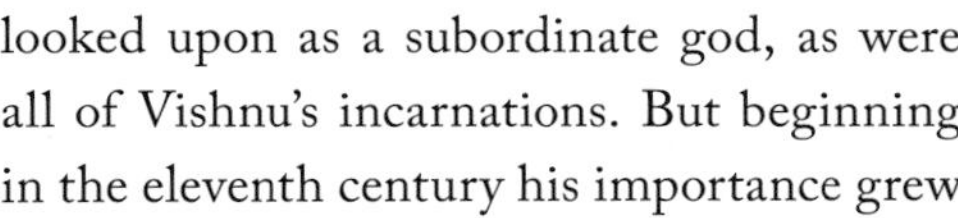

looked upon as a subordinate god, as were all of Vishnu's incarnations. But beginning in the eleventh century his importance grew to the point that he was the object of worship of his own cult. At the same time Sita's stature and influence also increased. As the emblem of faithful womanhood, she became seen as the shakti of her husband. Soon many sects sprang up, such as Ramaism, grounded in the Ramayana but based on a vision of Rama as a personal and supreme god who came into the world to save humanity. Curiously Ramaism is fundamentally monotheistic. It does not make caste distinctions and has no rigid dogma. Some aspects of its belief system, especially the emphasis on incarnation, recall the Christian creed. In any event, Rama is the country's most popular deity. A famous Indian television series was based upon episodes from his life.

▲ *Lord Rama, one of the great heroes of Hindu literature.*

▲◀ *Hanuman, the monkey-headed divinity, frees Sita from her abductor. He is considered to be an aspect of Shiva.*

▶ Tantrism

Tantras

▲ *Scene from the Kama Sutra, a compendium of sexual positions that aid in achieving the fusion of duality.*

▲▶ *Shiva and his feminine aspect, Shakti.*

One of the great creations of Hindu religiosity is Tantrism, a spiritual movement based on books called tantras. Their complex representations of psychological and spiritual realities include a baroque profusion of faces and arms, terrifying depictions of fearsome deities, and the frequent use of sexual imagery. They are the source of much of the canonical iconography of India for the last thousand years. In addition, the use of its diagrams (yantras and mandalas) and its sacred phrases (mantras) for meditation have been adopted by many seekers in the West.

> *The world that you inhabit depends upon your state of consciousness.*
>
> KULARNAVA TANTRA

Magic Formulas

▲ *Durga fighting the* asura *Mahishasura, who can only be defeated by the goddess.*

The Tantras (Sanskrit word meaning "loom, warp or weave," thus signifying an integrated system of beliefs) are texts written anonymously starting in the fourth century of the Common Era. They contain magical, alchemical and yogic formulas that were initially intended to serve in the worship of a divinity, but were also employed to solicit all kinds of boons from the gods, from material well-being or the destruction of one's adversaries, to final liberation from the cycle of reincarnation. Many of the Tantras are difficult to understand. Most are structured as dialogues between Shiva and his shakti, his feminine aspect manifested as Parvati, Durga or Kali.

Although at the beginning, Brahmins looked upon the Tantras as ill-written gibberish reflecting the superstitions of the lower classes, soon they began to collaborate in their composition, providing them with the refinement that they originally lacked, adding symbolism and prescriptions for ritual practice. Over time these texts became handbooks for sects worshipping the feminine aspects of Shiva and infused Hindu and Tibetan culture with their unique perspective on spirituality. With its exposition of the symbolic meaning of color, the layout of temples, and the style of cult imagery, Tantrism has left its mark on a wide cross-section of the religious art of Asia, from the end of the first millennium until today.

▲ *Representation of the seven chakras.*

▲▲ *Erotic reliefs in stone adorn the Temples in Khajuraho.*

Kundalini

Tantrism is a path of personal realization. The adept can transcend human limitations thanks to the magical rites of the Tantras, the practice of yoga, or the creation or contemplation of sacred images. The primary target of tantric devotion is Shakti, the feminine aspect of God, as it believes that the masculine aspect as embodied by Shiva does not intervene in worldly affairs. Tantrism upholds Shakti as the faculty of individual transformation, represented by the serpent Kundalini, which lies dormant at the base of the spine within the genital chakra.

To activate the Kundalini force one needs the guidance of a guru. By means of a series of exercises one can raise its energy up along the spinal column to the cranial chakra, thereby effecting the union between Shakti and her masculine counterpart. This process often consists of sexual practices and erotic ceremonies. By controlling sexual intercourse (ejaculation being avoided), the practitioner can obtain perfect dominion over superhuman cosmic forces, without seeking domination over other people. According to the Tantras, "the world one attains when the soul leaves the body depends upon the level of consciousness one has attained during one's time on earth."

▶ *Drawing of a mandala that contains the* Sri yantra. *Yantras serve as a focus for Tantric meditation.*

Mantras and Yantras

Tantric Hinduism has developed diverse practices of meditation. Often they entail the use of mantras. These are inwardly repeated formulae that are thought to arouse Shakti, putting the student in contact with divine energy, provided that the student has been initiated by a guru, who will then transmit a mantra. Each mantra sets forth in a concentrated fashion the verbal essence of the universe. The disciple receives a personalized mantra from his or her master, although there are elements common to most mantras. For example, the syllable most often recited is om, a sound that is considered to be a fundamental cosmic vibration.

▲ *The Sanskrit om, which is used as a mantra by Hindus and Buddhists alike.*

Other important vehicles for Tantric practice are the yantras, symbolic diagrams, which can be drawn on the floor, on stone or on cloth, and serve as a focal point for meditation. They usually consist of a circle inscribed in a square in which interlaced triangles appear, symbolizing masculine and feminine energies and offering a portal to transcendental realization. Yantras, geometric equivalents to the mandalas characteristic of Tibetan Buddhism, were considered by the great Swiss psychoanalyst C.G. Jung as psychic images of the cosmos emanating from the collective unconscious.

Akilathirattu Ammanai

▲ *The symbol of the Ayyavazhi religion is a thousand-petaled lotus with the sacred name of God written in white over the center of the flower.*

The sacred book of Ayyavazhi was written at the end of 1841 by Hari Gopalan, one of the worshippers of the great god Ayya Vaikundar. According to legend, the author awoke in the middle of the night. Impelled by a supernatural force he wrote down on palm leaves the words that the god spoke to him. The transmission of the message took many days. At the end of each day Gopalan would roll up the leaves and forget what he had just heard. At the god's command the palm leaves were gathered together and revealed their mysterious contents: the prodigious incarnation of Ayya Vaikundar and his war against the demons.

The Master's Way

The Ayyavazhi religion arose in South India and is principally found in the cities of Tuticorin and Tirunelveli and the state of Tamil Nadu. It has many beliefs in common with Hinduism, but there are significant differences in its conception of good and evil and dharma. There is no definitive agreement about the origin of the name "Ayyavazhi." One translation of it is "the master's way," but the Tamil words *ayya y vazhi* are polysemic. Depending on their literary or idiomatic context, they can mean "the father's way" or "the religious system of the guru." In any case *ayya* ("master, father, guru, superior, teacher, beloved. . . ") is the name given to its supreme god, Ayya Vaikundar, who is all this and more.

In fact Ayya Vaikundar incorporates numerous divine entities. One aspect is Ekam (supreme unity), the substance of the universe. In a passage from Akilathirattu Ammanai Ayya Vaikundar says: " I am he who created Ekam, and I am present in all phenomena." For this reason Ayyavazhi theology is considered to be monist (nothing exists other than the divine) and pantheistic (God is all that is real). In addition, Ayya Vaikundar manifests himself in three lesser figures: Vethan (the creator), Sivan (the destroyer) and Thirumalai (the protector), equivalent to the Hindu *trimurti*.

▲ *Monumental statue of Vishnu in Bali, Indonesia.*

▶ *Representation of Lakshmi in a Hindu temple. Lakshmi and her consort Vishnu are born of Ayya Vaikundar to defeat evil.*

▲ *According to the Ayyavazhi religion, Vishnu destroyed the demons that arose in the first* yuga*, one of eight periods that make up cosmic history. This image shows the goddess Kali with a necklace of skulls.*

Kali Yuga

The book dictated to Gopalan by Ayya Vaikundar is called Akilathirattu Ammanai, a name formed by the Tamil words *akilam* ("world"), *thirattu* ("collection") and *ammanai* ("ballad"). It also calls itself Thiru Edu ("The Venerable Book"). Its fifteen thousand verses, which abound in poetic figures, are grouped into seventeen chapters. Starting with the creation of the universe, they narrate Ayya Vaikunder's intervention on behalf of humanity.

The work commences with a dissertation by Vishnu to his wife Lakshmi about the evolution of the universe. This process goes through eight developmental stages or *yugas*. In the first *yuga*, Kroni, an evil genie, equivalent to Satan in the Abrahamic religions, comes into the world. Vishnu chops up his body into six pieces, but each fragment reforms as a demon. These are destroyed by the gods, one each in the first six *yugas*. We are currently in the seventh *yuga*, the Kali Yuga, a period of decadence, marked by the birth of the evil spirit Kali (distinct from the Hindu goddess of the same name), who is dedicated to torturing humanity with the help of Neesan, another horrible demon.

God in Human Form

To resolve this situation Vishnu decides that Ayya Vikundar (an avatar of Narayana, that is, of Vishnu himself) is to incarnate in the world. The Ayyavazhi believe that he took human form, adopting the name Mudisoodum Perumal. This spiritual teacher from south India was said to embody numerous gods and avatars: Ekam, Narayana, Vishnu, Vethan, Sivan, Thirumaly and of course, Ayya Vaikundar, who is the sum of all of these. In no other religion does the fragile human body contain so many divinities.

The ninth chapter of Akilathirattu Ammanai describes the fulfillment of the divine plan in great detail. Ayya Vaikundar, the son of Vishnu and Lakshmi, is born out of the sea and sent to earth to defeat the demon Neesan and bring an end to the Kali Yuga. The eight remaining chapters are devoted to an account of the adventures of the gods, which culminate in leading humanity into the eighth stage, the Dharma Yuga, a golden age in which moral and religious order is established. This progressive linear scheme differs from the cyclical conception of time developed in Hinduism. The mythological material of Akilathirattu Ammanai is complemented by the other sacred book of Ayyavazhi, the Arul Nool, which contains instructions regarding cultic practice, hymns and prophecies concerning the last judgment.

▲ *Ayya Vaikundar reveals himself to Vishnu.*

Granth Sahib

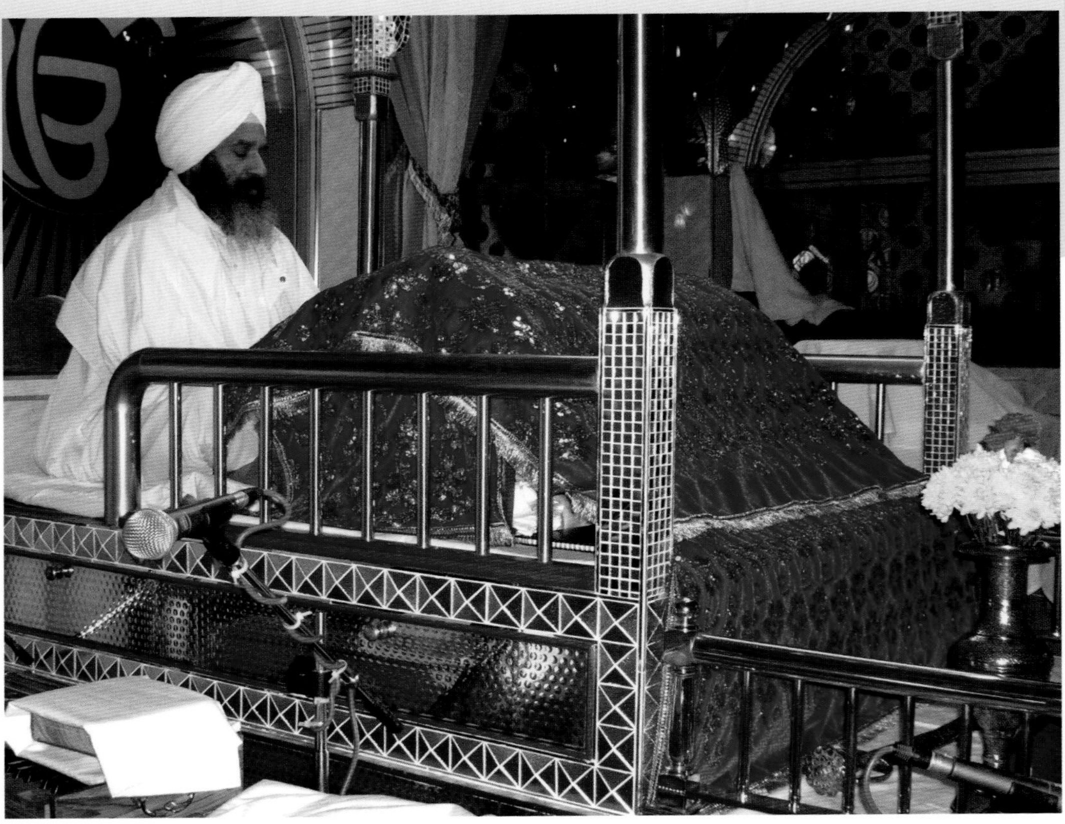

▲ *The final, eleventh guru for Sikhs is the Guru Granth Sahib, a sacred book that is found in every* gurdwara *(Sikh temple).*

The ultimate religious authority for Sikhs is not a person but a book, the Granth Sahib. Before his death the last of the ten gurus of Sikhism did not designate a human successor. Rather he chose as the perpetual and definitive leader of his co-religionists a sacred text composed by his predecessors, the Granth Sahib (also referred to as the Guru Granth Sahib). Historically, a sikh (disciple) is someone who follows the teachings of a guru. In reality the community is in charge of its own temporal affairs, while spiritual supremacy is maintained by the pages of the Guru Granth Sahib.

▲ *The Golden Temple of Amritsar.*

The Ten Gurus

Sikhism was founded in the Punjab region of northern India by Guru Nanak, a visionary spiritual master, at the beginning of the fifteenth century. In this region were a number of holy men influenced by different religions, including Hinduism, Yoga, and Islam. They disassociated themselves from the caste system, emphasizing personal devotion at the expense of ritual and ceremony. Guru Nanak followed their example and, before he reached the age of 30, renounced his possessions and devoted himself to spiritual practice. It is said that upon emerging from a profound mystical trance that had lasted three days, he uttered the following statement: "There are no Hindus, there are no Muslims; only man." Thus Sikhism was born.

Guru Nanak was the first link in an unbreakable chain. Each guru was designated by his predecessor and in turn chose his successor, until the tenth and final human guru. Each guru was the leader of the Sikh community and shared the same conception of God. They established the doctrines of the Sikh religion over the course of time, valuing inner experience over outward forms of piety. The goal of human existence, according to the Sikhs, is submersion in the ocean of love of the Supreme Being, referred to by many different names: Nam (The Name), Ikk (The One), Parmeshur (The Eternal), or Vahiguru (Wonderful Teacher). Sikhs strive to end the cycle of rebirth and death by becoming one with God.

▲ *Bathing in the waters surrounding the Golden Temple. Ritual ablutions play an important role in Sikhism.*

Music and Hymns

The first edition of the Sikh's holy book was published in 1604 by Guru Arjan, the fifth guru. He gave it the name Adi Granth. Afterwards the tenth guru, Gobind Singh, added the mystical hymns of his father, Tegh Bahadur, the ninth guru. This enlarged version became the Granth Sahib, the definitive text of Sikhism. From that time on, it has served as the eleventh guru, the highest spiritual authority of the religion.

▲ *Page from the Guru Granth Sahib with text by Guru Gobind Singh.*

The poetry and hymns that make up the book were the work of various gurus, as well as some Hindu and Muslim saints. The authors employ medieval language that is a blend of North Indian dialects but also includes Sanskrit, Persian and Arabic phrases. It is written in Gurmukhi, a Punjabi dialect, used solely for religious purposes. Guru Nanak believed that God revealed himself to humanity through *shabad* (words), so the poems contained in Guru Granth Sahib are referred to as *shabads*. These are set to music and recited or sung. Each begins with an indication of the key in which it was composed and the name of the author. Thus in addition to its sacred function, the book constitutes the foundation of the Sikh music.

◀ *Guru Nanak meeting with guru Gobind Singh, who holds a falcon.*

> *When the Giver of peace grants His Grace, the mortal being meditates on the Lord, the Life of the Universe.*
>
> GRANTH SAHIB

From Birth to Death

Granth Sahib plays a crucial role in all of the Sikhs' important ceremonies. For example, to baptize a baby, he is brought to a Sikh temple (*gurdwara*), which is considered a sacred place in that it houses a copy of this holy book. The newborn is set down next to the book, a page is opened at random, and a word is chosen from it. This becomes the child's name with the addition of the suffix *singh* for a boy and *kaur* for a girl.

During the marriage ceremony, the bridal pair sits before the book as they listen to verses from the text on the obligations of marriage and, holding a scarf, turn around each other. At the hour of death, the dying man is prepared with the five distinct emblems of the Sikhs. His long hair (*kesh*) is thoroughly washed; he wears his knee pants (*kaccha*); he takes hold of his short sword (*kirpan*), his comb (*kangha*), and his iron bracelet (*kara*). At death as he is burned on a funeral pyre, his loved ones recite hymns from Guru Granth Sahib or the poems of Dasam Granth, the other holy book of Sikhism, which was written by the tenth guru, Gobind Singh.

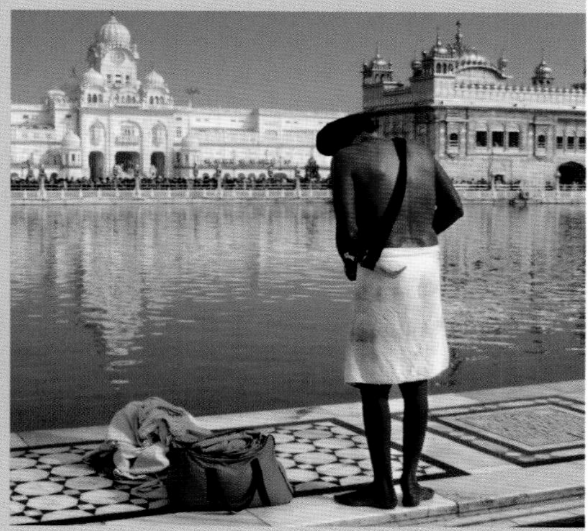

▲ *A Sikh pilgrim prays in front of the Golden Temple. The waters that surround it are referred to as the Pool of the Nectar of Immortality.*

Tattvartha Sutra

▲ *Depiction of Mahavira by an unknown artist dating from 1900. Like the Buddha, Mahavira was of noble birth and the founder of a new religion.*

For Jainism, there is no supreme being, but rather a series of masters or spiritual leaders who abandoned concern for material affairs to devote themselves to propagating the faith. They serve as models for Jain believers. The most important of these was Mahavira, who lived around the time of the Buddha. He established the foundations of the religion. Its principle tenets are nonviolence (*ahimsa*) and rigorous asceticism. Its ideas about the soul (*jiva*), karma, and *moksha* (that is, liberation from the cycle of reincarnation) are set down in the Tattvartha Sutra, one of Jainism's sacred texts.

> « *Cause no harm to living beings.* »
>
> MAHAVIRA

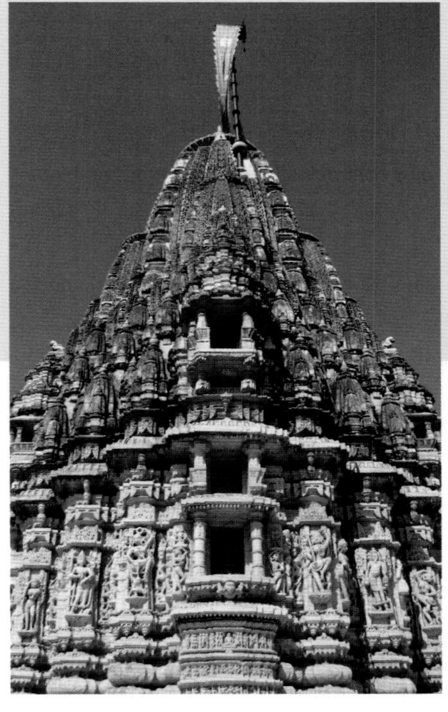

Mahavira

Despite its similarities to Hinduism and Buddhism, Jainism does not recognize the authority of the Vedas, the Brahmanas, or the Buddha. It is a nontheistic religion that takes an agnostic position regarding an absolute creator of the world. Jains look upon time as eternal, consisting of an infinite number of cosmic cycles in which periods of spiritual elevation alternate with decadence. When the faith is at a low point, there appears a *tirthankara* ("forger of a path or bridge") or a *jina* ("conqueror"), a man sent to indicate the way to a spiritual revival.

The last *tirthankara* to come to earth, in this the twenty-fourth cycle, was Mahavira ("Great Hero"), who lived in the sixth century BCE. Like the Buddha he was of royal birth. In his youth he chose to embrace asceticism to look for the true nature of things. Having achieved illumination, he spent the rest of his life urging Jains to lead holy lives. His followers spread out from Bihar in the north of India, Mahavira's birthplace, carrying his message. The life and teachings of the founder of Jainism are the subject of the Kalpa Sutra ("Book of Ritual"), a text that both of the religion's sects consider authentic. The two sects are the Svetambara, "white clad," and the Digambara, "sky clad" (i.e., naked).

▲ *High ornate façade of an Indian Jain temple.*

▲▲ *Ranakpur is famous for its marble Jain temple.*

▲ *Jain festival in Ranakpur.*

▲▲ *There are thirty-four caves in Ellora containing temples carved out of rock. Five of them are Jain.*

Jiva and Karma: Body and Soul

After the death of Mahavira, Jainism was in danger of disappearing because there did not exist a systematic work that presented its fundamental doctrines. In the third century of the Common Era, a Jain monk named Umasvati undertook the work of unifying various scattered texts and ideas. The result was the Tattvartha Sutra ("Book of the True Nature [of Things]"). It comprises 350 aphorisms written in Sanskrit that articulate the metaphysical and ethical vision of Jainism.

According to this work the universe is composed of an infinite number of incorporeal substances (*jiva*) that are omniscient and morally perfect. The human soul is one these. As a result of our actions, karma, which in Jain philosophy becomes an equivalent of material reality, binds the soul and subjects it to the physical world and the cycle of reincarnations. The soul can reside in a human being, an animal, even a plant, and become ever more distant from the prospect of liberation. It can only achieve *moksha* when it discharges all of its karma. To arrive at this state it is necessary to practice asceticism and the discipline of the "three jewels": right awareness, right belief and right conduct.

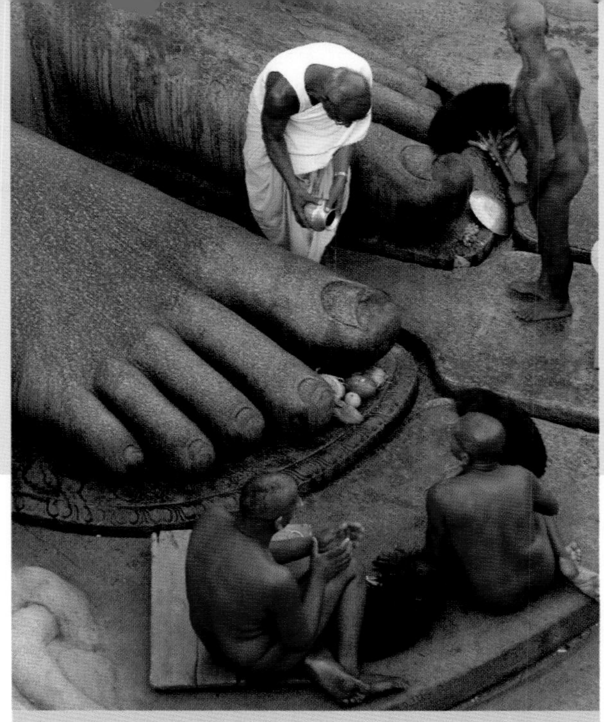

Extreme Non-Violence

In addition to the Tattvartha Sutra, the Jains follow the precepts set down by Mahavira and transmitted by his disciples. The first of these states: "This is the quintessence of wisdom; not to kill anything. All breathing, existing, living sentient creatures should not be slain, nor treated with violence, nor abused, nor tormented, nor driven away. This is the pure unchangeable Law. Therefore, cease to injure living things." The fulfillment of this principle of nonviolence (ahimsa) applies to all areas of life. Not only must one abstain from hurting another or exploiting another's labor, but also actively help those who are hungry or in need. Jains go beyond simple vegetarianism, even beyond veganism. They proscribe roots, since digging them up may harm animals that dwell in the soil. Jain monks and other very devout believers remain at rest after dark and don't rise until dawn, lest they inadvertently cause harm to animals or insects in the dark.

The Digambara

Members of the Digambara ("sky clad") sect renounce material possessions. They do not wear clothing. They believe that washing and taking care of clothing can lead to immodesty, and then to violence. Their only possession is a whisk broom made from fallen peacock feathers to brush the ground as they walk or sit so that they do not accidently harm any insects.

▲ *Digambaras at the feet of a giant statue of the Buddha.*

▲◀ *An open hand with a wheel is a symbol of Jainism. The wheel represents the cycle of rebirth; the open hand, the Jain creed of nonviolence.*

Buddhism

The Sermon at Benares

▲ *Statue of the Buddha, Sukhothai National Park, Thailand. The Buddha portrayed in this posture with his hand pointing downwards (the* bhumisparsa *mudra) calls on the earth to witness his Enlightenment and solution to the problem of suffering.*

The first preaching of the Buddha that is recorded took place in Sarnat, around Benares (today called Varanasi) in a park that still exists. In importance it has been compared to Jesus' Sermon on the Mount. Each explains the fundamentals of the religions named after them. The words of the Enlightened One have been faithfully reproduced in detail in different places in the Pali Canon (discussed in detail in the next section), and in Buddhist texts written in Sanskrit as well, which, according to experts ,demonstrates their authenticity.

▲ Prayer wheels. For the faithful each turn of the wheel is accompanied by a prayer.

▲▶ The great Dhamek Stupa in Sarnat was completed in the fifth century CE. It stands in the Deer Park marking the site where the Buddha gave his first sermon.

▼ The Buddha's footprint was an early Buddhist ymbol of It often contained a stupa,a lotus flower, and the Wheel of the Law.

The Two Extremes

After attaining enlightenment the Buddha rejoined the five companions who had engaged in ascetic practices with him. They would form the nucleus of the Buddhist monastic community. The group convened in the vicinity of Benares, from where the master would travel into the center and north of India to announce his message of salvation. The place chosen was the Deer Park at Sarnat, a woody and quiet locale, appropriate for contemplation and meditation, which can still be visited. The opening paragraph of the text gives the precise location where the sermon took place: "Thus have I heard: at one time the Blessed One dwelt at Benares at Isipatana in the Deer Park. There the Blessed One addressed the five monks."

Then the Buddha began his famous dissertation referring to the two extremes of opulence and self-mortification that he experienced prior to his enlightenment. "These two extremes, monks, are not to be practiced by one who has gone forth from the world. What are the two? That conjoined with the passions and luxury, low, vulgar, common, ignoble, and useless; and that conjoined with self-torture, painful, ignoble, and useless. Avoiding these two extremes the Tathagata [the Perfect One; that is, the Buddha] has gained the enlightenment

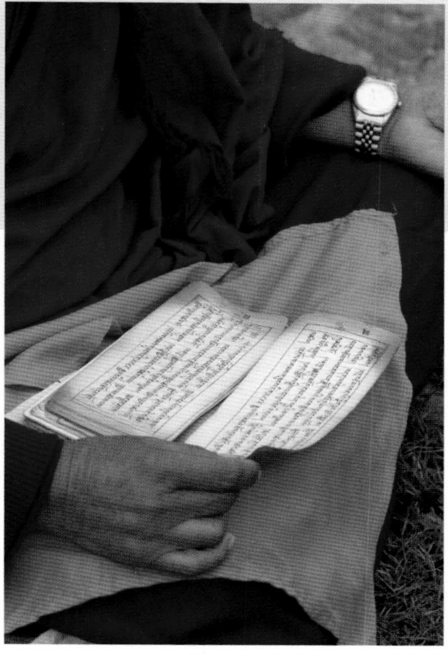

of the Middle Way, which produces insight and knowledge, and tends to calm, to higher knowledge, and enlightenment, nirvana."

The Middle Way Leads to Nirvana

▲ *Monk reading a sacred text in Sarnat, a Buddhist pilgrimage site in India.*

▲◀ *While journeying to Varanasi, the holiest city in India, the Buddha stopped in the Deer Park in Sarnat to deliver his first sermon.*

The sermon then explains The Four Noble Truths that constitute the foundation of the Buddhist worldview: 1. Suffering is a universal fact. All sentient beings suffer. 2. The origin of suffering is craving and ignorance. 3. By eliminating craving and destroying ignorance, which is based upon illusion, one can destroy suffering. 4. Suffering can be ended by following the Middle Way between the two extremes of self-indulgence and self-mortification. The Middle Way avoids both extremes, renouncing unchecked sensuality and fanatic asceticism. Buddha reproached both those who wallowed in luxury and those embarked on cruel privations. Not unlike Aristotle some centuries later, he situated virtue at the midpoint. Of course nirvana is a radical solution, a state in which desire is extinguished like a candle flame when blown

> *Think of me as someone who has disappeared.*
>
> Buddha, First Affirmation

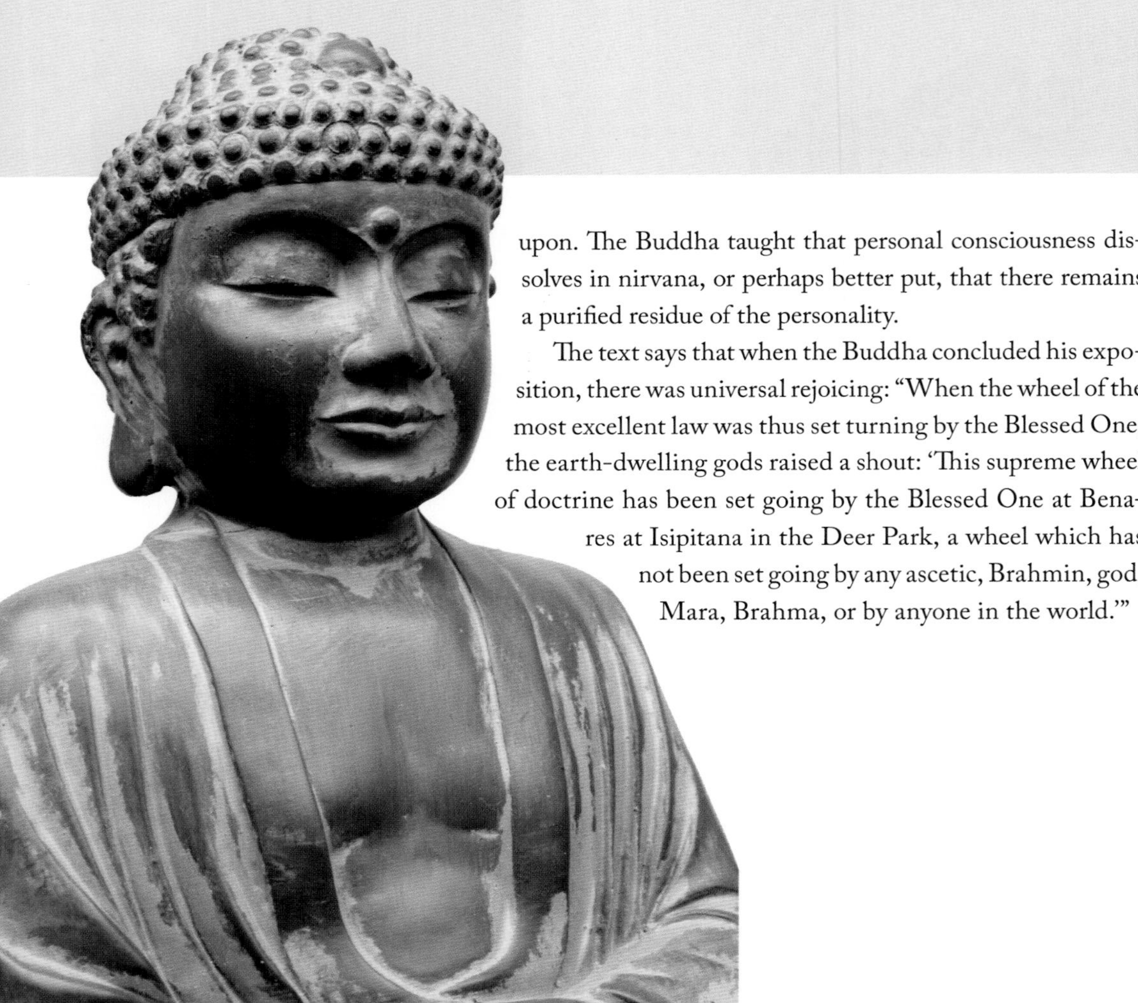

upon. The Buddha taught that personal consciousness dissolves in nirvana, or perhaps better put, that there remains a purified residue of the personality.

The text says that when the Buddha concluded his exposition, there was universal rejoicing: "When the wheel of the most excellent law was thus set turning by the Blessed One, the earth-dwelling gods raised a shout: 'This supreme wheel of doctrine has been set going by the Blessed One at Benares at Isipitana in the Deer Park, a wheel which has not been set going by any ascetic, Brahmin, god, Mara, Brahma, or by anyone in the world.'"

▲ *Statues of Amida Buddha are often found in gardens. They are considered to have a calming influence.*

The Dharma

The Dhammacakka (Sanskrit: Dharmachakra) is the Wheel of the Law, a key Buddhist symbol. The eight spokes symbolize the Eightfold Path: right understanding, right thought, right speech, right conduct, right livelihood, right mental attitude, right awareness and right concentration. The perimeter manifests the circular perfection of the teaching and its hub, the discipline of meditation. As it turns, the wheel disseminates the true doctrine throughout the world. All believers agree that the first turn of the wheel occurred when the Buddha gave his sermon to the five monks in the Deer Park. For this reason the sermon is also called the Dhammacakkappavattana-Sutta ("The Setting in Motion of the Wheel of Dharma Sutra"), and representations of the wheel commonly show it flanked by two deer.

At the end of the sermon the Buddha's message of illumination was celebrated with a kind of celestial fireworks, proclaiming the ascendency of Buddhism over Hinduism. "Thus at that very time, at that moment, at that second, a shout went up as far as the Brahma-world (the highest region), and this ten-thousand-fold world system shook, shuddered, and trembled, and a boundless great light appeared in the world surpassing the divine majesty of the gods."

▲ *The iconographic significance of the Wheel of Dharma (or* dhamma*) depends on the number of spokes in the wheel. It can symbolize the twelve* nidanas *or the chain of cause and effect (karma).*

Tipitaka

▲ *In Pagan, the ancient capital of present-day Burma, there is an important collection of manuscripts that includes the Tipitaka.*

Buddhism does not have just one sacred book, like the Bible or Qur'an, accepted by the entire community of the faithful. In fact, the scriptures venerated by the diverse strands of Buddhism are more extensive and varied than those found in any other religion. However, the old school, Theravada ("ancient") Buddhism, believes that it possesses a faithful reproduction of Buddha's actual teachings, memorized by his disciples and finally set down in the writing in what is known as the Pali Canon or the Tipiṭaka (Sanskrit: Tripitaka) five centuries after the Buddha's death.

The Three Baskets

The Buddha did not set down his teachings in writing, nor did he name a successor. After his death disagreements threatened the unity of his original message. Monks convened various councils and decided to create an authoritative collection of his sermons that had been preserved orally. This collection, completed in about 35 BCE, is called the Tipitaka, a Pali word meaning "three baskets." It is so named because its contents fall into three categories that would normally have been kept separate.

Pali is an Indian dialect used by the early Buddhists, for which reason the Tipitaka is also referred to as the Pali Canon. Today it constitutes the fundamental text in those countries in which the majority of Buddhists belong to the Theravada school (Sri Lanka, Burma, Thailand, Laos and Cambodia). Many adherents consider this tradition the only genuine one, but one cannot state with assurance that the Titpitaka represents the actual thinking of the Buddha. In any event, its pages contain a wealth of spiritual wisdom that can speak to all of humanity.

A Model of Austerity

The first basket, Vinayapitaka or "Basket of Discipline," is a thorough listing of the precepts governing the life of the Buddhist monastic community (*sangha*). It relates the history of the first monks and the monasteries they founded. To attain the proper attitude of detachment toward the world, the Buddha adopted for himself, and prescribed for his followers, an austere and solitary life style. They were to live from begging, from which they received the name *bhikku* ("mendicants"). Initially the monks lodged in temporary shelters, but later they were allowed to build their cells in abandoned gardens. This led to the formation of monasteries, but their simple way of life continues to be practiced to this day.

The text sets down ten rules with which Buddhists monks must strictly comply:

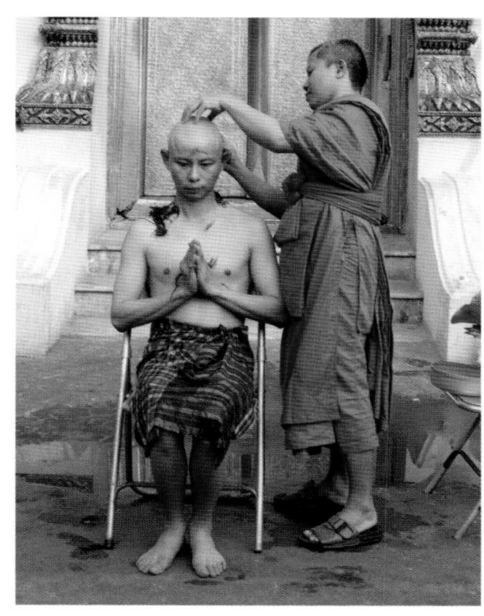

▲ *Shaving the head of a novice during the initiation ceremony.*

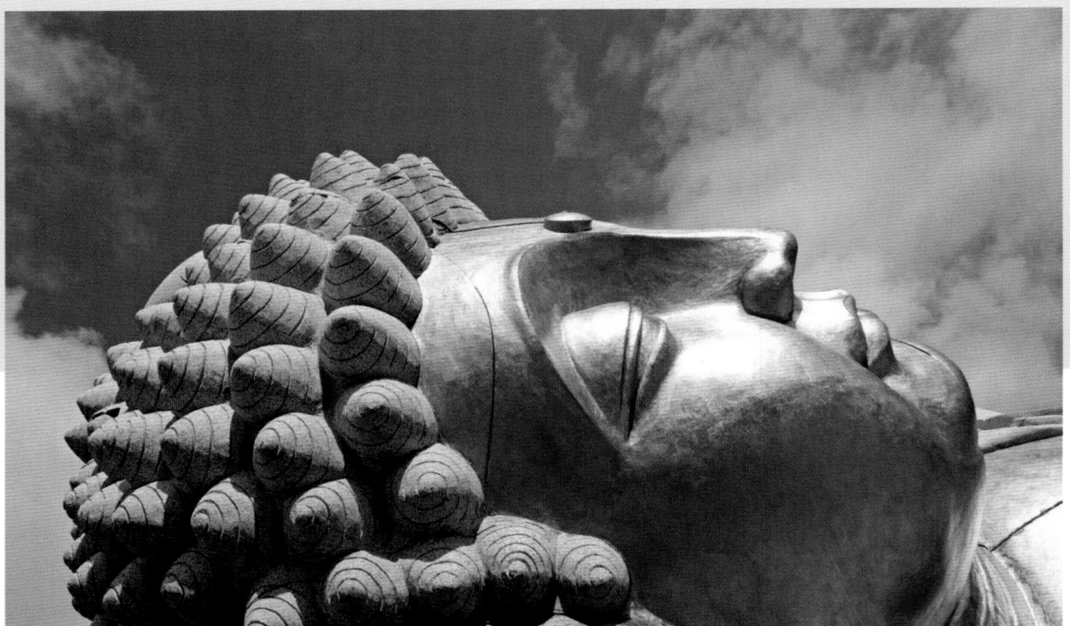

▲ *Reclining Buddha. This posture represents his death, definitive separation from the material world, and entrance into Nirvana. Once this state has been reached, one is liberated from the cycle of reincarnation.*

1) Refrain from killing living creatures.
2) Refrain from stealing.
3) Refrain from unchastity (sensuality, sexuality, lust).
4) Refrain from lying.
5) Refrain from taking intoxicants.
6) Refrain from taking food at inappropriate times (after noon).
7) Refrain from singing, dancing, or playing music.
8) Refrain from wearing perfume and cosmetics or garlands of flowers.
9) Refrain from sleeping on luxurious, soft beds.
10) Refrain from accepting money.

The Tipitaka enumerates 227 ways that one can break these rules, which apply to nuns as well as monks. Each member of the *sangha* has to publically confess his errors, twice a month, and the community imposes the appropriate penalty. Any delay in acknowledging one's faults increases their gravity and the severity of the punishment.

« Let no one deceive or despise another at any time. »

Tipitaka

The Discourses of the Buddha

The second basket, Suttapitaka or "Basket of Sermons," is formed by an intricate combining of long, medium and short texts, grouped and subdivided in ways that are more or less arbitrary. They include some of the most important teachings directly attributed to the Buddha: the Dhammacakkappavatna-Sutta ("The Setting in Motion of the Wheel of Dharma Sutra"), the Dhammapada ("Verses on the Dharma") and the Mahaparinibbana-Sutta ("Great Sermon on the Final Extinction"), all of which we will look at in the following pages. They describe the vision of the Enlightened One and contrast it with other contemporaneous philosophical ideas. They describe the steps one must take to achieve nirvana, the supreme state of plentitude.

The third and last part of the Tipitaka is the Abhidhamma Pitaka or "Basket of the Supreme Doctrine," where the contents of the preceding two baskets are outlinedin a systematic fashion. However, it substitutes the clarity and poetic poignancy of the sermons attributed to the Buddha with a philosophical subtlety that is well-nigh incomprehensible. The last of the tracts, known as the Patthana, which takes up six thick volumes in the Thai edition, is especially indecipherable, so much so that there has never been a translation of it into any Western language.

▲ *A fairly common Chinese image known as the "Laughing Buddha."*

▲▲ *During his meditation under the Bodhi Tree, the Buddha saw a continually turning wheel that contained all sentient beings and represented the seven mental states and the process in which one passes from one state to another.*

Dhammapada

▲ *The Korean Tipitaka dating from the twelfth century CE consists of 81,340 wooden leaves in 6,568 volumes. It was discovered in a Buddhist temple.*

▲▶ *This lovely image shows the Buddha in the lotus position with his head hiding the sun.*

The best-known work of Buddhist religious literature is, without doubt, the Dhammapada. No other text has had such wide circulation or has been so highly praised for its poetic beauty and profound wisdom. Its 423 proverbs are a selection from the sayings that the Buddha pronounced over the course of forty-five years of preaching. Memorized by his disciples, they remained part of a living oral tradition until they were collected and written down in the Tipitaka. This wonderful compendium of poetry and insight, the jewel of Buddhist ethics, still dazzles today's readers.

« *Hatred never quenches hatred.* »

DHAMMAPADA

The Historical Buddha

▲ *Temple of Mahabodhi at the site of the Buddha's attainment of illumination.*

▲▲ *This interlaced geometric pattern (the* shrivatsa*) represents longevity and the connection between wisdom and the cosmos.*

What do we know of the real-life Buddha? He was named Siddhartha Gautama and was born to a noble family in the middle of the sixth century BCE near Kapilavastu in present-day Nepal. His aristocratic family belonged to the Sakya clan, from which his surname Shakyamuni (the ascetic of the Sakyas) is derived. A famous Brahmin visited his family soon after his birth and predicted that the child would grow up to be a great ruler or a great spiritual teacher. We also know that at the age of 29, the young prince had a life-changing response to seeing the three principal causes of human misery: sickness, old age, and death. He abandoned his social position, his wife and son, and embraced the life of a wandering ascetic. But neither the teachings of the different spiritual masters that he followed nor the extreme self-mortifications to which he subjected himself provided him with the answers that he was looking for.

However, through the medium of intense meditation, he discovered that the only way out of the impasse of human suffering was to free oneself from the domination of one's desires. In this way he achieved illumination and awakening (bodhi) and arrived at a true understanding of dharma. He surrounded himself with a nucleus of followers, and from that moment he dedicated the rest of his earthly existence to extending his message of salvation. In addition to his extraordinary personality, which won over hearts and minds, he added the gift of oratory, which moved and persuaded his listeners, as is evidenced by the aphorisms in the Dhammapada.

▲ Scene showing the birth of the Buddha painted on the wall of a Laotian temple.

▲▲ Face of the Buddha wedged between the roots of a tree in Angkor.

▲▶ The Buddha's footstep is considered one of the eight favorable symbols of Buddhism.

The Legendary Buddha

Naturally, people filled in this sketchy biography with numerous legendary details that augmented the Buddha's mythic standing. It was said that ten months before his birth, his mother, Queen Maya, dreamed that a white elephant entered her womb; that the newborn child immediately started walking and announced: "This is my last incarnation. I am the Greatest of All Beings." And other prodigies surrounded his birth as well: sight was restored to the blind; birds stopped in mid-flight; rivers changed direction; and everywhere flowers of sublime colors bloomed.

According to tradition, there existed other Buddhas, whose births were accompanied by similar miracles. To determine whether the reports surrounding the birth of the child were correct, an old man named Asita traveled to Kapilavastu to inquire about the matter. Right away he saw on the infant's body the thirty-two signs that proved he was a supreme Buddha (forty teeth, a well-retracted male organ, the imprint of the wheel of dharma on the soles of the feet, among others). While prophesying the Buddha's glorious future, Asita wept that he would not live long enough to fully enjoy his light.

▶ *Foot from a giant sculpture of the Buddha in Leshan, China. The stature is over 200 feet high. It was carved into the side of a mountain in the eighth century CE.*

The 423 Aphorisms

The title Dhammapada comes from the Pali term *dhamma* (equivalent to Sanskrit dharma): the eternal law, absolute and universal truth that the Buddha discovered for himself. As pada signifies "way" or "path," Dhammapada can be taken to mean the "True Way" or "Path of Righteousness." It is one of the main discourses of the fifth and last division of the Suttapitaka (one of the three baskets of the Tipitaka) that comprises the best-known writings of Theravadan Buddhism.

The brief utterances contained in the book treat varied themes, such as: the mind, necessity, evil, self-control, the world, happiness, disgrace. It's easy to explain the contents of the Dhammapada, but it's better to let the Buddha, whether historic or legendary, speak for himself:

- Mind precedes all mental states. Mind is their chief; they are all mind-wrought. If with an impure mind a person speaks or acts, suffering follows him like the wheel that follows the foot of the ox.
- As rain breaks through an ill-thatched house, passion will break through an unreflecting mind.
- Hard to hold down, nimble, alighting wherever it likes: the mind. Its taming is good. The mind well-tamed brings ease.
- If a traveller does not meet with one who is his better, or his equal, let him firmly keep to his solitary journey; there is no companionship with a fool.
- Should you find a wise critic to point out your faults, follow him as you would a guide to hidden treasure.
- Greater in battle than the man who would conquer a thousand-thousand men, is he who would conquer just one — himself.
- To avoid all evil, to cultivate good, and to cleanse one's mind — this is the teaching of the Buddhas.

▶ Theravada Buddhism

Mahaparinibbana-Sutta

▲ *Buddhist center in Monywa, Burma. This important commercial enclave boasts a 300-foot-high statue of the Buddha.*

For a long time the Buddha was an itinerant preacher, spreading his message as much by his example as by his words. He died at the age of 80, by which time his community had become well established. A little before his death, he appeared transfigured to his disciples and said to them: "Behold now, Bhikkhus, I exhort you: All compounded things are subject to decay. Strive with diligence!" These were his last words according to the Mahaparinibbana-Sutta, which provides a wealth of detail about the final hours of the Enlightened One.

▶ *Pagodas in Pagan, Burma. Theravada Buddhism flourished in Southeast Asia.*

End of Wandering

▲ *This gigantic statue of the Buddha stands in a rice field.*

The Mahaparinibbana-Sutta (Great Sermon on Final Extinction or Great Sermon of the Perfection) is one of the most important Buddhist texts belonging to the Pali Canon. It is a part of the second basket, the Suttapitaka (Basket of Sermons). Although the text recounts the last period of the Buddha's life, his illness, and death, it is devoid of any trace of sentimentality.

The last wanderings of the Buddha's earthly existence led him from Rajagriha to Patali (which later become the city of Pataliputra), to Vaishali and then later to the village of Belwa, where during the rainy season he was seriously stricken with an illness that he was only able to withstand by force of will. However, the sickness that led to his death was brought on by a dish of pork that was offered to him by a blacksmith named Chunda. According to the Mahaparinibbana-Sutta he faced his final hours with serenity and fortitude and surrendered his missionary labors. But despite his weakened state, before death took him, he gave his disciples a final message of hope and inspiration.

The Death of Buddha

Though his health was severely compromised, the Buddha was still able to travel to Pava in the vicinity of Kusinagara, where his health utterly failed him. The Mahaparinibbana-Sutta tells us that he "died

▲ *Representation of* parinirvana. *The guardians of* dharma *lament the passing of the Buddha.*

with serenity and perfect control over himself." This took place in 480 BCE. His disciples gathered his ashes from his funeral pyre and preserved them with great respect in ten funerary monuments (stupas). In the following decades the early Buddhists created new stupas to contain relics of their master, decorating the stone monuments and adorning them with Buddhist symbols. The places in northwest India through which he had traveled became the sites of shrines dedicated to his cult and to prayer.

The Buddha had entered the peace of complete extinction (*parinibbana* or *parinirvana*) where attachment to worldly things, fear, suffering, and the cycle of reincarnation come to an end. This transition was accompanied by extraordinary manifestations, which led to further speculation about the deceased spiritual teacher. For example, it was said that six Buddhas preceded Gautama (according to other sources, this number is twenty-four, fifty-four, or even more than one hundred), and that he will be followed by an eighth Buddha, Maitreya, who will complete the work of spreading the doctrine of the dharma. In this way Buddhists dealt with the loneliness and vacuum left by the disappearance of their teacher.

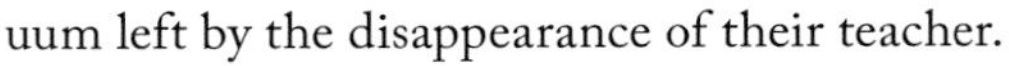

▲ *Every monastery in Southeast Asia has a statue of an elephant. The mother of Siddhartha dreamt of a white elephant before his birth.*

He died with serenity and perfect control over himself.

MAHAPARINIBBANA-SUTTA

◄ *Golden Temple in the Doi Suthep Monastery near Chiang Mai, Thailand. The parasol symbolically connects heaven and earth.*

Descent into Hell

Other narratives recount the past lives of the Buddha. He was a compassionate bear, the king of antelopes, a beneficent elephant, the prince Visvamatara, and in his penultimate existence, the king of the gods of heaven from where he descended into his sleeping mother's womb. During these lives he performed many miracles. "The blind regained sight; the deaf hearing, and the dumb speech. The mad regained reason; the naked were clothed; the hungry fed, and the thirsty given drink. The sick recovered, and empires were put in order."

The most heroic deed performed by the Buddha after his death was a visit to hell. The journey is described in various minor works of popular devotion. "The Buddha smiled. The law is when a Buddha smiles, blue, yellow, red and white rays of light flow from his lips. Of these some descend and others ascend. Those that descend travel to the very depths of hell and relieve the suffering of those condemned, so that they are transformed into devas [supernatural beings]. The rays that ascend traverse the twenty celestial realms, and the gods, filled with admiration exclaim: 'Let us leave here and apply ourselves to the dharma of the Buddha, annihilating the armies of death like an elephant crushes a house made of reeds.'"

▲ *Giant image of a reclining Buddha at Wat Po, in Bangkok, Thailand.*

Visuddhimagga

▲ *Thuparama Stupa in Anuradhapura, Sri Lanka, is the most important destination for Theravadan Buddhist pilgrims.*

▲▶ *Inner peace radiates from the countenances of these Buddhist statues.*

The most important of all the commentators on the Pali Canon was Buddhaghosa, a Hindu sage who traveled through India debating on religious subjects with the most learned men of his time. Renowned for his knowledge of the Vedas, he believed himself to be in possession of the truth, until he met a monk named Revata, who revealed the teachings of the Buddha and inspired him to immerse himself in the wisdom of the Theravadan school. The fruits of his intense study was the Visuddhimagga, a complete and systematic exposition of Buddhist doctrine. Although it is not officially part of the canon, it is considered as such in many countries.

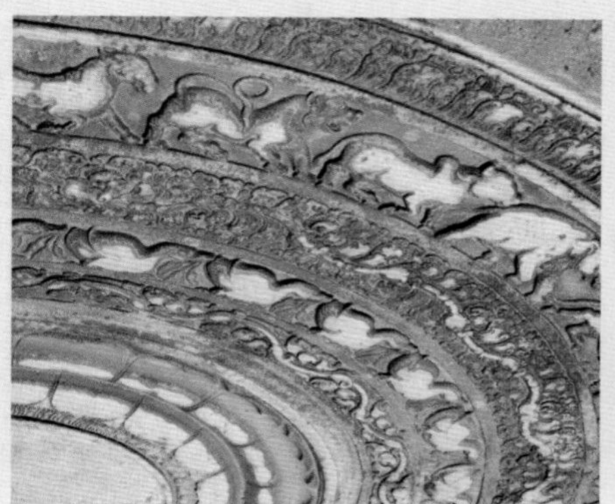

> *Mortals purify themselves by leading virtuous and noble lives, not by money.*
>
> VISUDDHIMAGGA

Buddhaghosa's Quest

It is difficult to separate historic facts from legendary anecdotes in the biography of this great teacher. It is well accepted that he was born toward the end of the fourth century CE to a Brahmin family in the old Indian kingdom of Magadhi. He was immensely learned in Hinduism; in fact, it was agreed that no one knew the Vedas better than he. He traveled widely, engaging in debates on the highest intellectual levels. It is believed that during one of these debates he was bested by a Buddhist monk named Revata, an expert in the subtle ideas of the Abhidhamma Pitaka and was converted to the religion of the Enlightened One. Buddhaghosa moved to Sri Lanka to study the sacred books held in the Mahavihara (Great Monastery) of Anuradhapura, the principal enclave of Theravada Buddhism.

Buddhaghosa worked his way through the voluminous commentaries on the Tipitaka found in the monastery and requested permission to synthesize the teachings in one volume written in Pali, the language of the early Buddhist texts. To test his abilities the monks invited him to expand the doctrine of dharma based upon a few brief verses, but Buddhaghosa brought in all of the commentaries and composed the Visuddhimagga.

Legends say that the gods destroyed his finished work twice, forcing him to start from the beginning again, but upon finding that each time he produced the identical work, they were forced to acknowledge its veracity and authority.

▲ *Buddhaghosa offering the Visuddhimagga to his superior in the Mahavihara Monastery.*

▲◀ *Moonstone symbolizing the Wheel of samsara that leads to nirvana.*

The Seven Purities

In one of his discourses the Buddha expounded the celebrated parable of the seven purities. They are like a man who travels by cart and needs to make various connections to arrive at his destination. Similarly, if one wished to attain nirvana, one must take various steps, known as the seven purifications. Each one leads to the next.

Buddhaghosa was inspired by this image to explain each stage. One begins with the purification of discipline, that is, rules and austerities that the monk is required to observe. For example, one should wear only three pieces of cloth, eat only once a day and only what is put in his begging bowl, and live in the open air. These practices lead to the purification of concentration (techniques of meditation), and successively, the purification of vision, the purification that consists in freeing oneself of doubt, the purification that allows one to distinguish between true and false, the purification of leading a right life, and finally the ultimate purification of enlightenment, leading to the anteroom of nirvana. These coincide with stages on the Eightfold Path.

▲ *Monk entering a temple of Angkor Tom, Cambodia.*

◀ Group of monks on their weekly shopping expedition.

◀◀ Young monk in Pagan, Burma.

The Five Precepts and the Eightfold Path

▲ Buddhism, like Hinduism, has a deep respect for all sentient beings.

When the Visuddhimagga was completed in CE 430, scholars considered it to be a magnificent compendium of Buddhist ideas. In fact, the author had done little more than bring together (admittedly with remarkable clarity) the principal moral teachings that all practitioners needed to fulfill. This begins with the Five Precepts: cause no harm to living creatures (the reason for Buddhist vegetarianism and pacifism); do not appropriate what does not belong to you (i.e., do not steal); abstain from sexual activity; avoid speaking ill of others, lying and cursing; and do not consume alcohol or other mind-altering substances.

Buddhaghosa's book centers on his exposition of the Buddha's Eightfold Path: the fundamental teaching on the way to eliminate human suffering. The eight steps, which make up an ideal way of life, coincide in large part with the purificatory steps described above:

1. Right view
2. Right thinking
3. Right speech
4. Right conduct
5. Right livelihood
6. Right effort
7. Right mindfulness
8. Right concentration

The first two steps correspond to wisdom, the next three to morality, and the last three to meditation, which will leads to detachment from materiality and the world of the senses, and to the ultimate realization.

Milindapanha

▲ *The ancient Greeks had some awareness of Indian religion because of Alexander's conquests. The Milindapanha consists of a dialogue between Menander, an Indo-Greek monarch, and a Buddhist monk.*

The ancient Greeks had an idealized picture of the exotic Orient. They thought of India as a country of nude wise men. After the conquests of Alexander the Great, who reached as far as the Indus River, the encounter between the two cultures assumed a reality that produced important written testimonies. One of these is the Milindapanha, a Buddhist text written anonymously that recounts a curious dialogue between the Indo-Greek king Menander I (Pali: Milinda) and the monk Nagasena, a faithful follower of the Buddha.

▲◀ A seemingly infinite line of Buddhas in Kek Lok Si, Malaysia.

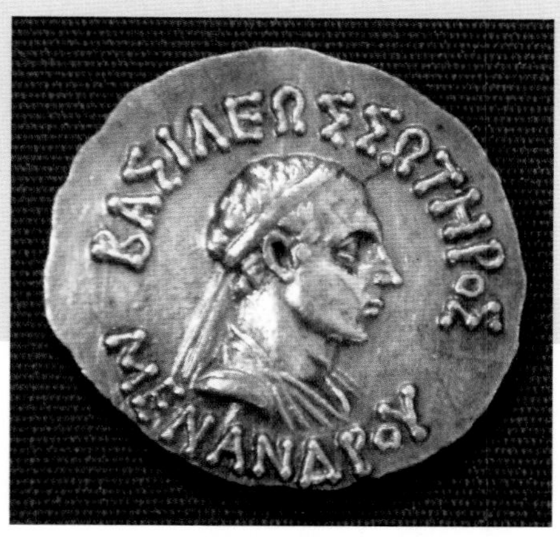

▲ Coin showing the bust of Menander, ruler over the Punjab from 160 to 140 BCE.

Conversation with a King

We do not have any details of the life of Nagasena aside from what is revealed in the Milindapanha, since there is no other mention in Buddhist tradition of a monk of that name. Regarding Menander I, known as Milinda in India, we can say with some assurance that he reigned in the second half of the second century BCE, and that he was one of the heirs of the Asian empire founded by Alexander. He was the ruler of Bactria (present day Pakistan and the Punjab), establishing his capital in Sakala. His reign was long if the coins he minted are any guide, since some depict him as a young man and others in advanced age. He was probably a convert to Buddhism and had a reputation for justice, since Plutarch states that after his death cities fought over the privilege of keeping his ashes, and as with the Buddha, monuments were raised to house these precious relics. In any event he is the only historical figure of India referenced in ancient Greek literature. Regarding his probable conversion, there is little doubt that it was politically advantageous to assume the religion of his indigenous subjects, but it has been suggested that his interest in Buddhism went beyond mere political calculation. Skilled in the art of rhetoric like all educated Greeks of the period, it is certainly plausible that he should engage in a debate with learned Indians, who also were no strangers to philosophical disputation.

▼ Nagasena in a picture from Ratnashri in Malaysia.

> *Fear is born from intimacy, Dust is from a house arisen. Homeless, free from intimacy, This is the sage's vision.*
>
> MILINDAPANHA

▲ *Gandhara Buddha. This style of statuary shows a definite Hellenistic influence.*

Continuity in Change

The setting of the book is the capital of the kingdom: "Sakala, the famous ancient city, where its king Milinda visited Nagasena, the most illustrious wise man in the world." The form of the dialogue does not vary. The king asks the monk a question, and he answers. To understand more fully, the king then asks for an example, and the monk immediately produces numerous examples; the subject of discussion concludes with an explanation. Milinda does not dispute the monk but assents to all of his propositions. At the end of their dialogue the two interlocutors part as friends. Milinda assures Nagasena that he feels like a captive lion who has been given the chance to stretch his neck through the golden bars of his cage to the freedom of the jungle.

The topics of the dialogue include: the reality of the individual, the identity of the personality, the existence of the soul, reincarnation, karma, samsara (the world of illusion), and nirvana. In one of the most famous passages, the king poses the key philosophical question of the concept of reincarnation. "He who is reborn, Nagasena, is he the same person or another?" To which Nagasena responds, "Neither the same nor another." The king asks Nagasena for an explanation and the monk replies, "You were once a child, a tender little thing lying on his back. Are you still that, now

that you've grown?" Milinda replies, "No, I am another." Then the monk says, "If you're not that child, it follows that you have not had a mother or father . . . " The conclusion: "Precisely, O king, thus the continuity of a person or thing is maintained. One is reborn and extinguished simultaneously."

▲ *Buddha displaying a mudra representing the Wheel of Dharma.*

A Non-Canonical Classic

It is not known exactly when the Milindapanha was written. The version that comes down to us is from CE 420 in Chinese, but the original is certainly several centuries older. As a religious text it is one of the best expositions of the essential teachings of Buddhism, but it is not part of the Pali Canon. This fact doesn't diminish its value, but it has hampered its transmission and translation. Not being held in as a high esteem as the canonical works, it has sometimes been passed along by careless or unscrupulous interpreters or copyists who have introduced serious alterations to the original text. Its very popularity has led to plagiarism and arbitrary additions.

As a prose work it is considered a masterpiece of Indian literature for its clear and accessible style, very different from most of the Tipitaka. In its vivid colloquial language and its formal and stylistic characteristics, it suggests Hellenic influence, echoing the Socratic dialogues of Plato.

Mahayana Sutras

▲ *Borobudor in Indonesia was a great Buddhist center. It was built in the ninth century. The site contains more than 2,500 reliefs and 500 statues of the Buddhas, as well as numerous stupas.*

Like Socrates, Confucius, and Jesus, the Buddha did not write down his own teachings. According to the Theravada tradition, after his death his disciple Ananda recited them at the first council at Rajagriha. Accordingly, the sutras always begin with the phrase "*evam me suttam*" (This I heard). Centuries afterward Mahayana Buddhism introduced new sutras that did not figure into the original canon, claiming that they contained more advanced teachings that had to be passed down in secret until there were enough of the faithful with the capacity to understand them. This explains their late appearance.

◀ *The lightning bolt or diamond scepter (vajra) is a common symbol of realization in Mahayana Buddhism.*

▲ *This statue of the Buddha from Hong Kong shows him holding a lotus flower.*

The Great Vehicle

Mahayana Buddhism emerged at the beginning of the Common Era in reaction to the older approach of the Theravada (ancient) school. Its followers considered themselves progressives. They called their movement Mahayana ("The Great Vehicle") and called Theravada Hinayana ("The Little Vehicle"). Mahayana teaching recognizes the validity of the Pali Canon but believes that it is addressed to a less advanced audience. The Mahayana teachings are directed to more spiritually elevated hearers. The Lotus Sutra explains this using the parable of the burning house: Some children are playing in a house that catches fire. Their father wants them to flee, but they are unaware of the fire and are immersed in their play. So the father tells them that their favorite toys are waiting for them outside. The children rush out to find that they have all received the same beautiful toy. Can the father be blamed for deceiving his children about the toys he had promised them? Certainly not. He did it to save their lives. In the same way the Buddha employed tactics (skillful means) to lead his followers to salvation, transmitting truths that were commensurate with their understanding.

Illumination for All

Curiously the principal innovation of Mahayana Buddhism consists in its extending the possibility of illumination to all sentient beings. One does a disservice in classifying the sutras into those written for the people versus those written for the elite. Salvation was no longer

◀ *Early Mahayana relief showing bodhisattvas and a monk at the far right.*

▲ *It is said that Mahayana Buddhism spread throughout Southeast Asia with the help of* nagas*. Representations of these nine-headed serpents can be found on bridges throughout Cambodia.*

considered to be the monk's exclusive domain. Anyone could achieve it. Furthermore, Mahayana presents as its ideal the bodhisattva (a future Buddha), someone who has achieved illumination but chooses not to enter into Nirvana. Rather he decides to remain in the world to help others achieve enlightenment. Thanks to these ideas Mahayana spread rapidly through China, Tibet, Nepal, Vietnam, Korea and Japan.

The numerous Mahayana sutras, some six hundred in all, were written by and large in the early centuries of the Common Era. Followers of the Great Vehicle consider them to have been spoken by the Buddha but transmitted in secret, sometimes with the help of fantastic animals such as *nagas*, who mediate between this world and the next. Among the most important texts are the Lotus Sutra, the Heart Sutra, and the Diamond Sutra. We will be looking more closely at the first two of these in the succeeding pages.

Sarvashura, countless are the rebirths of those sentient beings who misprize the Dharma.

Sanghata Sutra

The Virtues of the Bodhisattva

The Diamond Sutra is the abbreviated form translating Vajracchedika Prajnaparamita-Sutra ("The Diamond Sutra of the Perfection of Transcendent Wisdom"). Its primary theme is the emptiness and ephemeral nature of all phenomena. The diamond, as a precious and coveted jewel, can have a negative sense, symbolizing that which impedes the wisdom that leads to enlightenment. The sutra narrates a dialogue between the Buddha and Subhuti, an old monk, who inquires about the nature of perception. The text is prolix, repetitive, and difficult to understand, but it contains one passage of exceptional clarity. In it Buddha enumerates the virtues of a bodhisattva (generosity, morality, patience, courage, concentration, and wisdom) and affirms that the first of these is the greatest, since the future Buddha will radiate compassion without boundaries or hope of reward, solely to help others along the path.

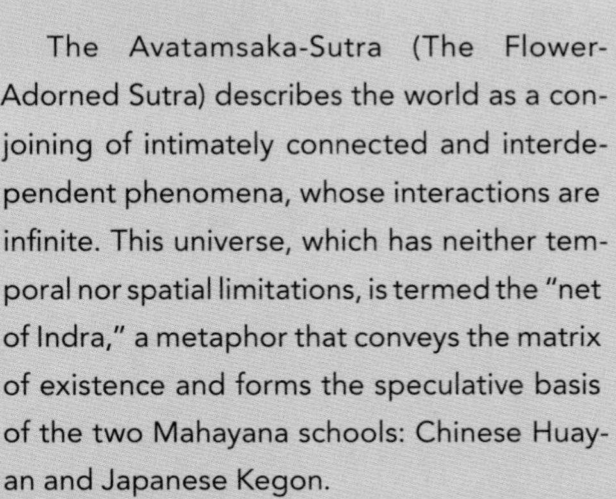

The Avatamsaka-Sutra (The Flower-Adorned Sutra) describes the world as a conjoining of intimately connected and interdependent phenomena, whose interactions are infinite. This universe, which has neither temporal nor spatial limitations, is termed the "net of Indra," a metaphor that conveys the matrix of existence and forms the speculative basis of the two Mahayana schools: Chinese Huayan and Japanese Kegon.

▶ Mahayana Buddhism

The Lotus Sutra

▶ Thangka *on paper. This painting represents White Tara, one of the twenty-one forms of Tara, daughter of Avalokitesvara.*

The lotus flower, symbol of the Buddhist monk, is considered in India to be the most beautiful flower. It is rooted in dark mucky ponds, and yet its blooms are pure and perfect, and its petals spread immaculately in the sun. This is an apt metaphor for the essential message of the Lotus Sutra: although humans live in a painful reality, filled with lies and darkness, they can pass through it without becoming corrupted and reach a state of spiritual freedom.

> *For those who have not gained deliverance, I will deliver them.*
>
> The Lotus Sutra

This I Have Heard

Among the Mahayana sutras written in Sanskrit, the Saddharm Pundarika-Sutra holds a decisive importance. Its full title can be translated as "The Sutra on the White Lotus of Sublime Dharma." It is believed to have been composed in the second century of the Common Era, a considerable time after the Buddha's death, and versions in Chinese and Japanese appeared many centuries later. Its success was such that it soon became the fundamental text of many different currents of Buddhist thought, such as Tientai in China and Tendai and Nichiren in Japan. These sects saw the totality of Buddhist ideas concentrated in its pages.

As with many other great Buddhist sutras, it begins with the words: "This I have heard." It continues with an extraordinary gathering of tens of thousands of disciples, bodhisattvas, celestial beings, warrior gods, and human and nonhuman witnesses, all of whom have gathered in the city of Rajagrha to listen to the Buddha's discourse. While the assembled multitude contemplate the Enlightened One, a series of prodigies take place. Flowers fall from heaven, the earth trembles, and a column of light is projected from the Buddha's forehead that "illuminated all the eighteen thousand worlds in the east, down as far as the lowest hell." All of these signs confirmed the extraordinary power of the sutra's teachings.

▼ *Reclining Buddha made of granite in a temple in Xinchang, Zhejiang Province, China.*

▲ Guanyin, the bodhisattva embodying compassion, is the Chinese form of Avalokitesvara. In Tibet the figure is masculine, while in China she adopts a feminine form.

▲▶ White pagodas in Xining, China.

A Revolutionary Message

What the sutra teaches was not only innovative, but in many ways contradicted many earlier sutras. These generally held that there were three paths to enlightenment: the path of those who "have heard the voice" (i.e., disciples), those who "have understood" (advanced disciples who seek enlightenment for their own benefit), and bodhisattvas. This recognizes that there are different levels of the ability to understand and learn. However, here the Buddha teaches that there is only one path to Buddhahood, and it is open to all. This is the radical message of the Lotus Sutra.

To illustrate the point, the Buddha offered the example of Devadatta, his first enemy, who tried to supplant him and hatched a plan to kill him, but afterwards achieved enlightenment. The sutra also claims that the way is open to women. The story of the dragon princess is cited. She is told that she can attain enlightenment immediately. In fact any individual can reach the supreme state, provided he or she believes in the Lotus Sutra. Or to put it another way, if you have faith in the possibility, the possibility will be transformed into a certainty.

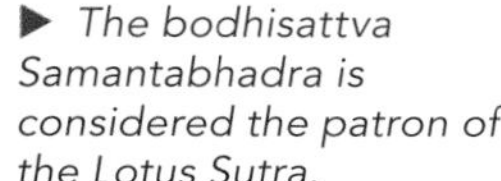

▶ The bodhisattva Samantabhadra is considered the patron of the Lotus Sutra.

An Airborne Assembly

Marvelous and paradoxical phenomena appear throughout the twenty-eight chapters of the Lotus Sutra. An enormous seven-jeweled stupa surges from the ground. The Buddha Shakyamuni rises into the air and enters the stupa, and then elevates all of those gathered to hear his words. Some now ask who will propagate the sutra after the demise of the Enlightened One, and how they ought to proceed. The answer of the master is at once precise and ironic. Each of those present will be responsible, and he instructs them how they can do this, offering six difficult tasks and nine easy ones. The six difficult tasks are as follows: to spread the sutra; to copy it or have others copy it; to recite it even if in brief; to teach it, even if only to one person; to listen and accept it and inquire into its meaning; and to maintain faith in the sutra. All of this looks simple. The congregation asks if these are the difficult tasks, what are the easy ones. The Buddha very cleverly responds with a series of impossible tasks (to move a mountain, to shake loose the manifold cosmos, to grasp empty space and wander around with it, among others). All these are easy. What will be difficult will be to believe in the Lotus Sutra in the turbulent times that will follow after the Buddha enters Nirvana and leaves the world.

The Heart Sutra

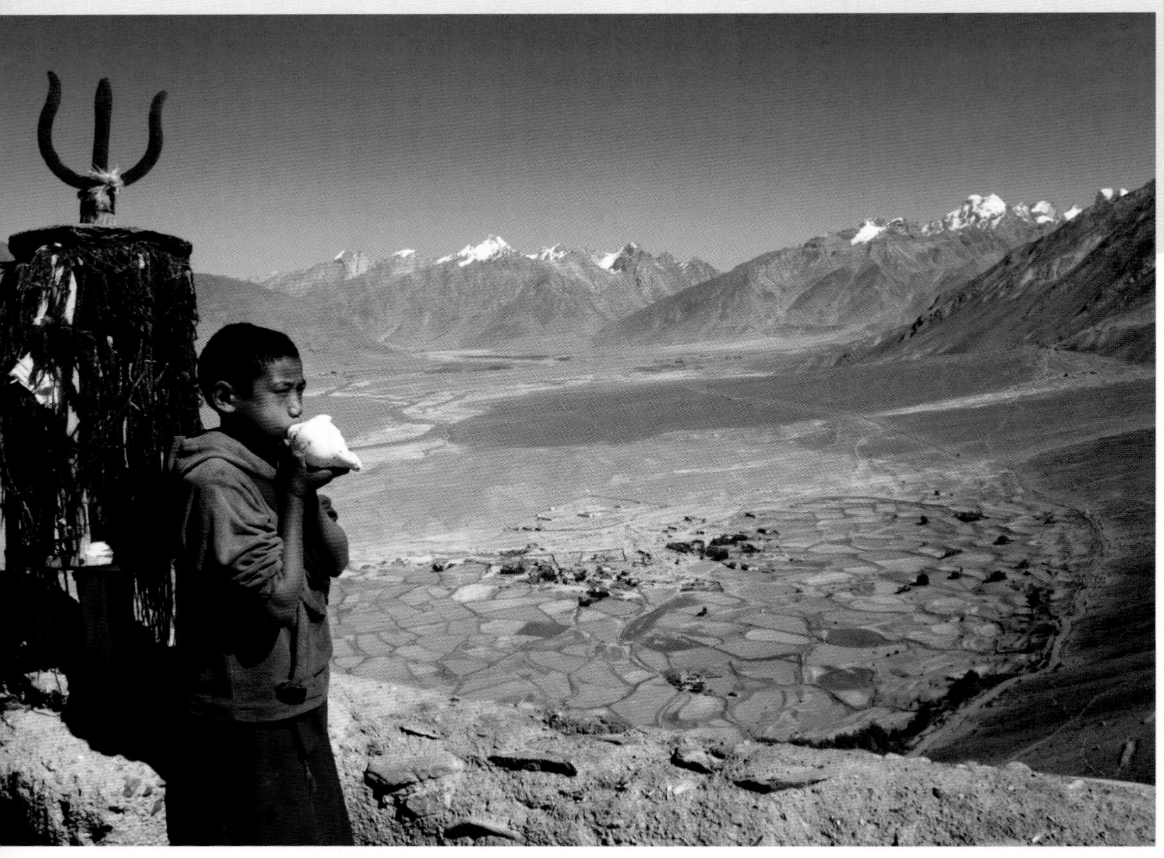

▲ *A young monk in a valley in Tibet. Vajrayana or Tantric Buddhism developed in the Himalayas.*

Of all religions one can say that Buddhism is the only one that offers a lucid critique of itself. It arrives at the point on the road to enlightenment at which the religion per se needs to be left behind. The Heart Sutra tells us that doctrine, writings, meditation and rituals are necessary for a time, but then one must transcend all of these limitations to achieve the "perfection of wisdom." And at its conclusion it offers us a mantra that conveys the essential message of the sutra.

The Greatest Wisdom

Just as with the Diamond Sutra, the Heart Sutra belongs to the *prajnaparamita* (Perfection of Wisdom) literature. It is here that the Mahayana reaches its ultimate profundity, although the subtlety of the teaching can seem almost impenetrable. The book is remarkable for its antiquity, its profundity, and its length, since the Sanskrit version with its fourteen verses of 280 words is one of the shortest of all sutras. (Some sutras contain more than 100,000 verses.)

Its title, Hridaya Sutra in Sanskrit, reflects that it is the heart or essence of *prajnaparamita*, since it transmits in an extremely condensed form the fundamental significance of all the texts that this rubric comprises. It is hardly surprising that this text is recited in all those countries in which the Mahayana Buddhism is the dominant form, since in a sense it conveys the entirety of this tradition.

▲ *Prayer flags in Hong Kong.*

▲▲ *Prayer wheel used in the devotions of Tibetan Buddhists.*

▲◀ *Tibetan monk shown with prayer wheels.*

Emptiness

The Heart Sutra is a dialogue between the bodhisattva Avalokitesvara (Lord who looks down upon the world) and Sariputra, one of the Buddha's main disciples. The latter represents the limited wisdom of the Lesser Vehicle (Hinayana), while the former embodies the higher wisdom of the Greater Vehicle (Mahayana) and sweeps away the

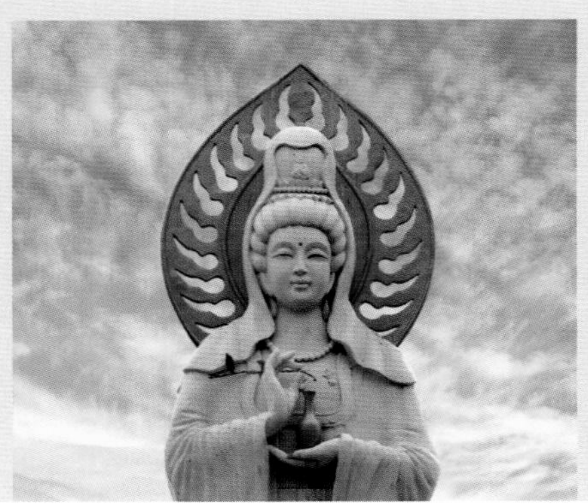

◀ *Statue of Avalokitesvara emphasizing feminine qualities of compassion.*

▲ *Monk of the Gelugpa sect of Tibetan Buddhism.*

doubts and hesitations of his interlocutor. To begin with, Avalokitesvara declares the emptiness of all phenomena, including the five *skandhas* (aggregates) that form each being (body, senses, ideas, will and consciousness), as well as the philosophy of the religion itself. "There is no ignorance, no extinction of ignorance … There is no decay and death, no extinction of decay and death. There is no suffering, no origination, no stopping, no path. There is no cognition, no attainment and no non-attainment." The emptiness (*sunyata*) to which Avalokitesvara refers does not mean that phenomena do not exist; however, they lack any fixed, unchanging or substantial character. Phenomena do not contain the essential attribute of being.

In other words, if we wish to attain perfect wisdom, we need to abandon Buddhism, since the religion is a vehicle that can convey us only so far. In this regard, the Heart Sutra demonstrates its connections to Zen, which seeks detachment from traditional religious forms. Accordingly, when the student asks the Zen master, "What should I do if I meet the Buddha along the path?," his brusque reply is, "Kill him." In this way he tells the student that religion is simply a means to an end, and that one should not mistake one for the other.

> *Hear O Sariputra, form is emptiness, and the very emptiness is form.*
>
> HEART SUTRA

The Final Mantra

The Heart Sutra ends with the mantra of the "perfection of wisdom," closing the circle of complete awareness. In the same way as the sutra condenses the prajnaparamita literature, so does the mantra condense the teaching of the sutra. It goes as follows: Gate gate paragate parasamgate Bodhi svaha.

The simple translation does not convey its full significance: "Gone, gone, gone beyond, gone altogether beyond, O what an awakening, all hail." But it is possible to decipher its transcendent meaning. This audible, quasi-magical formula, proposes that one must pass over the world of phenomena as we know it, to go beyond the dualities that theology insists upon (for example, between nirvana and samsara) and religious dogma, including the concept of emptiness. One must leave behind everything that is commonly considered "reality," whether material or immaterial, and dive into Buddhahood, the ultimate awareness. Only then, when one has awakened to the light, when one becomes Buddha, will one be blessed with all favor.

This supreme wisdom, concentrated in a phrase of six words, is chanted constantly in Zen ceremonies in China, Japan, Korea and Vietnam, to liberate the faithful from the weight of the sacred and usher them into the heights of omniscience.

▲ *Zen sand and rock garden.*

Infinite Life Sutra

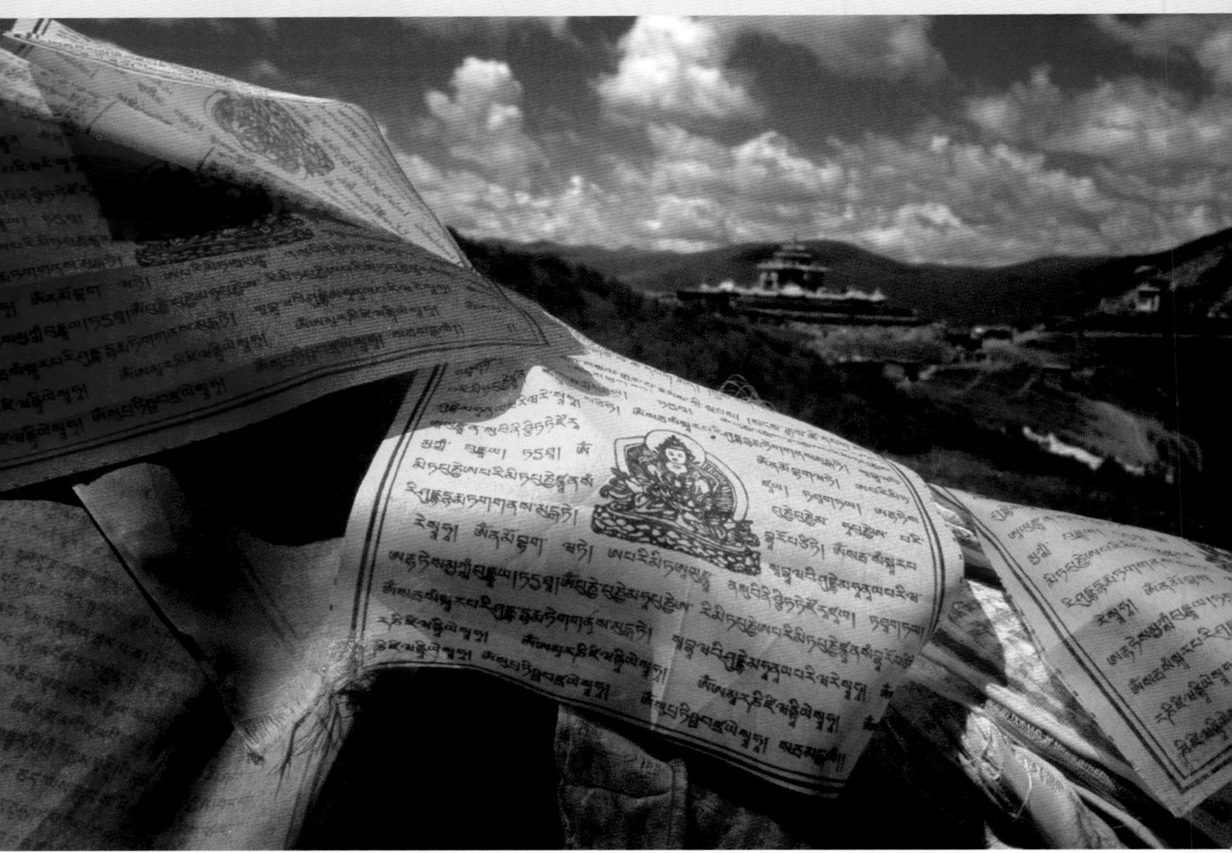

▲ *Amitabha (Japanese: Amida) is well known in places where Tibetan Buddhism is practiced. It is believed that the Panchen and Shamarpa lamas are his reincarnations.*

▶ *This statue of Amida Buddha in Kamakura, Japan, radiates tranquility.*

Eons ago there lived a monk named Dharmakara who took a vow to achieve illumination and create a marvelous world for all who invoked him with complete confidence, so that they could enjoy a blissful existence before entering into nirvana. Dharmakara attained his goal and was transformed into the Buddha Amitabha. He created Sukhavati ("Land of Bliss"), where no hint of suffering exists. This accomplishment is recounted in the Infinite Life Sutra, the fundamental scripture of the Pure Land tradition of Buddhism.

> *There are as many Buddhas as there are grains of sand in the Ganges.*
>
> Amitabha Sutra

◀ *Amida Buddha.*

All Can Enter Paradise

The devotion to Amitabha ("Infinite Light"), also known as Amitayus ("Infinite Life"), was born in India. However, it flourished in China where it was adopted by adepts in Mahayana Buddhism, and there the Pure Land school developed. According to the proponents of this teaching, salvation is not to be achieved by one's own efforts, but through the grace of Amitabha. One needs to recite his name wholeheartedly, and conduct oneself with a quantum of morality in order to be reborn into his paradise.

From China the cult traveled to Japan, where it became identified with the Jodo school. The Japanese contributed their own twist on the doctrine, asserting that only faith, not works, guarantees salvation. It is only through the compassion of Amida (the Japanese form of Amitabha) that one can attain nirvana. It follows that sinners have a better chance of illumination than the just, since owing to their lack of spirituality, they will offer less resistance to Amida's redemptive power. Shinran, one of the Japanese masters of Pure Land, observed: "The good can get to paradise, but even more so the wicked."

When I Become Buddha

The Infinite Life Sutra (Sukhavati Vyuha Sutra, literally "The Great Sutra of the Ornaments of the Land of Bliss") begins with a dialogue between Shakyamuni and his disciple Ananda, who asks him about past, present and future Buddhas. The Enlightened One responds that there have been and will be others like himself, and relates the history of Dharma kara ("Treasure of Doctrine"), who upon seeing the resplendent face of Lokesvararaja Buddha ("Sovereign of the World") vowed that he would attain Buddhahood, "practicing with diligence all the virtues of the Bodhisattvas: generosity, good conduct, patience, energy, contemplation, and wisdom."

▲ *The Bayon temple in Angkor was built during the reign of the Mahayana Buddhist king Jayavarman VII.*

▲▶ *Buddhist monk in Angkor. For many years Buddhist monks were the only inhabitants of the ruins of this great city that was being swallowed up by the jungle.*

His ultimate goal was to create a miraculous world where happiness reigns, that is, Sukhavati: "When I become a Buddha, my land shall be most exquisite, and all its people wonderful and unexcelled; the seat of Enlightenment shall be supreme… Those who come from the ten quarters shall find joy and serenity of heart; when they reach my land they shall dwell in peace and happiness." His devotees believe that his dream has become a reality. "The monk Dharmakara achieved incomparable illumination and became a perfect Buddha. From then on his name became Amida. His light extends in all directions and knows no obstructions. It is impossible to calculate the duration of his life, since it has been prolonged indefinitely out of his compassion for all sentient beings."

▶ *Two young monks from a monastery in Ladakh, India.*

Next Stop, Nirvana

The Pure Land of Amida, also called the Western Paradise, is seen as proximate to Nirvana, and the sutra describes it in great detail. It is ornamented with seven buildings covered in precious stones and avenues of wish-granting trees populated by rare species of birds. In crystalline lakes float lotus blossoms. It is a kind of Eden for those fortunate to be reborn there. The major virtue of those happy beings was to have repeatedly invoked the name of Amida, to the exclusion of all other disciplines or personal striving. Now they too become bodhisattvas, and their supreme happiness consists in hearing the *dharma* from the lips of Amida himself, who resides in the center of Sukhavati.

Thanks to the intervention of Amida there is no need to accumulate merit or practice asceticism over the course of thousands of rebirths. All one needs to do is continually chant the formula "Homage to Amida Buddha," and one will achieve a penultimate rebirth in Sukhavati. "Those reborn in my pure land will only be reincarnated one more time, to experience the supreme state of Buddhahood, unless they decide to return to the world out of compassion for other beings." It is no wonder that the Pure Land school is extremely popular, since it is not interested in complex or subtle doctrine, nor does it present the road to enlightenment as an interminable obstacle course.

▲ *The Great Buddha of Kamakura is a monumental bronze statue of Amida Buddha. It is forty feet high. The Buddha's hands display the* dhyani *mudra, symbol of meditation.*

▶ Tibetan Buddhism

Bardo Thodol

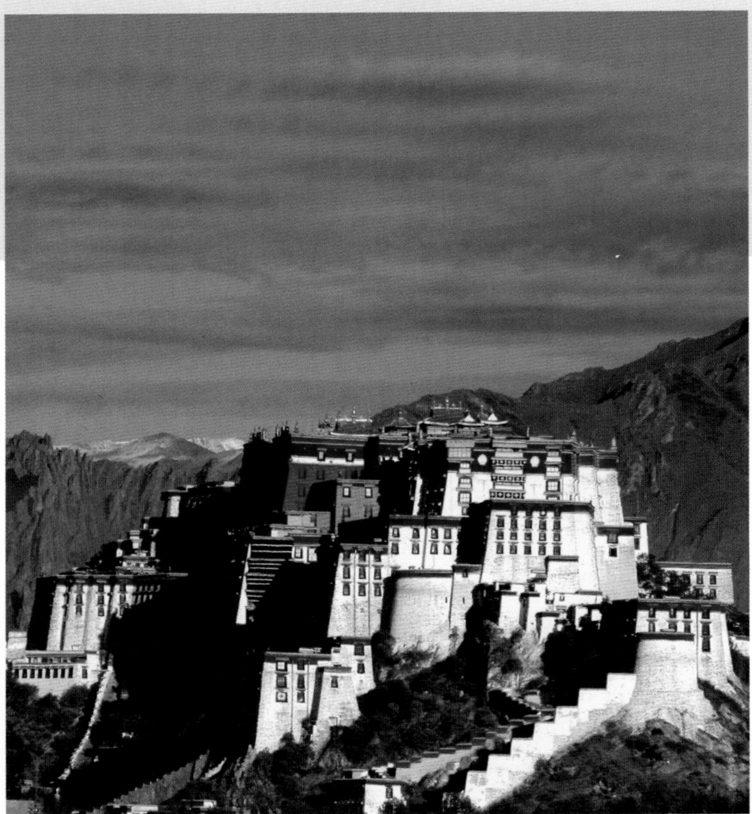

▶ *Potala Palace in Lhasa, capital of Tibet.*

▼ *Tibetan prayer wheels.*

The Bardo Thodol, also known as Tibetan Book of the Dead, is a handbook that Tibetan lamas utilize for fulfilling funeral rites. Its pages describe the perceptions of the dead during the period between rebirths. This lasts between twenty and forty-nine days. The study of the Bardo Thodol serves as a preparation for death, and if a lama recites it to the believer during his final hours, or immediately after death, it can help him to escape from the cycle of reincarnation, or at the very least assure him of an auspicious rebirth.

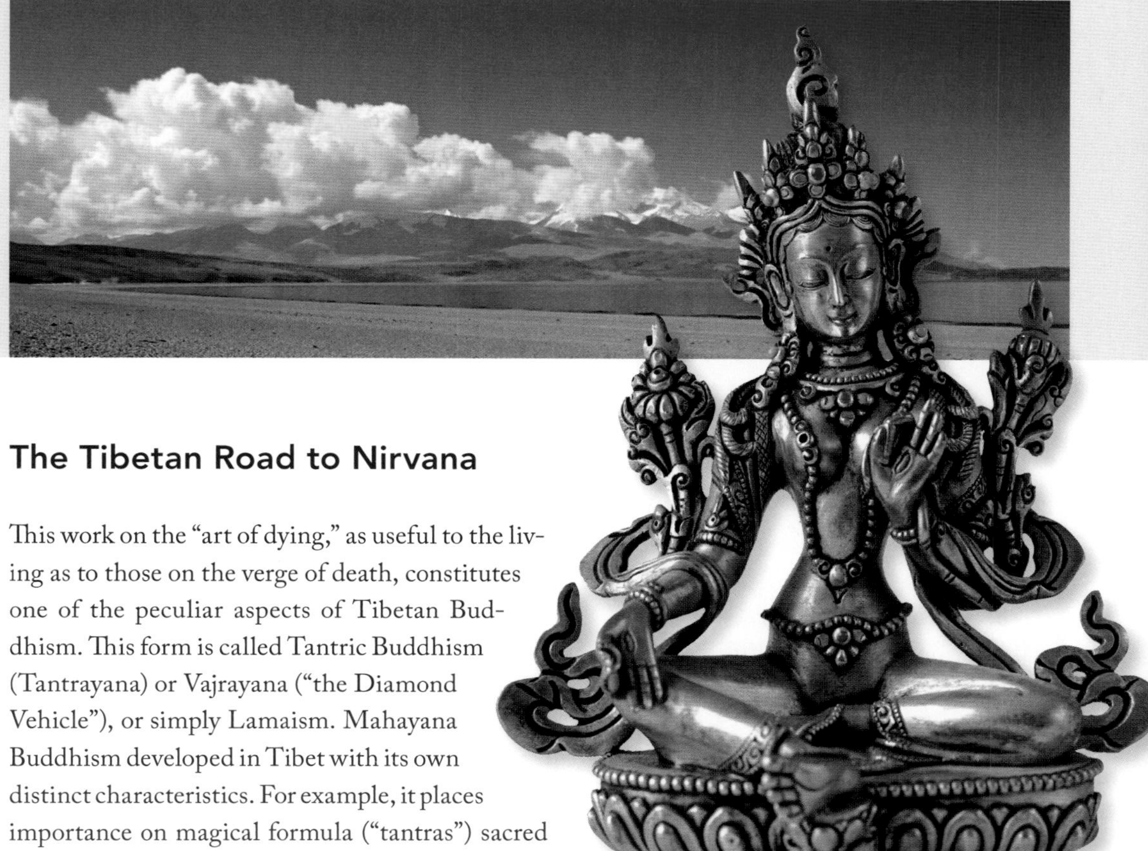

The Tibetan Road to Nirvana

This work on the "art of dying," as useful to the living as to those on the verge of death, constitutes one of the peculiar aspects of Tibetan Buddhism. This form is called Tantric Buddhism (Tantrayana) or Vajrayana ("the Diamond Vehicle"), or simply Lamaism. Mahayana Buddhism developed in Tibet with its own distinct characteristics. For example, it places importance on magical formula ("tantras") sacred phrases ("mantras"), mystical diagrams ("mandalas") and ritual gestures ("mudras").

Buddhism flourished in Tibet thanks to eminent religious teachers from India, such as Padmasambhava, who is considered to be the founder of Lamaism. This great sage, sometimes referred to as Guru Rinpoche, lived in the seventh century of the Common Era. It is believed that he was born from a lotus flower. He was invited to the Land of the Snows to combat the demons that were impeding the spread of the Buddha's message. Thanks to his efforts, many Tibetan monks traveled to India to learn Sanskrit and translate the principle tantras, which convey the essence of Tantric Buddhism. The Tibetan tradition believes that one must combine the Buddhist sutras with the tantras to reach enlightenment.

▲ *The Tantric Buddhist deity Tara represents compassion and liberation.*

▲◀ *Lake Rakshas along with Lake Manasarovar adjoins Mount Kailas. Rakshas represents the dark side of the psyche, while Manasarovar represents the light.*

◀ Mount Kailas is considered holy by Buddhists. It was the home of Demchok, the Buddha of happiness.

▶▶ Portable prayer wheels that Buddhist pilgrims carry, turning them as part of their prayers and chanting.

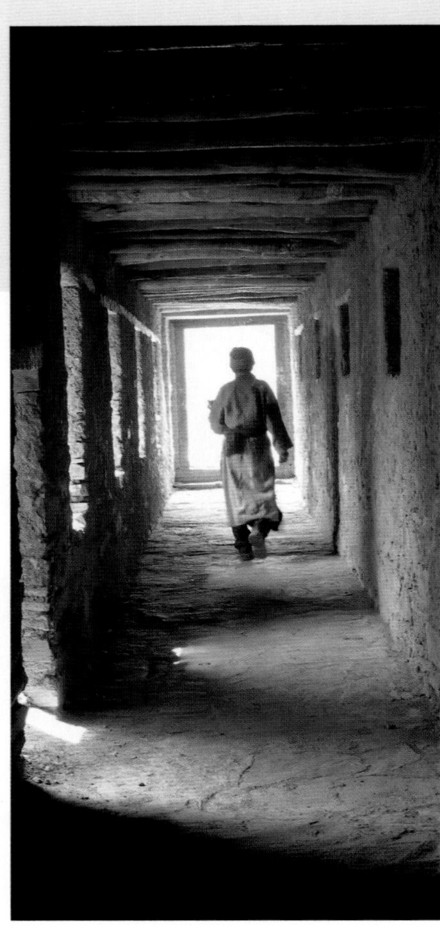

▲ Buddhist pilgrim in Ladakh, India.

A Lost and Found Treasure

Tibetan Buddhism preserves the words of the Enlightened One in extensive collections: the Kanjur, which roughly coincides with the three baskets of the Tipitaka, and the Tanjur, extra-canonical texts from the Hindu tradition. These treatises make up hundreds of fat volumes and are of great religious significance. But there are some to which the lamas are especially devoted. The most celebrated among these, and most widely read in the West, is the Bardo Thodol.

The Bardo Thodol is attributed to Padmasambhava. It was hidden for several centuries to preserve it from destruction when the cruel and impious King Land Darma banned all Buddhist practices from his kingdom. The Bardo Thodol was from then on referred to as a *terma* ("treasure"). It was later recovered by Lamaist spiritual masters called *terton* ("discoverers of the hidden treasure").

The work's title is composed of *bardo* ("intermediate state"), *tho* ("to hear") and *dol* ("liberation"), so it can be translated as "Liberation through hearing in the intermediate state." Effectively, hearing and remembering the text recited will free the dying from the necessity of continuing reincarnation.

Encounter this penetrating vision as a mother who is reunited with her son.

BARDO THODOL

Stages Of Transit

The Bardo Thodol explains the mysterious crossing of the solitary soul after death. When separated from the body, it is abandoned to itself and exists like a feather blown in the wind. Tibetan Buddhists believe that its wandering lasts not less than twenty and no more than forty-nine days. Mourners observe that period with prayers, rituals, and offerings.

What does the soul see on this hallucinatory journey? In the first phase or stage of transit following death, *chikhai bardo*, a brilliant light appears. For a person of highly developed spirituality, this provides the opportunity to escape from the cycle of rebirth and enter into Nirvana. Otherwise, one is totally lost for seven days until the next phase commences. The lamas call this stage *chonyid bardo*, the experience of reality. The soul awakens before a mandala of forty-two peaceful deities. That is then replaced by another mandala consisting of fifty-eight terrifying deities. If the soul is capable of realizing that these differences simply reflect different forms of awareness, it can follow its own path and prepare for an auspicious rebirth.

Then comes the stage of rebirth, *sidpa bardo*, during which the soul acquires a mental body endowed with the five senses. Here he or she is tested by Yama, the god of the dead. Finally comes the moment of reincarnation, although there is one last chance for the soul not to return to samsara. This is termed "closing of the door of the womb," which prevents the soul from materializing in one of six possible states: god, lesser god, human being, animal, hungry ghost, or damned soul.

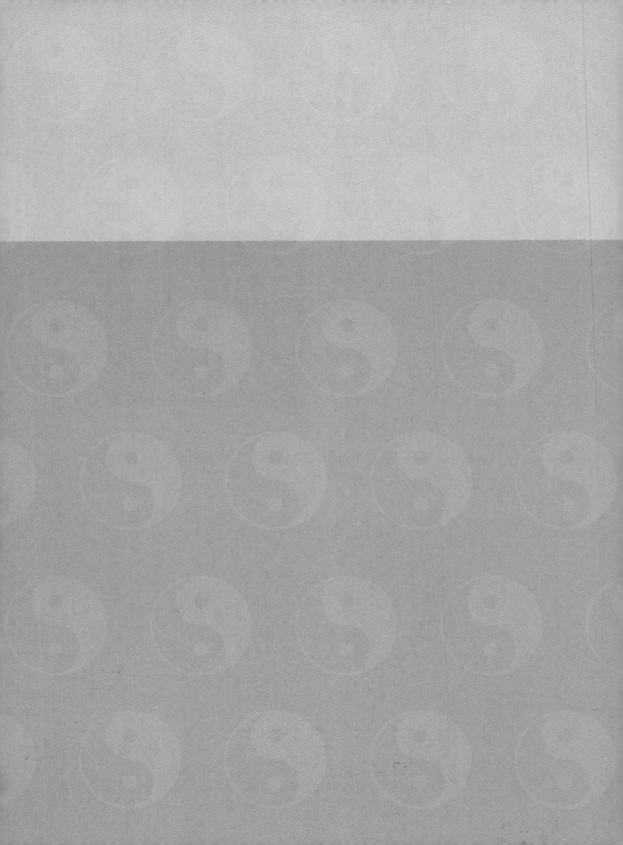

Confucianism, Taoism, and Shinto

氣備四時與天地鬼神日月合其德
教垂萬世繼堯舜禹湯文武作之師

▶ Confucianism

The Five Classics

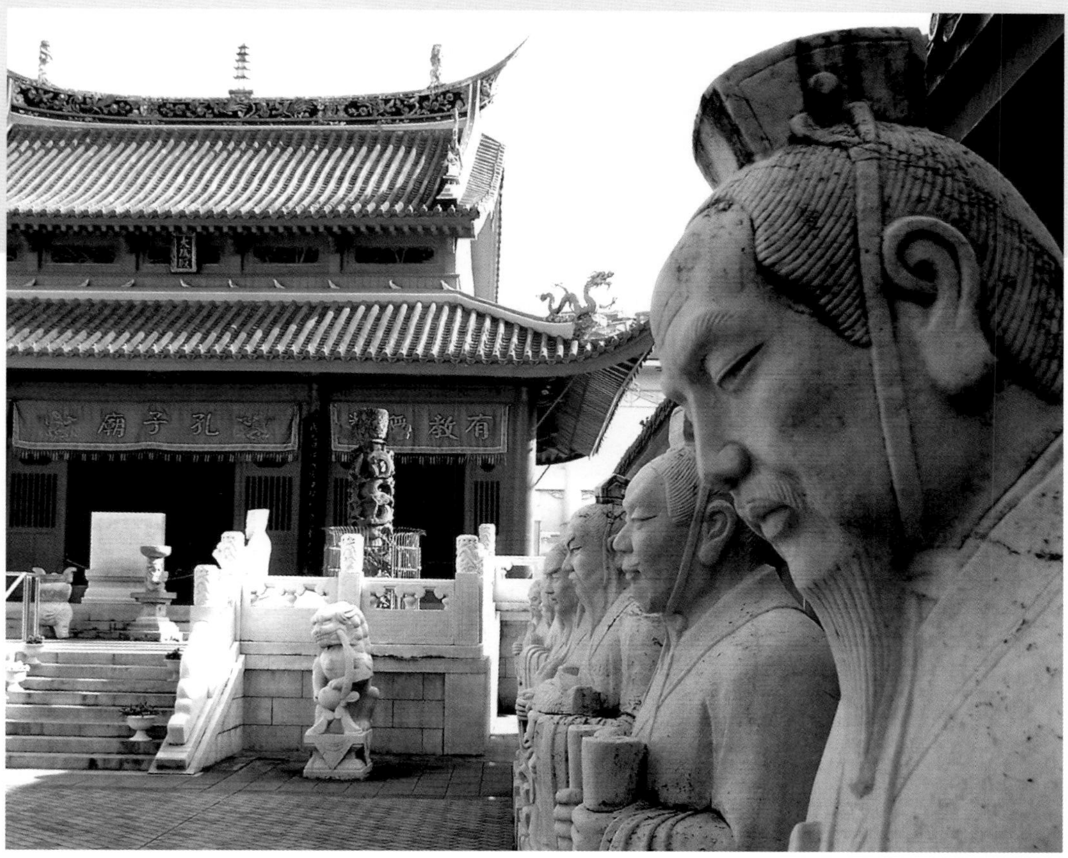

▲ *Statue of Confucius in front of Japanese Temple, along with other figures.*

◀ *Engraving of Confucius.*

The great Chinese sage Confucius never intended to found a religion. His main objective was to restore the traditional virtues of the past, when the sovereigns behaved as superior men. To do this he compiled and anthologized old documents. "I transmit; I do not invent. I love and seek to spread what is longstanding." These collections make up the Confucian canon called the Five Classics. These books were revered in China for centuries until the fall of the last Chinese emperor in 1911.

▲ *In 213 BCE the Emperor Qin Shi Huang ordered the writings of Confucius to be burned.*

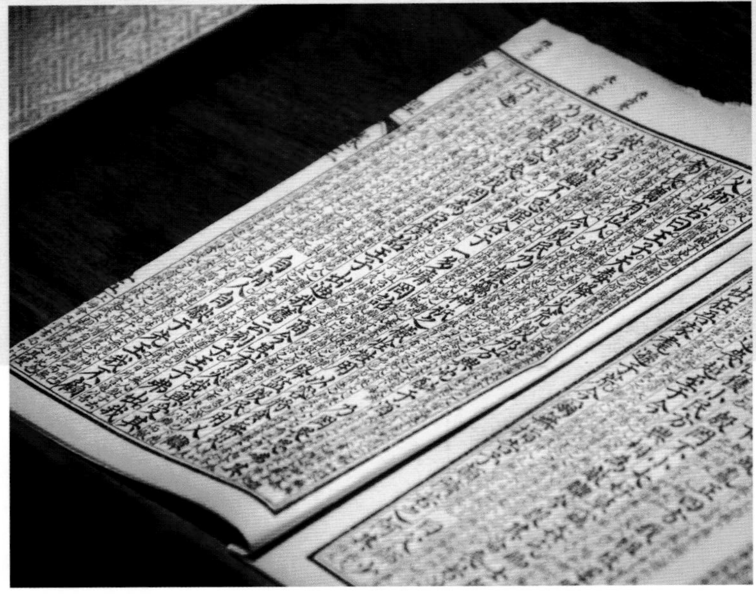

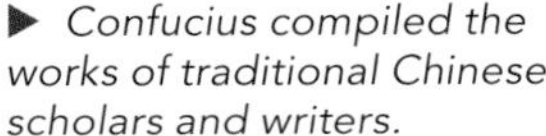

▶ *Confucius compiled the works of traditional Chinese scholars and writers.*

Return to the Old Ways

The contents of the Five Classics (Wujing), which were created long before the lifetime of Confucius, constitute the oldest literary work of China. There are five books: the Classic of History (Shujing), the Classic of Poetry (Shijing), the Classic of Rites (Liji), the Classic of Changes or the Book of Changes (I Ching), and the Annals of Spring and Autumn (Chunqiu). Together they constitute a library of knowledge about ancient Chinese customs that Confucius deemed worthy to pass on for the edification of his contemporaries.

▲ *Door knocker from a Confucian temple in Shanghai.*

The first of these works, the Classic of History, contains a series of selections gathered from the dusty archives of the Zhou Dynasty, which held power starting in the year 1122 BCE. Confucius used them in teaching his disciples. Its pages summarize two millennia of Chinese history, starting from the philosophical and political antecedents of the Zhou Dynasty and proceeding back to the time of the earliest mythical rulers of the state. Along the way they touch on a wide range of subjects such as geographical data and descriptions of canal construction, albeit in an uneven and spotty manner.

A knight eats without filling his belly.

SHUJING I, 14

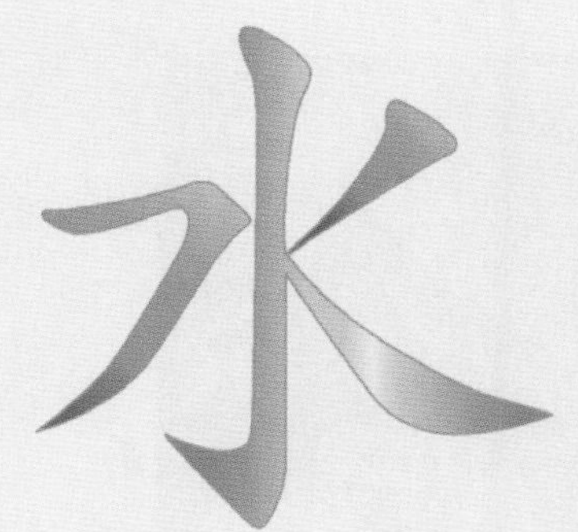

Book Burning

In 213 BCE, centuries after the death of Confucius, the emperor Qin Shi Huang ordered that all ancient texts, especially those of the Confucian school, be destroyed, charging that they taught the past to discredit the present. The Shujing was consigned to the flames, as were many other books of ancient wisdom that were considered dangerous. In fact, at one time there were six, not five classics. The text dedicated to music (Yuejing) disappeared in the fire.

A few years later when a new dynasty, the Han, seized the throne, an attempt was made to remedy this catastrophe. The new ruler sent out investigators through the whole country to look for copies of the lost works. In the case of the Shujing, an old scholar named Fu Sheng set down from memory twenty-eight chapters of the book, and that was all that survived. Later on, however, an incomplete copy was found in the walls of Confucius' house, and over time other fragments turned up, which were carefully pieced together with the existing material. In the end the entire volume was reconstructed, and the emperor in his frenzied attempt to destroy China's literary heritage suffered a posthumous defeat.

▲ *The teachings of Confucius came back into favor when the Han Dynasty assumed power in 206 BCE.*

PHILOSOPHORUM SINENSIUM
PRINCIPIS
CONFUCII
VITA

▲ *Confucian temple in Tai'an, Shandong, China.*

▲▶ *Title page from* Principis Confucii *(Life and Works of Confucius) by Prospero Intorcetta, 1687.*

▼ *Confucian temple in the traditional style.*

Poetry and Rites

Fortunately this kind of effort was not necessary for the second of the Five Classics, Shijing, which has poetry as its subject. Originally there were as many as three thousand compositions, some written as long ago as the eighteenth century BCE. From these Confucius chose 305, which are preserved intact. Most of the poetry was written to be recited, some with musical accompaniment. Courtesans would sing these at banquets, and they would figure in festivals held in the home and military celebrations. Some are exquisite, simple poems that express with

▶ Representation of Confucius with the Chinese characters for the Five Classics.

admirable brevity some easily recognized human emotion:

The willow tree is full of leaves at
the East Gate
An appointment at sunset
The stars shine brightly.

The third classic, the Liji, is dedicated to cultic practices and provides valuable information about ancient Chinese customs, morals, institutions and education. It was drawn from codes that were in force in the feudal states of the Zhou Dynasty. The rites discussed deal with private and public conduct and the relationships between fathers and sons, rulers and subjects, and older and younger brothers. "The ruler should behave as a ruler, the minister as a minister, the father as a father, and the son as a son." For Confucius it was vitally important that each member of society fulfill his proper role. Fathers should educate their children to become good citizens; children should honor their progenitors; kings should treat their ministers fairly; subjects should remain loyal to their sovereign, and so on. Only collective observance of such norms, which seemed to have been forgotten in the period in which Confucius lived, could guarantee lasting social justice and order. The other two books in the Five Classics are the famous I Ching and the Annals of Spring and Autumn, which we turn to now.

▲ Confucius taught that harmony would exist when everyone fulfills his proper place with honor and ethical behavior.

I Ching

▲ *Entrance to a Chinese garden.*

▲▶ *Three gold coins. These can be used for consulting the I Ching.*

The I Ching is a truly mysterious and, according to some, incomprehensible book. It is not the work of a single author, or of one time period, but the result of very ancient traditions. It sees human fortune for good or ill as inextricably linked to natural phenomena, and for that reason by understanding the laws governing nature, one can prognosticate over human affairs. In the West there have been attempts to translate and interpret the oracular text, inspired by a romanticized orientalism. The results, however, distort its significance. One ends up with esoteric rigmarole.

▲ *Nuwa and Fu-Hi, two of the three mythical sovereigns who created mankind.*

Change Is the Only Constant

The I Ching had a long gestation period. It seems that the initial nucleus of the work dates from the epoch of the mythical emperor Fuxi, who lived around 2400 BCE. It was later completed by a king named Wen and his son, the Duke of Zhou, around the year 1100 BCE. Finally Confucius and his disciples added commentary, known as the Ten Wings, which are usually published at the end of the book. Although it is said that the I Ching is solely an arcane exposition of Confucian ethics and is one of the Five Classics, the work owes much to Taoist thought. For example, its conception of the world and its evolution is very similar to that expressed by Lao Tzu in the Tao Te Ching.

The title I Ching can be literally translated as the "Book of Changes." It includes the Chinese character "I", which can arguably denominate a species of chameleon (an animal that adapts its color to its environment). This implies three apparently incompatible ideas: change (since natural and human affairs are continually in the process of transformation), immutability (since these changes have fixed rules), and simplicity (since the rules are not complex). The book considers change to be the only reality, with form and matter manifestations of something more profound.

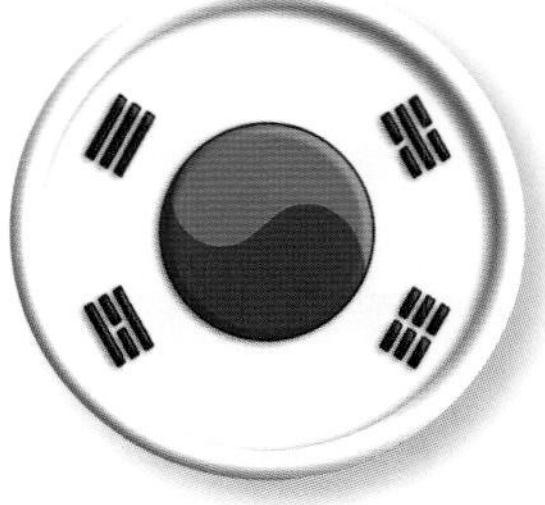

▲ *Korean symbol from the Olympic Games based upon the country's national flag. In the center is the yin-yang symbol surrounded by the trigrams for air, water, earth and fire (clockwise starting at the upper left).*

Yin and Yang

What is the constant principle that fills the universe? According to Chinese philosophy all phenomena consist of two opposing and com-

Advancing and retreating, the righteous persistence of warriors brings advantage.

I Ching, Hexagram 57

▲ *The yin-yang symbol surrounded by the eight trigrams in the colors of water and fire.*

plementary forces, yin and yang, which reveal themselves successively or simultaneously. Yin is the feminine pole: receptive and negative. Yang is the masculine pole: active and positive. If one divides nature into yin and yang, the earth, moon and darkness are yin; the sky, sun and light are yang. With respect to time, autumn, winter and night are yin. Spring, summer and daytime are yang. With respect to humanity, the son, subject and wife are yin. The father, ruler and husband are yang.

The I Ching presupposes that change is a dialectical relationship between yin and yang. Every situation is dominated by one or the other with the complementary force governing the state into which it will change. As changes succeed one another in a cyclical and predictable manner, much like the seasons of the year, divination can help us live harmoniously with these changes and avoid misfortune.

◀ *Fuxi in a drawing by the painter Ma Lin.*

◀◀ *Traditionally the oracle is read with stalks from the yarrow plant.*

Trigrams and Hexagrams

"Study the past to predict the future," said Confucius. To accomplish this, the sages and seers who created the I Ching included in its text a method of divination that has been practiced for more than three thousand years in the court of China and among its educated class. The method entails throwing yarrow stalks upon a flat surface (sometimes coins are used in their place) to form a diagram of two sets of three lines (trigrams), one placed over the other. The lines can be unbroken (symbolizing yang) or broken (symbolizing yin).

Each trigram provides a quality, an image and a place in the social order. For example, the trigram of three unbroken lines (qian, "the creative") indicates the quality of strength, the image of heaven and the family figure of father. According to the configuration of the thrown yarrow stalks, each trigram is combined with another. In this way one of sixty-four possible hexagrams (six-lined figures) is formed. Each hexagram has its own meaning.

When the interpreter is competent, the result of the reading will be a picture of the present state of the inquirer and a possible future scenario. The key to interpretation is the ability to deduce the dynamic forces hidden behind appearances and the orientation toward more or less resistance to the changes that will occur. To predict the possible future effects of actions may appear to be a magical operation, but the authors of the I Ching considered it an entirely reasonable undertaking.

Annals of Spring and Autumn

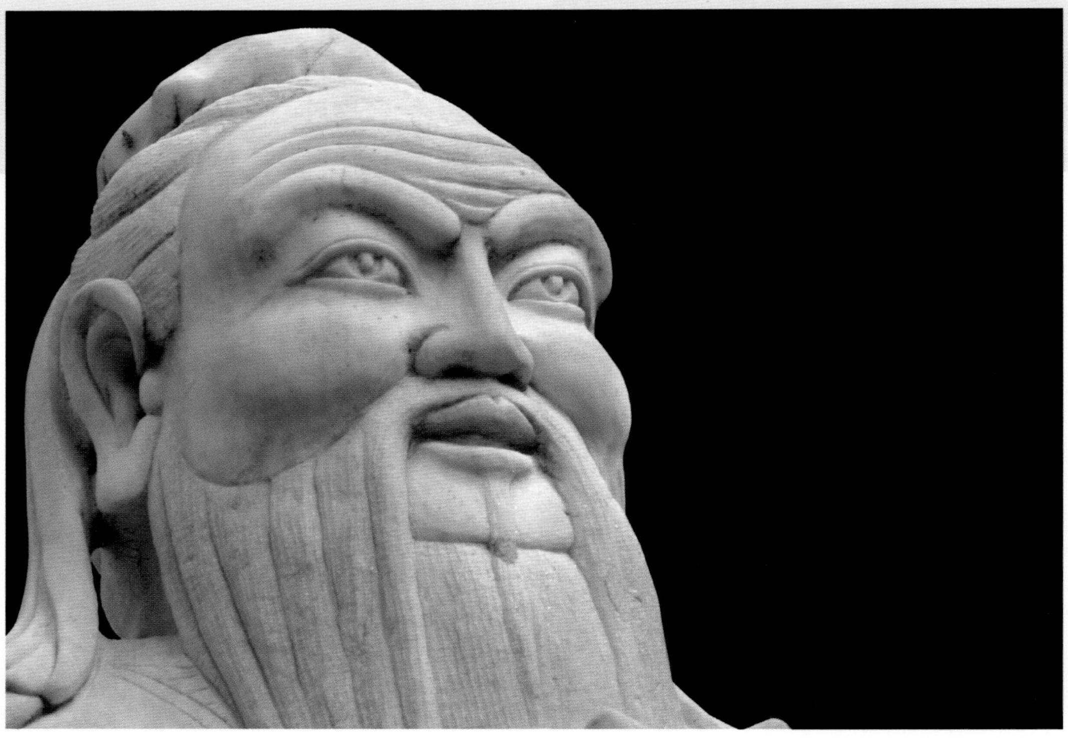

▲ *The name Confucius is the Western version of the Chinese name Kong Qiu.*

Confucius drew up plans for a perfect state, just as Plato was to do two hundred years later. Unlike Plato, however, Confucius did not envision a strictly regimented society, but rather one that functioned as an extension of the family. The relationship between the prince and his subject would echo that of a father and his sons. He did not subscribe to the idea of a hereditary aristocracy but asserted that all men were naturally equal. He elaborated these ideas in the Annals of Spring and Autumn, Chunqiu, one of the Confucian Five Classics.

> *Do not do to others what you don't want done to you.*
>
> CONFUCIUS

A Decadent Era

▲ *Incense burner from the time of the writing of Annals of Spring and Autumn.*

▲◀ *Statues of Confucius and the Buddha in a temple in Lingyin, China.*

The true name of Confucius (551–479 BCE) was Kong Qiu. From the appellative Kong Fuzi (literally, Master Kong) was derived the Latinized form Confucius, which was used by the early missionaries to China. He was born in the village of Qufu, in the ancient state of Lu, and belonged to the Kong clan, prosperous landowners. However, his father died when he was only three years old, leaving his family in poverty. Despite this, the child received a superb education.

The China that Confucius knew was divided into several feudal states, all battling for supremacy. The Zhou Dynasty, which during the early years of its reign had established peace and stability, showed itself inadequate to control the power of local warlords. The governing class was dominated by intrigues, the mechanisms of government had fallen into disarray, and the common people lived in misery. This period of decadence is called the Period of Spring and Autumn, taking its name from the chronicle of the years 722 to 481 BCE written by Confucius.

Confucius lamented the chaos of his time and the lost moral values that had characterized earlier epochs. His solution was to return to the virtue expressed in the Chinese word *ren* (humanity). Practice of this quality would result in the end of aggression and lead people to resist their resentments and inclinations toward greed. Furthermore, Confucius believed that individual graciousness could transform society: "Do not do to others what you don't want done to you."

▲ Depiction of daily life in China during the Song Dynasty.

In Search of the Ideal Government

Confucius looked upon *ren* as love of one's neighbor that extended from the individual to the family, to the people and to the sovereign, the father of all his subjects. In addition, he developed the concept of the "Superior Man" (*junzi*), whose cultivated personality was both just and moderate in its desires, standing out among the mass of common people. The Superior Man could transcend his personal preoccupations in the interests of the state and of his fellows. To find or to nourish this superior individual, Confucius sought to harness the ideal principles of the feudal order, hoping that would lead to the reforms he envisioned.

Unfortunately, reality proved less malleable than the world of ideas. When Confucius was 50, the governor of Lu named him Minister of Justice. For a brief time he able to administer the law impartially and mitigate the atmosphere of violence. But times soon returned to normal, and a plot was hatched against him. Dismissed by his lord, Confucius had to leave Lu, accompanied by a nucleus of disciples. Convinced that he had failed, he retreated from public service and dedicated himself to teaching, traveling from one feudal court to another. In 481 BCE, he composed the Annals of Spring and Autumn.

▲ Emperor Yao drawn by Ma Lin, court painter of the Song Dynasty.

Interpreting Confucius

In this work, Confucius reviews the principal occurrences in the

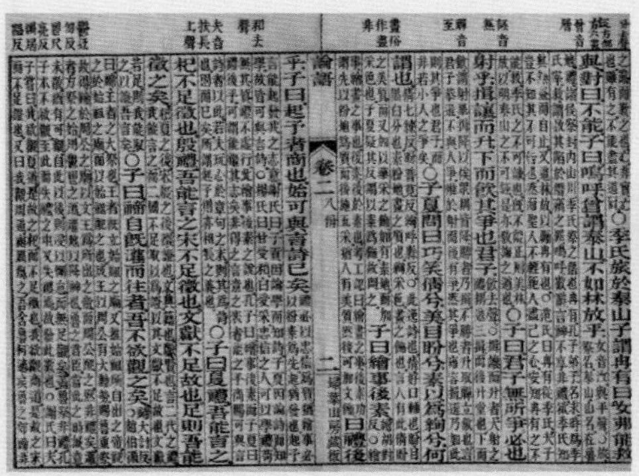

State of Lu over the course of two and a half centuries, which he called the "period of spring and autumn." He drew from his own experiences as well as from official archives. His recounting of events, many of them anecdotal, was designed with moral or political lessons in mind, since he proposed to show the necessity of a strong central government, as once existed with the early monarchs of the Zhou Dynasty. The style of the work is arid and concise, a recital of facts, as befits a work written in service of the state. But for a full understanding, one should read later commentators, according to whom Confucius synthesized his thought to conceal deeper meanings that the reader needs to discover. For example, the master writes: "In the month of February in the fifth year of his reign, Prince Lin of Lu was in Tang contemplating fishing." On the face of it a simple statement. But interpreters observe that it contains a hidden critique, since unimportant things (such as fishing) should demand no more than that they be seen. Contemplation should be reserved for rituals of important matters of state. From which it is deduced that the Superior Man ought to devote his attention only to important things. Such is the subtlety of Confucian thought.

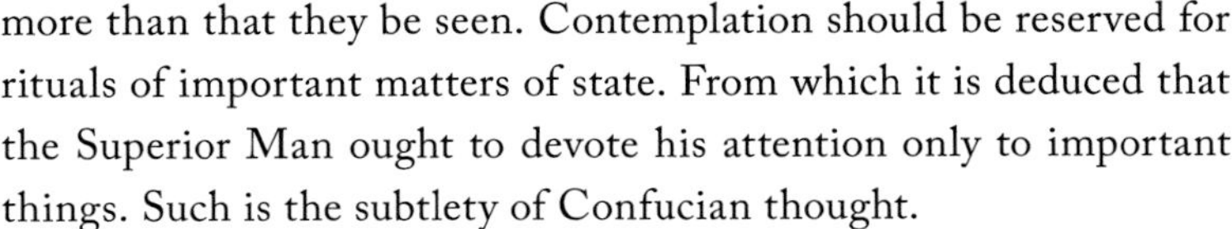

▲ *Painting from the Qing Dynasty period shows Confucius presenting a baby Buddha to Lao Tzu.*

▲◀ *Ancient manuscript containing a fragment of the Analects.*

The Four Books

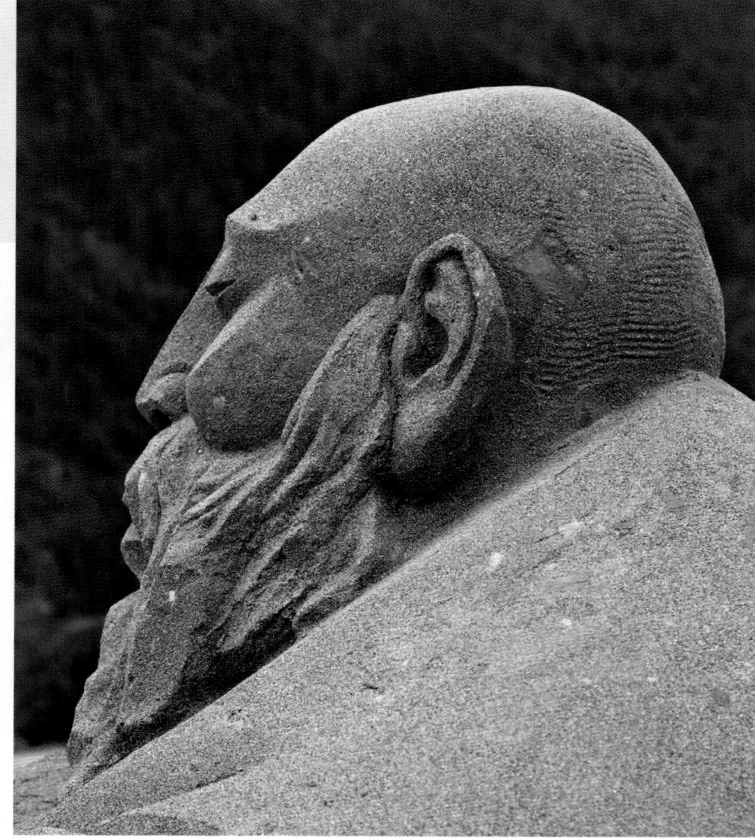

▲ *Watercolor of a house in the mountains painted in traditional Chinese style.*

▶ *Bust of Confucius in meditation.*

The Four Books (Sishu) present all of Confucius' thoughts on the subject of ethics. They were set down in writing by his disciples not long after the master's death. Their pages are filled with valuable insights. The figure of the wise man is expanded to incorporate the ideal perfection of the Superior Man, who controls his passions, submits to the forces of nature and contributes to universal harmony by suiting his deeds to his words. Confucius says of him: "The best indication of wisdom is concord between one's words and one's acts."

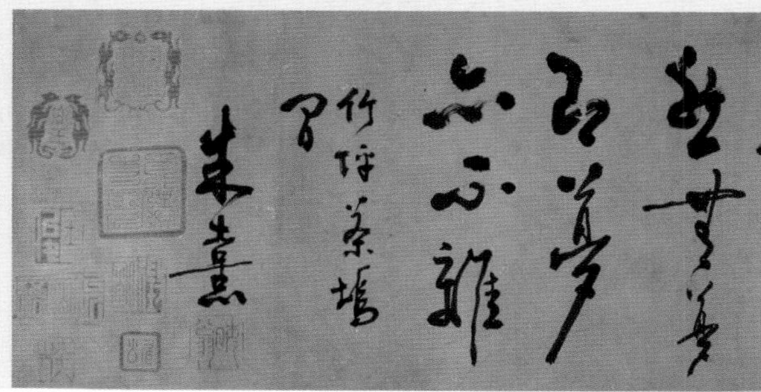

Humanity Is a Heavenly Virtue

▲ *Text from a scroll by Zhu Xi, an erudite Confucian of the Song Dynasty who interpreted the Four Books.*

▲◀ *Delicate painting on silk from the Song Dynasty.*

The Four Books were compiled between the fourth and third century BCE. Their titles are Analects (Lunyu), Mencius (Mengzi), Great Learning (Daxue) and Doctrine of the Mean (Zhongyong). The two last of these were integrated into the Classic of Rites (see above), but to establish them as indisputable parts of the canon, they were eventually edited as separate volumes and are considered to belong to the Four Books. In any event, the first two books are far more interesting, since each presents a systematic investigation of Confucian ethics through dialogue and maxims.

The Analects (a florilegium or anthology of selected passages) is of capital importance in understanding Confucianism. The disciples of Confucius were scrupulous in setting down their conversations with him, providing us with a faithful record of his thinking. Thanks to them, we know that the master derived his idea of *ren* ("humanity") from the traditional concept of heaven (*tianming*), the intelligent power that guides the world with justice and beneficence, for he never questioned the fundamental elements of the ancestral traditions. He did not believe in progress; just the reverse, he wanted to regress to the golden age of ancient China. His recipe for restoring this lost paradise consisted of a series of virtues: altruism (*ren*), equity (*yi*), respect (*shu*), loyalty (*zhong*), sincerity (*xin*), filial piety (*xiao*) and especially study (*zhi*), since old writings were the source of modes of conduct worthy of imitation.

▲ *Portrait of a Chinese astronomer. For Confucius wisdom arises from study and the development of one's will.*

The Ideal of Wisdom

Confucius avoided metaphysics. His message was not concerned with "being" but rather with the individual's relationship to society, that is, ethics and politics. He believed that will (*qi*) when married to reason could free the person from a host of undesirable effects. He himself had risen to his eminent position through force of will: "At 15 my heart was set on learning; at 30 I stood firm; at 40 I had no more doubts; at 50 I knew the will of heaven; at 60 my ear was obedient; at 70 I could follow my heart's desire without overstepping the boundaries of what was right."

In the dialogues in the Analects, Confucius appears as the preeminent moralist of the Eastern world. His words have been quoted for over two millennia, preceded by the formula *zi yue* ("the master said"), equivalent to the Aristotelian *ipse dixit*. Here are a few of his well-known aphorisms:

- When we see men of worth, we should think of equaling them; when we see men of a contrary character, we should turn inward and examine ourselves.
- Expect much of yourself and little of others. This will save you a lot of trouble.
- The Superior Man is aware of Righteousness, the inferior man is aware of advantage.
- When I walk along with two others, from at least one I will be able to learn.

> *To study and not think is a waste. To think and not study is dangerous.*
>
> Analects

◀ *Mencius (372-289).*

Justification of Regicide

The second important text of the Four Books is the work of Meng Ke, the most distinguished thinker after Confucius. He is also known as Meng Tzu or Mengzi (Master Meng) and is called Mencius in the West. As with his predecessor this ethical philosopher traveled throughout China looking for a prince who would put his ideas into practice. His success was no greater than that of Confucius. This book tells the story of his many meetings with aristocrats and philosophers, in whom he tried to inculcate a disdain for material goods, since he considered the desire for them to be a dangerous source of disorder. His ideas are based on his conviction of the innate goodness of man and that one must cultivate those inner qualities that allow one to accomplish good in the world. That means keeping one's emotion and desires within the bounds of moderation. For this reason, Mencius justified killing a king who becomes ruled by a mania for power and acts in a perverse fashion.

▶ *Guardian of a temple in Malaysia.*

▶ Taoism

Tao Te Ching

▲ *Statue of Lao Tzu in Quanzhou in the Chinese province of Fujian.*

So very little is known about Lao Tzu (Laozi), the founder of Taoism, that some scholars doubt whether he actually existed. The few snippets of information passed down have a legendary character. It is said that he decided to abandon the world and, mounted on a water buffalo, he traveled to the western frontier toward the paradise of the immortals. Before all trace of him was lost, the guardian of the border asked about the manuscript he was carrying. It was the eighty-one chapters of the Tao Te Ching (Tao Te Ching), the sacred text of Taoism (Daoism).

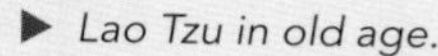
▶ Lao Tzu in old age.

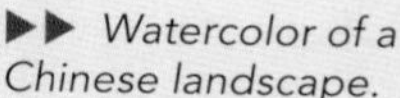
▶▶ Watercolor of a Chinese landscape.

The Enigma of Lao Tzu

▲ *Bamboos bending in the wind. From the Yuan Dynasty period, Museum of Shanxi.*

The name Lao Tzu means "great philosopher." It designates a mythical person who is venerated as a god by the followers of his teachings, which in reality do not constitute a philosophical system as such. Ancient historians give his name as Lao Dan or Li Er and date his birth to 570 BCE, about twenty years before that of Confucius. According to tradition both philosophers displayed intellectual gifts at an early age. Lao Tzu worked as an archivist at court, until the political situation began to deteriorate. Soon thereafter he disappeared. The border guard Yin Xi, the last man to see him alive, as far as we can tell, preserved his book, passing it down as Lao Tzu's legacy to posterity.

The book, whose title can be translated as "The Classic of Life and Virtue," is probably an anthology of ancient texts that were brought together after the death of Lao Tzu. Its five thousand characters are distributed over eighty-one chapters or paragraphs — as many years, legend has it, as he spent in his mother's womb. The work is written in an obscure and lapidary style that has left centuries of translators and commentators puzzled, if not baffled. Its brief passages in rhymed prose or verse are primarily descriptions of the Tao ("The Way"), the source of everything.

The Tao: A Black Hole

The Tao Te Ching describes the absolute principle that has existed for all time, prior to heaven and earth, invisible, inaudible and inexpress-

ible. Taoism substitutes the idea of a creator god with a universe that creates itself, a species of black hole, that is called "self-sufficient reality," "the gate of all wonders," and "the mystery of mysteries."

But the Tao is not only a metaphysical idea. It is also the path that each person, especially those in government, ought to follow. How should one lead the people and bring happiness to one's subordinates? The response of the Tao Te Ching seems to be the dream of all libertarians. The best king is the one who does practically nothing. He allows things to take their own course.

Respecting the fluidity of the Tao, the wise ruler lets the forces of nature unfold according to their own internal dynamics.

Tao can be infused into the nature and put to use without being exhausted.

It is deep and subtle like an abyss that is the origin of all things.

It is complete and perfect as a wholeness that can
Round off sharp edges;
Resolve confusion;
Harmonize with the glorious;
Act in unity with the lowly.

Tao is so profound and yet invisible. It exists everywhere and anywhere.

▲ *According to legend, Lao Tzu crossed the border out of China mounted on a water buffalo.*

> *The Tao that can be spoken of is not the eternal Tao.*
>
> TAO TE CHING

◀ *This work from the school of Unkoku shows the eight immortals of Taoism.*

Non-action

There is an ancient copy of the book in which the title is inverted, Te Tao Ching rather than Tao Te Ching, and this reversal occurs throughout the text. Analysts believe that this change was not accidental, since it underlies the importance of te (de), "virtue", which can also mean "action." In contrast with the classic version of the Tao Te Ching, which condemns violence and war, an interpretation of this text can show that a good part of it is a manual of military tactics and strategy. Following this thesis, where the text praises the wisdom of retreating before one's enemy, it is really recommending an astute tactical withdrawal that will allow one to more easily achieve victory.

Seen from this vantage, the celebrated Taoist quality of non-action (wei wu wei), so highly thought of by Lao Tzu, may not be a way of abandoning the field, but rather of simulating passivity to get one's way: "One should know everything, be informed about everything, but act as if nothing is known." Many phrases in the Tao Te Ching display this paradoxical quality. "To be hollow is to be filled; to be battered is to be renewed." "A man of superior virtue acts without action in keeping with his true nature ... When Tao is lost, there is Te [virtue]. When Te is lost, there is humanity. When humanity is lost, there is justice. When justice is lost, there is etiquette."

▲ *Lao Tzu calmly writing the Tao Te Ching.*

Zhuang Zi

▲ *Zhuang Zi, one of the eight immortals. The picture is attributed to Liang Kai.*

▲▶ *Lao Tzu and disciple in a Chinese landscape.*

Zhuang Zi (Zhuangzi), Lao Tzu's most brilliant disciple, compared his life to a wonderful mirage: "Once, Zhuang Zi dreamed he was a butterfly, a butterfly fluttering about, happy with himself and doing as he pleased. He didn't know that he was Zhuang Zi. Suddenly he awoke and there he was, solid and unmistakable Zhuang Zi. But he didn't know if he was Zhuang Zi who had dreamt he was a butterfly, or a butterfly dreaming that he was Zhuang Zi." This lovely allegory, reminiscent of Lewis Carroll, is found in the book whose title is the author's name, one of the great philosophical works of ancient China.

> *One day Zhuang Zi dreamed that he was a butterfly.*
>
> Zhuang Zi

The Philosophical Poet

As is the case with the other two major Taoist figures, Lao Tzu and Lie Yukou, almost nothing is known of the life of Zhuang Zi (Master Zhuang). The work that bears his name was probably composed in the fourth or third century BCE. Later on it was called Nanhua Zhenjing (True Classic of the Southern Flower). Of its thirty-three chapters only the first seven are thought to have been written by Zhuang Zi. The rest of the book was probably the work of his followers. It consists of a series of parables, anecdotes and allegories with short explanations imbued with poetry.

▲ *Drawing of a Chinese river garden.*

▲▲ *Characters for* wu wei, *the Taoist concept of non-action.*

Peng and Yan

To illustrate the concept of the Tao, Zhuang Zi makes use of a series comparisons, such as that between two birds, named Peng and Yan. Peng is enormous. Its wings are like the clouds that line the heavens. Yan flies low and makes fun of the grandness of Peng. But in relation to the Tao, there is no difference between Peng and Yan. Or another example: In ancient times there was a tree with flowers that bloomed for eight thousand years and fruit that lasted for another eight thousand years. At the same time there were insects that were born in the morning and died in the afternoon. Then we have humankind. The most fortunate live for one hundred years, which is practically nothing, since in relation to the absolute, it is but a moment.

▲ The Tao is the way of harmony. This landscape from the south of China conveys a peacefulness that is hard to come by in the modern world.

Conformity with the Tao

In the same way, it is of little worth to distinguish between good and evil, since this dichotomy is meaningless in relation to the vast unknowable nature of the Tao. The substance of the universe can be compared to the wind, which is silent in itself, but sounds in different ways depending upon the effects it brings to pass. The same holds true for war and peace, righteousness and injustice, happiness and disgrace. One needs to detach oneself from these conventional dualities to find true freedom. The evils of the world exist because man considers them as such, and driven by fear, he classifies things as desirable and undesirable. When one ceases making these distinctions, one sees that everything that exists is an inevitable manifestation of the Tao.

Zhuang Zi proposed abandoning worldly pursuits in search of perfection, that is, by living in conformity with the Tao. This meant renouncing the active life, rejecting pleasure, forgetting oneself and devoting oneself to meditation. It doesn't matter that we cannot know everything. "A trap is for fish: when you've got the fish, you can forget the trap. A snare is for rabbits: when you've got the rabbit, you can forget the snare. Words are for meaning: when you've got the meaning, you can forget the words. Where can I find a man who has forgotten words? He is the one I would like to talk to."

▶ Some of the terracotta warriors that graced the tomb of the Emperor Qin.

Prolonging Life

Zhuang Zi's book contains many references to practices to extend one's lifespan. Taoism was not interested in longevity on earth, but rather the gradual replacement of corruptible organs with incorruptible ones, so that at the point of death one can "free the body" and easily transition the nonperishable body to paradise. This possibility is reserved for those exceptional individuals who have mastered various practices: respiratory (holding the breath for as long as possible), dietetic (strict vegetarianism) and spiritual (practicing virtue).

There is also a pill for long life created using alchemical processes that enables one to bypass intermediate stages and directly attain immortality. However, aspirants were often undone by the poisonous cinnabar required for the recipe. Other Taoist practices call for engaging in specific sexual practices that have a revitalizing effect. They involve *coitus prolongatus*, in which the ejaculation is delayed or even avoided altogether, so that the nutritive sperm, which according to Chinese medicine originates in the brain, is not dispersed.

Book of Perfect Emptiness

▲ *Ma Yuan,* A Walk on a Mountain Path in Springtime. *Ma Yuan was a twelfth-century painter at the Song Dynasty court.*

Along with the metaphysical Tao Te Ching and the lyrical Zhuang Zi (which bears its author's name), the Lie Zi (Liezi), or Book of Perfect Emptiness, completes the sacred trilogy of Taoism. This tract is a collection of fables in which the preoccupations of the people of China — their daily struggles, customs and idiosyncratic way of thinking — are vividly displayed before our eyes. That is to say, the book does not attempt to interpret life but rather to teach one how to live. As a result, some of the parables found in the book can be seen influencing the popular culture of China today. Mao Zedong drew on the fable of "The Old Fool Who Moved the Mountains" in his *Little Red Book*.

The Enigmatic Master Lie

▲ *Wood carving showing a master and his disciples seated at table.*

Authorship of the book has been ascribed to Lie Yukou, a legendary figure, who is thought to have been one of the early followers of the Taoist school. We know almost nothing about him. He probably lived before Zhuang Zi, in the fourth century BCE, since Zhuang Zi quotes him in his treatise. However, one part of the Book of Perfect Emptiness shows similarities to passages in the Zhuang Zi, leading many to believe that it is actually an anthology composed during the Qin and Han dynasties (third century BCE to fourth century CE), a period that also saw the rise and fall of the Roman Empire.

The only certain date associated with the work is much later. On March 31, 742, the Emperor Xuanzong, a great patron of the arts and friend to writers and musicians, catalogued the book in his library as a canonical Taoist work under the title "Classic of Simplicity and Emptiness." Its supposed author received the posthumous title "transcendent being." Some three centuries later another emperor renamed the book "The True Classic of Simplicity and the Emptiness of Perfect Virtue," from which the title by which it is known in the West is derived. In China the work is simply called Lie Zi ("Book of Master Lie").

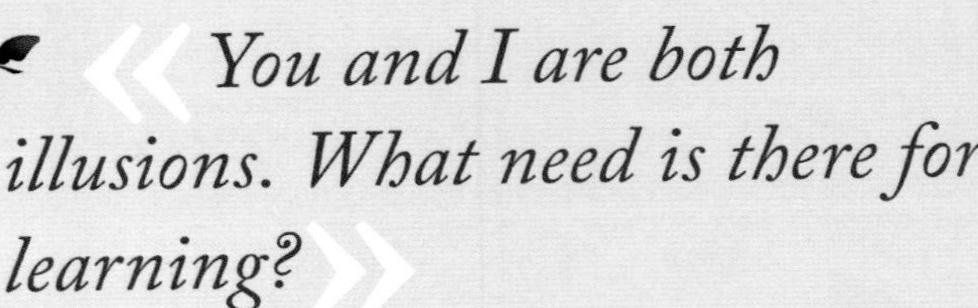

« You and I are both illusions. What need is there for learning? »

LIE ZI

The Epicurean Master Chu

The Lie Zi is much more accessible than other Taoist classics. It tackles themes such as the importance of renouncing worldly interests and detaching from emotions (for example, accepting the prospect of death without undo anxiety). It affirms the illusory nature of perception and counsels skepticism regarding religious teachings. One of its chapters has as protagonist Yang Zhu, a philosopher whom Mencius criticized as unwilling to sacrifice a hair on his head for the good of his country.

Although Yang Zhu declared himself an adept in Taoist doctrine (embracing the simplicity of one's natural state), he actually advocated a fatalistic epicureanism, consisting in enjoying the pleasure of existence to the fullest extent. His reasoning seems impeccable. If we consider that at most one person in a thousand will live to 100, and then subtract half of that spent as a youth and in old ages, subtract another third for time spent in dreams and distractions and then in sickness and suffering, there is left at best ten years for happiness. From this he deduces that to squander this little precious bit on superficial matters makes no sense whatsoever.

▲ *Lie Zi taught that one should renounce the pleasures of the flesh and become detached from one's emotions.*

◀ *Ma Lin,* Old Man Contemplating a Mountain, *12th century.*

▼ *Mao Zedong added dedication to collective labor to achieve his objectives.*

Yugong and the Mountains

The Taoism of the Lie Zi is not in question. However, some episodes in the book display elements of Confucianism. For example the fable known as "Yugong moves mountains," comes from an adage attributed to Confucius: "Move a handful of dirt every day and build a mountain." This is the story of Yugong, an old man whose house faced two high mountains that blocked his path. Yugong enlisted the help of his children and decided to use his hoe to move the mountains. Another old man, seeing him hard at work, made fun of him saying, "What do you think you're doing? You'll never be able to accomplish it." Yugong replied, "When I die, my children will continue the work, and when they die they will be succeeded by their children and the endless generations that follow. For no matter how high the mountains are, they will get no higher, but they'll diminish with each bite of the hoe." Yugong continued with his unwavering digging until heaven was moved by his perseverance and sent two genies who shouldered the mountains.

Mao Zedong copied this encomium to persistence, while introducing significant changes. In "The Old Fool Who Moved Mountains" divine intervention disappears. Instead all of the inhabitants of his village help the aged Yugong. Thus individual enterprise is subsumed into collective will and succeeds in accomplishing a Herculean task right before the eyes of perfidious capitalists.

Kojiki and Nihonshoki

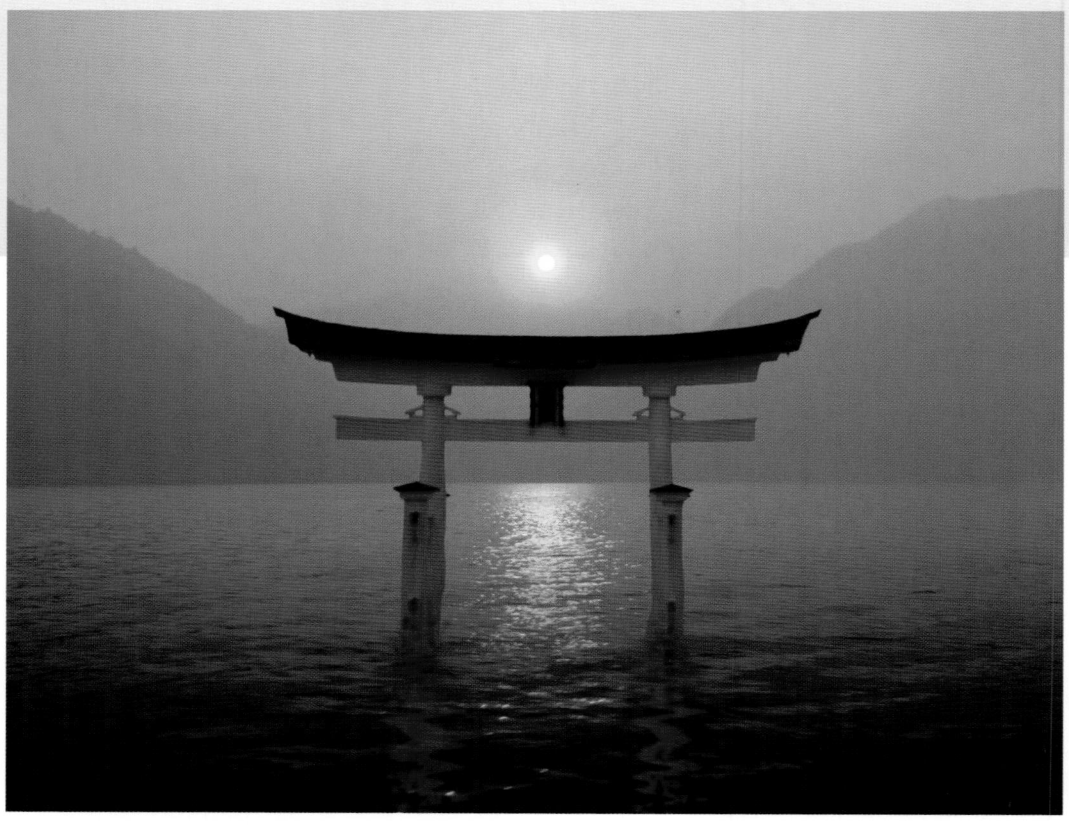

▲ *The* torii, *shown here in the ocean, is a symbol of Shintoism. This traditional gate, usually painted red, is most commonly found at the entrance of Shinto shrines.*

Shinto is the ancient religion of Japan. It is practical rather than theoretical. It has not created precise dogmas, but rather enjoins certain rituals on its followers that express the traditional styles and values of the Japanese people. Shinto's numerous festivals encourage communal cohesion. Its adherents celebrate these with optimism, without preoccupying themselves with metaphysical questions. What is important is the harmony of the moment and the purity of action as manifested in the simplicity of the Japanese esthetic and its admirable delicacy.

◀ *Kami can reside in any object, for example, in a tree.*

▼ *Ono Yasumaro, author of the Kojiki, the most important Shinto text.*

Belief in the Kami

The two most important sources for Shinto belief and practice were compiled during the Nara period (CE 710–794). They include descriptions of the divine origin of the Japanese imperial family. The Kojiki ("Chronicle of Ancient Matters") is a collection of myths put together by the historian Ono Yasumaro in 712. Eight years later, the Nihonshoki or Nihongi ("Annals of Japan") was completed under the supervision of Prince Toneri. The objective of both works, written at the request of the court, was to connect Japan's mythical past with the imperial dynasty and thereby confirm its sacred character. There is no claim of revelation or that they were dictated by a deity. Rather they are genealogical narratives that recount the generations of gods and men from the creation of the world.

According to Shinto, the universe is filled with mysterious supernatural entities (*kami*). The most important of these are the primordial gods, but powerful natural phenomena can also be *kami*: mountains, waterfalls, rivers, animals, trees and human beings as well. The Kojiki recounts many fantastic adventures of the *kami* and links these divinities with the ancestors of the imperial Yamato clan.

▼ *Page from the Nihonshoki, which chronicles Japanese history from the creation of the world up to the beginning of the eighth century CE.*

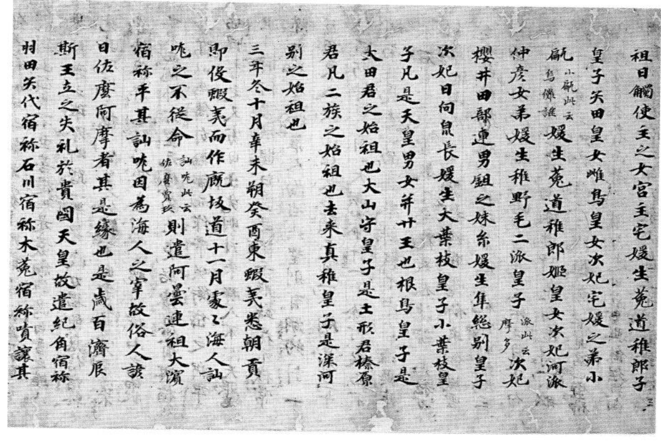

祖日觸使主之女宮主宅媛生菟道稚郎子
皇子矢田皇女雌鳥皇女次妃宅媛之弟小
甂（小甂此云烏儺誤）媛生菟道稚郎姫皇女次妃河派
仲彦女弟媛生稚野毛二派皇子（派此云摩多）次妃
櫻井田部連男鉏之妹糸媛生隼總別皇子
次妃日向泉長媛生大葉枝皇子小葉枝皇
子凡是天皇男女幷廿王也根鳥皇子是
大田君之始祖也大山守皇子是土形君榛原
君凡二族之始祖也去来真稚皇子是深河
別之始祖也
三年冬十月辛未朔癸酉東蝦夷悉朝貢
即役蝦夷而作厩坂道十一月處々海人訕
哤之不從命（訕哤此云佐摩賣玖）則遣阿曇連祖大濱
宿祢平其訕哤因爲海人之宰故俗人諺
日佐麼阿摩者其是縁也是歳百濟辰
斯王立之失礼於貴國天皇故遣紀角宿祢
羽田矢代宿祢石川宿祢木菟宿祢嘖讓其

> *In the beginning heaven and earth arose . . .*
>
> Kojiki

▲ *Eitaku Kobayashi,* Stirring the Sea with the Tenkei, *1885, Boston Museum of Fine Arts. This painting depicts the Japanese deities Izanagi (at right) and Izanami standing in the clouds. The tenkei is a kind of curved spear that the gods used in forming the earth.*

The Two Demiurges

In the beginning the earth was empty and gelatinous like "a jellyfish in the middle of the ocean." To populate it the primitive gods sent a masculine god, Izanagi, and a goddess, Izanami, provided with a spear decorated with precious stones. With it they stirred the ocean and created the island of Onokoro (First Land). Once settled there, they decided to unite in matrimony. Their first attempt, however, was a failure since the goddess took the initiative (a flagrant violation of correct protocol). Later they engendered the eight large islands of the Japanese archipelago and the *kami* of nature: the mountains, rivers, wind, forests, and so forth.

When Izanami gave birth to Kagutsuchi, the fire god, she suffered such serious burns that she retreated to the realm of the dead. He husband tried to rescue her, but she had begun to rot and gave off such a terrible smell that he took a huge rock to block the entrance to the land of the dead. Then after suitably purifying himself, he created Amaterasu, the sun goddess, who is the principal Shinto deity. She is the one who taught the Japanese how to cultivate rice and the art of weaving. She also sent her grandson Ninigi to govern the country. Thus began the imperial line of the Yamatos, which has econtinued without interruption to this day.

◀ *Southeast China abounds in beautiful scenery that can leave the traveler feeling that he or she is walking through a mythical landscape.*

Amaterasu and the Emperors

From this it can be gleaned that the emperors are owed the same devotion as the kami. In the Kojiki and the Nihonshoki, we pass with ease from one world to the other, from mythological episodes to historical accounts, from the gods to the rulers. The adventures of the former and the exploits of the latter seem indistinguishable, and the celestial pantheon is a faithful reproduction of the hierarchy of the imperial court. In this way the books use every means at their disposal, including religion, to establish the sacred nature of the Japanese throne.

▲ *The* yatagarasu, *a three-legged crow, is a common figure in Far Eastern mythologies.*

Buddhism and Shinto

To become the state's official religion, Shinto had to struggle against Buddhism, which traveled from China and easily found a home in Japan. The Buddhist monks accepted the kami, but considered them as bound to the wheel of reincarnation and consequently inferior to the Buddhas. Later, the ideas emerged that the Shinto deities manifested Buddhahood in a unique fashion and that both religions were based on the same doctrine. But in the end the Japanese priestly caste, under pressure from the emperors, declared that Shinto was more profound and original than Buddhism, Taoism and Confucianism, and that it alone represented the pure sensibility of the Japanese spirit.

Mythology and Hermeticism

▶ Mayan Mythology

Popol Vuh

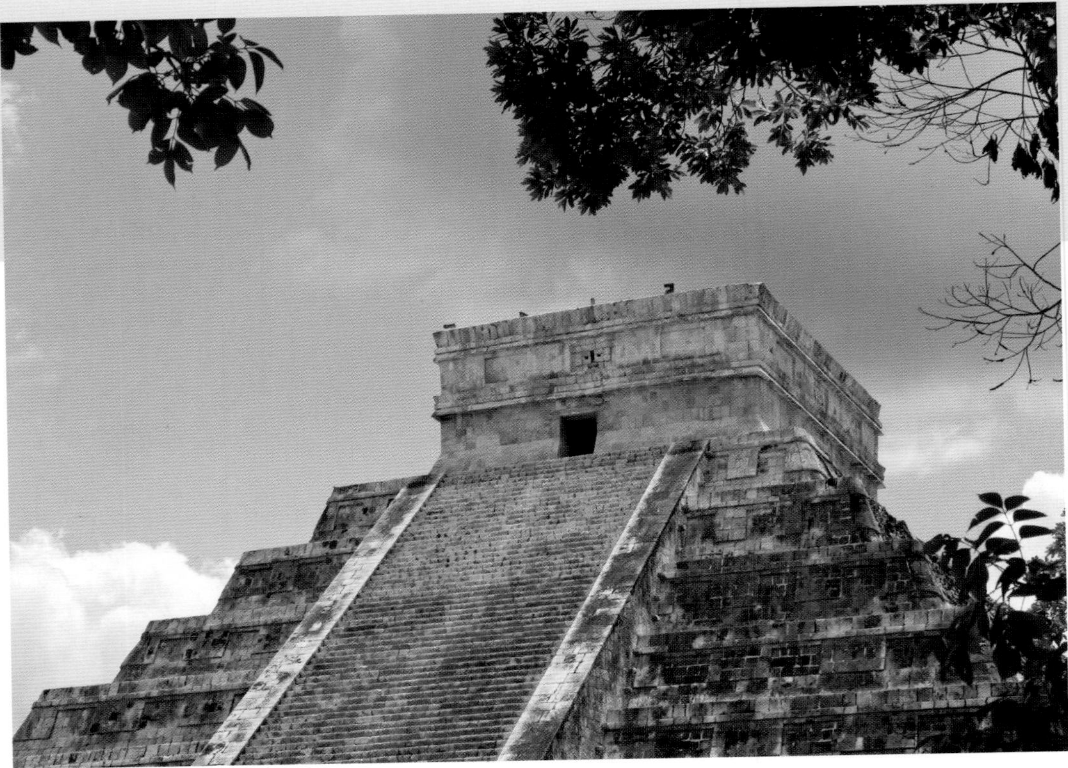

▲ *The Temple of Kukulkan in Chichen Itza is one of the most important Mayan constructions. From its rooftop one sees dense forest on all sides.*

The Maya elaborated a sophisticated system for measuring time and realizing complex astronomical calculations. They invented a hieroglyphic script with more than seven hundred signs, planned cities and created gorgeous art associated with ceremonial centers. This rich civilization was tinged with a religiosity that demanded human sacrifices by drowning, beheading, even ripping out the heart of the victim — all to curry favor with the gods. In this way they could ensure abundant rainfall, avoid natural disasters and maintain the cosmic order. The Popol Vuh is the most important document we have about their extraordinary mythology.

« *This is an account of how all was in suspense.* »

Popol Vuh, Chapter I

▼ *Mayan glyph from its golden age. The figure wears the headdress of the priestly caste.*

The Myth of the Progenitors

The Popol Vuh, which can be translated as the "Book of Counsel," belongs to the Quiché, an ethnic subgroup of Maya that inhabited parts of present-day Guatemala. The version that has come down to us was not composed in pre-Columbian times but after the Spanish conquest in the middle of the sixteenth century by an anonymous author. He was probably an indigenous religious figure who wanted to preserve a much older oral and pictographic tradition. The book is in the Quiché language written in Roman characters according the Spanish phonology of the period.

Corn People

The book opens with the gods creating the world out of nothing. "This is the account of how all was in suspense, all calm, in silence; all motionless, quiet, and empty was the expanse of the sky. This is the first account, the first discourse. There were no people, no animals, birds, fish, crabs, trees, rocks, valleys, grass or forests. Only the sky existed." It was then that the "creators and shapers, Tepeu and Gucumatz" (the "progenitors") originated life.These divinities wanted to be worshipped. At first they thought that animals would serve that purpose, but they found that they could only "screech, cackle and caw" in an incomprehensible language. So they condemned them to devour each other and set out to create other "obedient and respectful beings," humans, who would feed the animals. They first tried to make them out of mud, but that didn't work, since the new creatures fell apart when they got wet. Then they tried wood, but that resulted in soulless inert humans, with-

▼ *Title page of the oldest known copy of the Popol Vuh.*

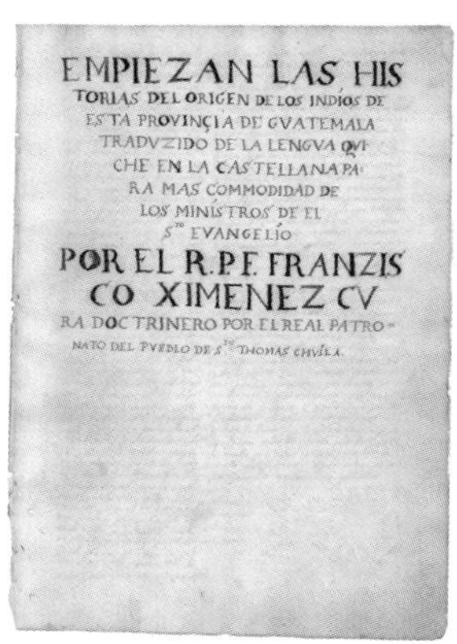

EMPIEZAN LAS HIS
TORIAS DEL ORIGEN DE LOS INDIOS DE
ESTA PROVINÇIA DE GVATEMALA
TRADVZIDO DE LA LENGVA QVI
CHE EN LA CASTELLANA PA
RA MAS COMMODIDAD DE
LOS MINISTROS DE EL
S.TO EVANGELIO
POR EL R.P.F. FRANZIS
CO XIMENEZ CV
RA DOCTRINERO POR EL REAL PATRO-
NATO DEL PVEBLO DE S.TO THOMAS CHVILA.

▲ *Tulum on Mexico's Atlantic Coast was one of the last Mayan enclaves.*

out feelings, who had no concern for the gods. So they destroyed most of them in a great flood. The descendants of the survivors became monkeys and lived in the forests. Finally they used corn: "Of yellow corn and of white corn they made their flesh; of cornmeal dough they made the arms and the legs of man. Only dough of corn meal went into the flesh of our first fathers, the four men, who were created."

In this way the first four men were born: Balam Quitzé, Balam-Acab, Mahucutah and Iqui-Balam. The gods were afraid these perfect beings might supplant them, so they limited their intelligence. They then had them mate with four women created for that purpose. From their unions were born eight men, who all spoke the same language and established a community. But in an episode reminiscent of the story of the Tower of Babel, the community was dispersed and scattered across the face of the earth.

The Popol Vuh includes a genealogy that connects the descendants of these forefathers with the rulers of the Quiché people. This section of the book is less mythological and more historical, and it provides numerous details about the political structure of Quiché society and its internal rivalries. It ends with a magnificent funeral dirge in which everything described in the book disappears, including the Quiché nation.

Hunahpu and Ixbalanque

The second part of the Popol Vuh narrates the heroic adventures of the twin brothers Hunahpu and Ixbalanque, god-heroes of Maya mythology. The story of their birth is very curious: Hun Hunahpu, their father, was assassinated by the evil lords of Xibalba (the underworld).

◀ *Representation of the Mayan creation myth from San Bartolo in Petén, Guatemala.*

▶ *Mayan mask. The majority discovered are funerary masks that come from the tombs of kings and nobles.*

They buried his body, after first beheading him, and hung his head on a tree as a warning. One day, however, curiosity led Xquic, one of the assassin's daughters, to approach the head, who asked her to open her hand. The head then spit in her palm, impregnating her. Her father was incensed and forthwith expelled her into the intermediate human realm. Xquic hid herself in the house of the children's grandmother, Xmucane.

After the children were born they had to leave their grandmother's house because she was also raising another set of twins, earlier sons of Hun Hunahpu, who made their younger brothers' lives miserable. Nonetheless, the story ends well: The twins descend to Xibalba, the realm of shades, and avenge their father by defeating its inhabitants on the ball court and at other tests. Eventually, they are transformed into the sun and the moon.

▲ *Page 9 of the* Dresden Codex, *which along with the Popol Vuh, is the best known Mayan text. It contains a collection of rituals and astronomical observations.*

Chilam Balam

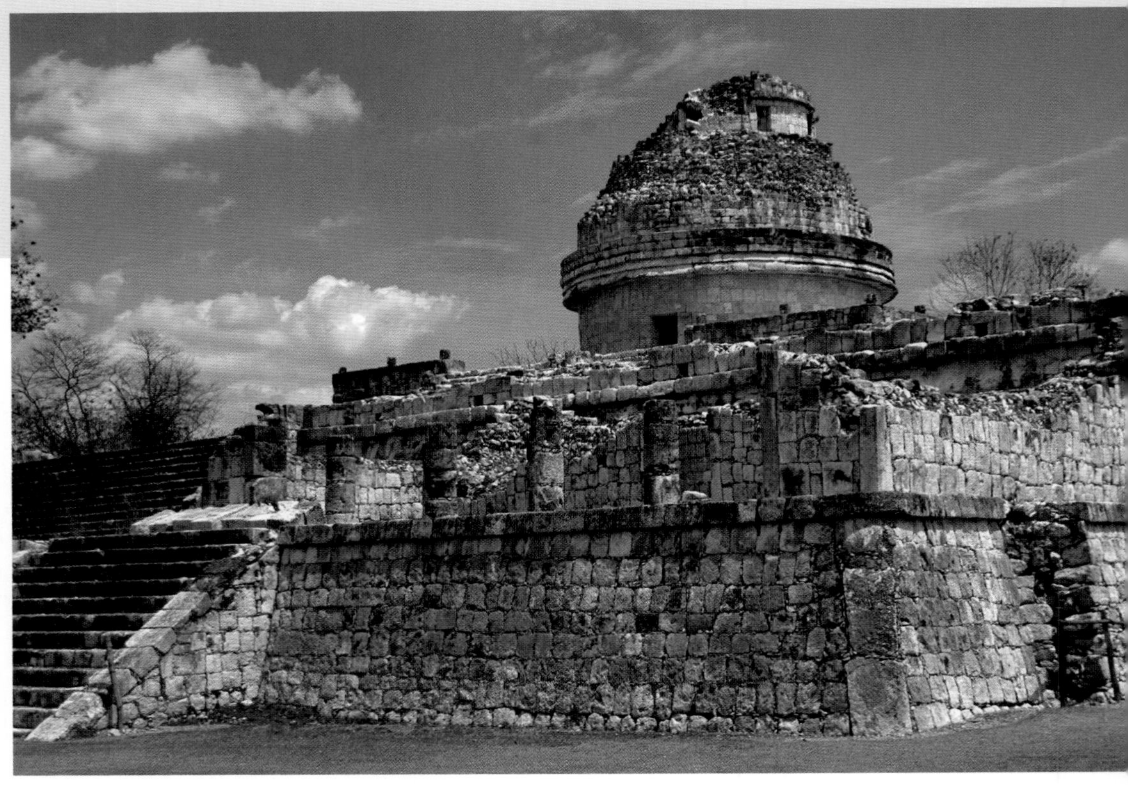

▲ *The Observatory at Chichen Itza. The Maya were skilled astronomers with an impressive knowledge of celestial phenomena.*

When the Maya looked into the skies, they were contemplating their past and their future, since the gods had written the history of the world in the heavens. To decipher this divine language they carefully observed celestial phenomena and created diverse calendrical systems. Since for them time was cyclical, and everything reoccurred after a fixed period, foretelling the future was almost as simple as remembering familiar facts. The different versions of the texts referred to as Chilam Balam are echoes of these prophetic visions. They contain ritual instructions coupled with wide-ranging medical and astronomical knowledge that far surpassed that of every other pre-Columbian civilization.

▶ *Bas-relief showing a king and priest engaged in a ritual.*

Many Different Books

There is not a single version of Chilam Balam. The title is given to many different texts, each resembling the others but with definite local variations. Its literal translation is "what is in the mouth," that is, the speech of the Mayan priests (*chilames*) who interpreted the ancient writings and based their prophecies upon them. *Balam* can mean "jaguar" but also "sorcerer." It probably refers to a mythic figure dating from before the conquest. Although the compiled texts were suppressed by the Spanish, who considered them pagan works, some were preserved and jealously guarded by various Mayan communities, whose priests added new material to them in secret. Thus each settlement elaborated its own version, and there is a Chilam Balam of Chumayel (the best known), and others from Tizimin, Mani, Kaua, Ixil, Tekax, Nah and Tusik, although some of these have not been translated from Mayan.

▼ *Mayan calendar showing May 5, 2009.*

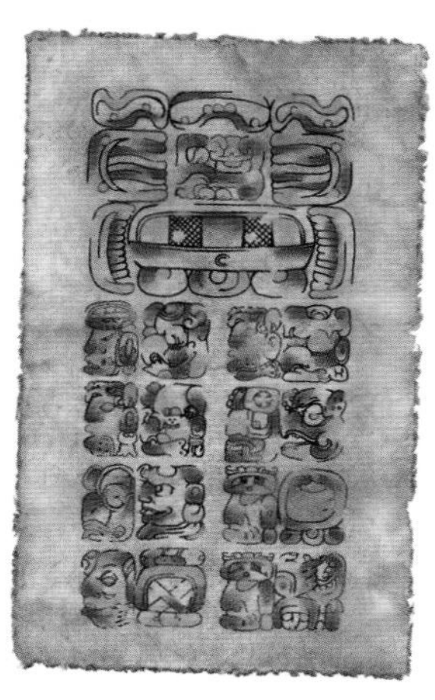

All of the versions are closely connected to the Mayan calendar, since every present or future event is registered in these temporal computations. Starting from the first day, which begins the calendar system and this cycle (according to Mayan calculations, the equivalent to August 13, 3114 BCE, probably chosen for a significant event of which we have no knowledge), there are various calendars, such as the Haab, in which the astronomical year is divided into eighteen months

> *This was the* katun *when the foreigners arrived. They came from the east when they arrived.*
>
> Chilam Balam

▲ Bas-relief of an important personage. A relief discovered near Palenque has led some to speculate that the Maya were acquainted with astronauts. Were their gods actually travelers from another planet?

of twenty days (with the addition five "nameless" days) and the Tzolkin ("serpentine road of the gods"), a sacred cycle of 260 days. In addition, the Maya's grasp of mathematics and their intimate acquaintance with the heavens allowed them to precisely measure the solar year to 365.2422 days and to note other astronomical phenomena such as the phases of the moon and the movements of Venus, and other stars and constellations.

Prophecy of the Spanish Conquest

To untangle the prophecies contained in the Chilam Balam, one needs to know all of these particulars, since any given day in the Mayan calendar is inscribed in superimposed cycles that determine its characteristics. An adept priest could arrive at complete knowledge of each day and decide upon the most propitious time to celebrate a wedding, offer a sacrifice or launch a military campaign. Each period of time has to come full circle, and then over many cycles events reoccur. The predictions of the Chilam Balam announce phases of destruction and rebirth and anticipate the end of the Mayan people as victims of the conquistadors.

The original pictographic writing of the Maya, the most elaborate of all writing systems of the indigenous people of the Americas, expressed all of these ideas. Archaeologists continue to struggle to deci-

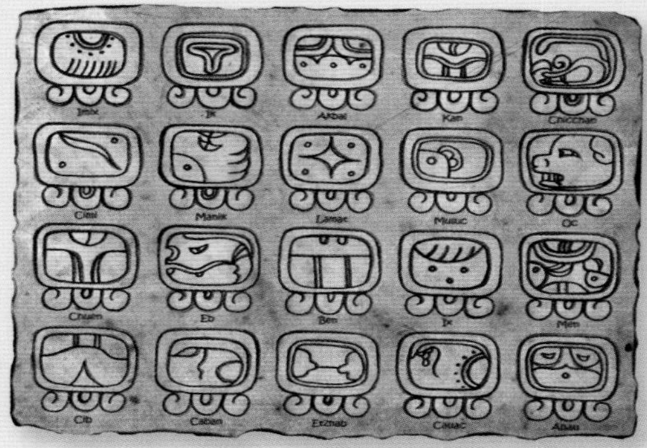

pher much of it, and even when successful the language remains strange and cryptic to Western readers. When translated it retains a magical quality.

The main version of Chilam Balam, that of Chumayel, relates in a manner replete with numerology the migrations of diverse Mesoamerican peoples. It also contains prophetic texts, the most noteworthy of which directs the reader's attention to the *katun 11 ahau* (the *katun* is a period of 7,200 days, and the *ahau* approximately a month). At this time "foreigners arrive from the east … When your younger brothers arrive, the cursed foreign barbarians will change the color of your clothes. Their priests adore an incarnate god who is worshipped throughout the world." And further it states: "We were downcast because of the great stone mounds. This *katun* was a *katun* of misery and of devilish strife."

Mayan Prophesy

According to the chronological system of the Maya, cyclical time will end when the sun completes its journey around the Pleiades. This was to have taken place on December 22, 2012. The Maya did not see this as the end of the world but of its transformation and regeneration. There was considerable concern in esoteric circles as the day approached, but when December 23 dawned and all was as before, only the most diehard believers returned to their calculators to refigure the involved computation.

▲◀ *A series of characters from the Mayan written language.*

▶ Norse Mythology

Eddas

▶ *Title page of the* Prose Edda *from an Icelandic manuscript of the eighteenth century.*

Early peoples of Scandinavia passed down over generations powerful poetry whose protagonists were Odin, Thor, Loki, and other gods and heroes, the main figures of a mythology the origins of which extend beyond the historical record. These stories, which were told around fires during the frigid northern winters, were finally gathered together and written down in the *Eddas* (edda is the Norse word for "great grandmother"), a name that alludes with some humor to their antiquity. Medieval manuscripts have preserved two related but separate texts: the *Poetic Edda* and the *Prose Edda*.

Norse Mythology

▲ *W.G. Collingwood, "Odin Rides to Hell," illustration from* The Elder Edda, *1908.*

The *Poetic Edda* (also known as the *Elder Edda*) contains various myths and legends written down by unknown authors copying ancient oral traditions. It is believed that the poems were originally composed in Norway or in the Norse settlements of Iceland and Greenland between the ninth and thirteenth centuries. Twenty-nine of the thirty-three lays that make up the *Poetic Edda* are preserved in a single manuscript, the *Codex Regius*, that was discovered in 1643 by an Icelandic bishop, Bryjolfur Sveinsson, who entitled the collection the *Saemundar Edda*, believing it to be the work of the Saemundar the Learned, a twelfth-century Icelandic priest.

The poems contained in the *Codex Regius* are an invaluable source of knowledge about the mythology and religious sentiments of the early Germanic and Scandinavian peoples. Most noteworthy are the *Hávamal* (Sayings of the High One) and the *Voluspá* (Prophecy of the Sibyl). Both are highly accomplished and powerful poetic works. Other important poems are: the "Lay of Vafthrudnir" in which the so-named giant answers Odin's questions about the creation and end of the world; the "Lay of Grimnir," which contains references to many supernatural beings and ends with a long list of the names of Odin; and the "Lay of Thrym," which tells the story of Thor and his search to recover his missing hammer, Mjollnir.

▲ *Adolf Lange,* Odin drinking from the Spring of Wisdom, *1903.*

« *There was in times of old, nor sand nor sea, nor gelid waves; earth existed not, nor heaven above, 'twas a chaotic chasm, and grass nowhere.* »

POETIC EDDA, VOLUSPÁ

A Guide for Poets

▲ *Loki, the god of conflict in Germanic mythology, taught men how to fish.*

▲▶ *Mjollnir, Thor's hammer, is the symbol of Asatru, a nineteenth-century revival of the ancient pagan religion of N\ north and central Europe.*

The *Prose Edda* is a work written by the historian and statesman Snorri Sturlson (1179–1241), who sought to preserve the traditional artistic tradition of Iceland, which was converted to Christianity in 999. Using the *Poetic Edda* as his starting point, Sturlson describes the religion of his pagan ancestors and at the same time offers a poetic handbook for the skalds (Norse court poets) that provides everything necessary about mythology and correct versification. The text is preserved in the *Codex Upsaliensis*, a manuscript dating from around 1300, which includes four copies of the lost original.

The book consists of four parts. In the Prologue, Sturlson explains ancient Norse beliefs in euhemeristic terms, that is, contending that the gods were originally historic figures. The next section, the "Gylfaginning," provides an account of Norse mythology in the form of a dialogue between King Gylfi and three gods. It concludes with some stories about Odin and Thor related by Bragi, the god of poetry, to Aegir, the sea god. The third part is the "Skaldskaparmal" ("The Language of Poetry"), in which the use of metaphor (*kenningar*) is explained as well as symbolic synonyms (*heiti*). The last section, the "Hattatal" ("List of Verse Forms"), is a hymn to the Norse king in one hundred stanzas, each stanza composed in a distinct verse form. The two last sections constitute an instruction manual for young skalds who were studying to practice traditional poetic styles.

▶ *Odin battling Fenrir, the wolf, during Ragnarok.*

Odín, Thor and Loki

▲ *This painting by Marten Eskil Winge shows Thor fighting to save the world at the battle of Ragnarok.*

The *Eddas* provide us with a detailed vision of ancient Norse cosmology. Asgard, the highest region of the heavens, is the home of the *aesir* ("gods") and *asynjur* ("goddesses"). The chief god is Odin, omnipotent mage and inventor of the runes. Odin forms a triumvirate with Thor, the thunder god who wields a hammer, and Freyr, a phallic fertility god. Another important figure is Loki, god of chance and chaos.

The Nordic peoples also venerated the *vanes* or *vanir*, peaceful gods of nature who are defeated by Odin. There are also many other supernatural beings: giants, Valkyries, elves and formidable monsters such as Fenrir, the giant wolf, Jormungandr, the sea serpent, and Ratatoskr, a squirrel who runs up and down the world tree Yggdrasil, which connects the nine worlds of Norse cosmology.

▶ Norse Mythology

Hávamál

One of the principal lays of the *Poetic Edda* is the *Hávamál*, a title that can mean "Discourse on the Highest Things" or "Sayings of the High One" in reference to Odin, ruler of the gods in Norse Mythology. The distilled wisdom in its verses conveys a vivid sense of the Viking mentality, which on the surface seems so distant from our own. On closer examination, however, its appeal is far broader. Its protagonist, Odin, raises questions and faces situations that are profoundly human and not unlike those we face in everyday life today.

▲ *W. G. Collingwood, "Odin's Self-Sacrifice," illustration from* The Elder Edda, *1908.*

◀ Odin with two crows and two wolves.

> *Let no man glory in the greatness of his mind, but rather keep watch over his wits.*
>
> HÁVAMÁL

Sound Advice

▲ Lorenz Frolich, The Sacrifice of Odin, *1895. After his ordeal Odin obtained the knowledge of the runes.*

It is believed that the poem, which has come down to us through the *Codex Regius*, was originally composed before 980 and underwent various revisions after that. Rather than a religious or dogmatic tract, it comprises proverbs and refrains, information about family customs and moral counsel, often in the form of anecdotes that provide a view of the ethical mores of the ancient Norse skalds, especially those of the Vikings. Its 165 stanzas were intended for the edification and spiritual enrichment of its listeners. It is a representative of an oral tradition that has been put down in writing.

The "Gestpattr"

The *Hávamal* opens with the seventy-nine stanzas of the "Gespattr," a gnomic poem (formed of brief sayings and moral observations) that are primarily devoted to the obligations of hospitality, the debts owed by guests to their hosts and the need for reciprocal welcoming, all of vital importance for travelers. Stanza 52 is a good example:

Not great things alone must one give to another,
praise oft is earned for nought;
with half a loaf and a tilted bowl
I have found me many a friend.

▶ *Viking tomb in northern Europe.*

▶▶ *"Odin Drives out the Sons of Loki," illustration from Victor Rydberg,* Teutonic Mythology, *1906.*

▲ *August Malmström,* Odin Hunting, *1901. In their imagination, ancient Germanic peoples saw Odin as an inhabitant of their lands. He is often depicted as traveling in the company of two crows and two wolves.*

One of the most famous stanzas is number 76:

Cattle die and kinsmen die,
thyself too soon must die,
but one thing never, I ween, will die,
the doom on each one dead.

Humor and Sacrifice

The romantic adventures of Odin, which are recounted in a lighthearted style, although not devoid of symbolism, serve to introduce the following section entitled "Loddfafnismal," which consists of a series of exhortations by Odin to Loddfafnir, who is otherwise unknown. Odin has much to say about amorous engagements, as in Stanza 112:

I counsel thee, Stray-Singer, accept my counsels,
they will be thy boon if thou obey'st them,
they will work thy weal if thou win'st them:
seek not ever to draw to thyself
in love-whispering another's wife.

Stanzas 138–165 constitute the "Runatal," Odin's "Song of the Runes." Here the lord of the gods reveals the secret of these magical signs and his self-sacrifice in the quest for knowledge (Stanzas 138 and 139):

I trow I hung on that windy tree
nine whole days and nights,
stabbed with a spear, offered to Odin,
myself to mine own self given,
high on that tree of which none hath heard
from what roots it rises to heaven.

The work ends with the "Ljodalok," a list of magical spells that transmit the knowledge of Odin's mysteries. Odin had stabbed himself with his own spear and bound himself to the world tree to obtain this hidden knowledge. After nine days gazing into its roots he discovered the language of the runes.

The Nine Viking Virtues

The historical form of the religion of the Norse polities, which dominated northern Europe until the Germanic and Scandinavian tribes were converted to Christianity, was revived in the nineteenth century under the name of Asatru (literally, "loyalty to the *aesir*"). Currently a new group of followers of Odin have launched a second revival, reconstructing the religion. Its adherents turn to the *Eddas* for inspiration. They communicate via the Internet, organizing meetings and ceremonies, and have elevated the nine virtues of the ancient Vikings: courage, truth, honor, loyalty, discipline, hospitality, industriousness, self-sufficiency and perseverance.

▲ *Viking with coat of mail, sword and shield.*

▶ Norse Mythology

Voluspá

▲ *W. G. Collingwood, "Odin's Last Words to Balder," illustration from* The Elder Edda, *1908.*

As a new millennium arrived and Christianity was beginning its inexorable encroachment into the heathen lands of the North, a Scandinavian author, who continued to profess the pagan religion of his ancestors, composed one of the most beautiful sacred poems ever written. Its sixty-three stanzas of alliterative verse present a *volva* (prophecy) to Odin relating the mythological history of the universe from its origin from chaos to the final apocalypse and ultimate rebirth. The *Voluspá* is part of the *Poetic Edda*, a part of the work contained in the *Codex Regius*.

▲ *Loki was the father of Hel, Fenrir, and Jormungandr.*

▲◀ *"The Wolf Fenrir Attacks Odin," illustration from H. A. Guerber,* Norse Myths, *1909.*

Creation Myth

Readers of the poem, whose title can be translated as "Prophecy of the Sibyl," will see that the poet was very familiar with Christian texts, but that he venerated above all the spirit of the ancient Norse gods and myths. His hope was to recover the glorious past of the Scandinavian peoples, not only in memory, but to reformulate it in Christian terms: to put the "old wine in new bottles" without spilling any of it.

The poem begins with an invocation and a request for silence from "the sons of Heimdall" (human beings). The sibyl asks Odin if he wants her to recount the ancient wisdom. She says she remembers the primeval giants who bore her. Then she begins her account of the cycle of universal history in a series of fantastic images that increase in intensity as the poem unfolds.

In the beginning there is chaos, described as a deep abyss situated between Niflheim, the misty realm of ice, and Muspillsheim, the burning region of fire. Out of the meeting of ice and fire emerges the giant Ymir, who engenders the first divine triad: Odin, vivifying spirit, Vili, energetic will, and Ve, religious sentiment.

> *At the dawn of time, in the days of Ymir, there was neither earth, nor sea, nor waves.*
>
> Voluspá

▲ *Georg von Rosen,* Odin as a Vagabond, *1886.*

An Eschatological Vision

Surging out of the night of time, the first *aesir* imposed order upon primordial chaos, regulating the passage of days and nights, and the movement of the sun, moon and stars. Now begins the Golden Age in which the first tools are forged, great treasures unearthed and palaces raised up. Happiness reigns on earth. The first ten stanzas conclude with a description of the race of dwarves, the creators of weapons for the gods and heroes.

After a long list of the names of the dwarves, the sibyl tells how the gods sculpted the first man and first woman out of wood: ash and elm. She also describes Yggdrasil, the world tree with roots that reach into the hidden depths of the cosmos.

Immediately, Ragnarok ("twilight of the gods") is ushered in. This is a world-shattering conflict between the *aesir* and the giants, led by Heimdall. The sibyl attributes the conflict to the vices, intrigues and rivalries between Odin's companions. This disorder carries over into the world and unleashes the forces of chaos: the serpent Midgardsormr, the wolf Fenrir and the terrible god Loki, who comes down from the north with an army of maddened warriors. The war ends with the annihilation of the cosmos and the tragic end of many of the *aesir* including Odin himself, who is devoured by Fenrir.

Valkyries in Valhalla

The gods are defeated, but the world is reborn out of the ashes. The

▶ *John Charles Dollman,* The Ride of the Valkyries, *1909, Art Gallery of Western Australia, Perth. The Valkyries rescued warriors from the field of battle and brought them to Valhalla.*

few survivors among gods and men populate a new world as the cycle comes round to the beginning. The fall of the aesir has been determined by the *norns*, female deities who reside in the roots of Yggdrasil and govern the destiny of all beings. Having departed from the world, the *aesir* receive the healing attention of the Valkyries in Valhalla, the warriors' paradise, while humanity is left to recommence its terrestrial adventures.

After the description of Ragnarok the poem returns to the majestic tone of its beginning, manifesting an inextinguishable hope in eternal beauty that has always existed and will return to govern a regenerated world. Balder, the son of Odin and god of beauty, will rule over an epoch of prosperity in the company of "the good gods." This conclusion, inspired by the newly emergent power of Christianity, presented in the *Voluspá* and seen in other parts of the *Eddas*, offers a vision of a world that exists after the end of time, or perhaps better put, as "a return to the ancient past at time's beginning."

▼ *Peter Nicolai Arbo,* Valkyrie, *1864, Nationalmuseum, Stockholm.*

Egyptian Book of the Dead

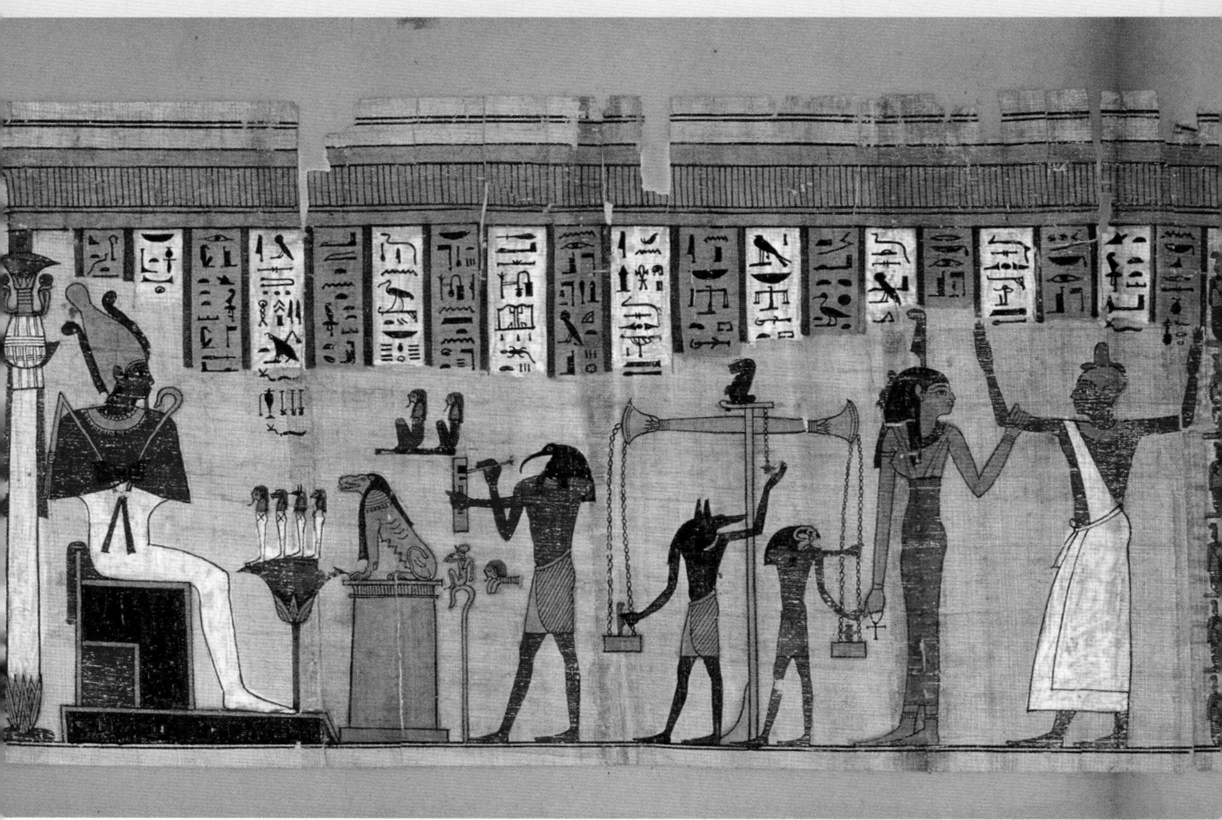

▲ Book of the Dead. *This scene depicts the "Weighing of the Heart." Osiris presides over the trial; the deceased is at the right; at his side is Maat, goddess of justice, who places his soul on the scale. Anubis and Horus stand beneath; Thoth records the verdict; and Ammut stands ready to devour him if he is found wanting.*

According to the ancient Egyptians the dead could attain eternal life after death if complex funerary rites were observed, beginning with embalming. This preserved the physical body until such time that it could be reunited with its soul and, if the verdict of the god Osiris was positive, ascend to the heavens. But before that happened the departed had to traverse the underworld, the Duat, a passage fraught with dangers that could only be avoided by employing the incantations from the *Book of the Dead*: a roll of papyrus that was placed in the sarcophagus that provided safe conduct to the next world.

▶ *The jackal-headed god Anubis guides the souls of the dead to the next world.*

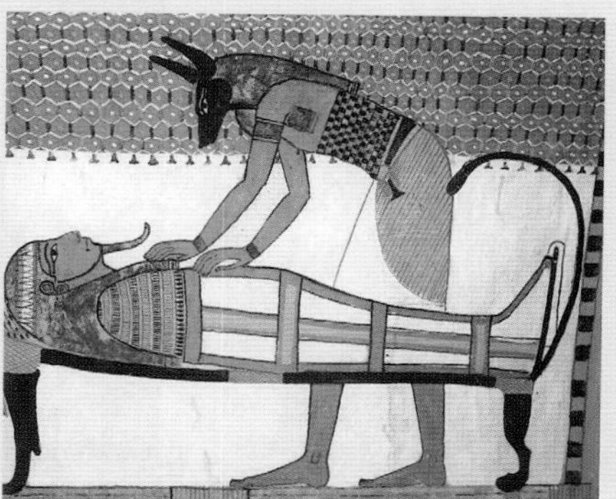

▲ *Pharaoh, flanked by Anubis at his left and Horus at his right.*

Anubis, God of Embalming

The origin of the magical formulas that enabled the deceased to pass through Duat to arrive at the judgment seat of Osiris is to be found in the Pyramid Texts, inscriptions reserved for the pharaohs that decorated the walls of their spectacular tombs. Later on, when the rituals for resurrection became more widespread and available to wealthy individuals, Coffin Texts that imitated the earlier Pyramid Texts came into circulation. In order to fulfill the demand they were reproduced on cloth or papyrus, and many different versions of the *Book of the Dead* appeared. One of the best known of these is the *Papyrus of Ani*, written and illustrated around 1300 BCE on three rolls that altogether measure close to seventy-five feet in length.

The emergence of the various versions took place over a period of millennia. The inhabitants of the Nile basin began burying their dead to preserve cadavers for a longer period of time. Seeing that jackals would dig them up to feed upon them, the belief arose that the soul would proceed to the next world in this fashion, and jackals were considered sacred. For this reason Anubis, the jackal-headed god, assumed the role of his hungry predecessors and became the guide of the dead and master of funerary rituals: symbolically embalming them, leading them through the underworld and protecting cemeteries. Embalming was performed in his name by a priest wearing a jackal mask.

▲ Book of the Dead. *Anubis opens the mouth of the deceased.*

> *Let there be prepared for me a seat in the boat of the Sun on the day wheron the god saileth.*
>
> PAPYRUS OF ANI

The Judgment of Osiris

▲ Osiris, god of the Underworld, is the judge at the tribunal that decides the fate of the departed soul.

All of the rituals, conjurations, hymns and magical formulas contained in the *Book of the Dead* are attributed to Anubis. As the god of transition he is also responsible for the amulets and talismans that were placed within the wrappings of mummies. Thanks to them the dead soul could make his or her way through the realm of Duat without getting stuck there for all time.

Anubis leads the soul to the Hall of Two Truths, where Osiris waits seated on his throne. In the middle of the hall there is an enormous balance. Standing next to it are Maat, the goddess of justice, and Ammit, whose role is to devour those found guilty. The heart of the deceased is placed on one of the scales, on the other, an ostrich feather representing Maat. Anubis oversees the "weighing of the soul" and attests to the result. If the scales balance the deceased is destined for eternal life, if the sinful heart outweighs the feather, Ammit devours it on the spot.

The *Book of the Dead* describes the labors incumbent on the newly arrived souls in paradise. They must till the fields of Osiris, carry sand, and construct irrigation channels. To help them accomplish their tasks, *ushabti* (answerers), wooden figurines, were placed in tombs. These were doubles of the deceased and were called upon to do the heavy lifting, as well as acting as reminders of one's good fortune.

▶ *Detail from the tomb of Thutmose III showing Ra crossing the domain of the god Seker in the Underworld.*

◀ *Relief of the pharaoh Menkaure with the goddess Hathor and a gnome, from the city of Diospolis Parva.*

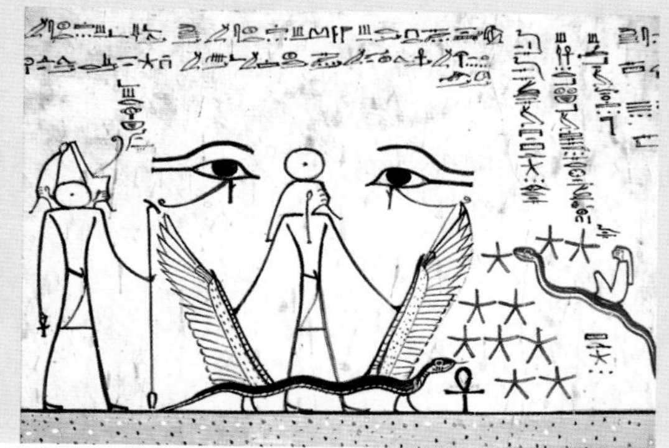

Kemetism

The faith practiced in ancient Egypt has recently been revived under the name of Kemetism. This comes from the Egyptian word kemet, "black earth," the name of the country around the shores of the Nile, which periodically overflows, covering the land with fertile black silt. It is not a New Age fancy mixed with the sonorous names of Egyptian gods and goddesses, but rather an authentic form of neo-paganism. Its adherents seek to faithfully reconstruct the religion of Osiris. Its spiritual leader, the "sovereign" Hekatawy I, was crowned in Egypt in 1996, although currently the group is centered in Europe.

The sacred book of the Kemetists is not surprisingly the Book of the Dead. Their main goddess is Maat, who represents balance and universal justice. Without her, the world would revert to chaos; thanks to her all is rational and orderly. At the same time all divinities are gathered around one primordial force named Netjer, who is believed to have created the universe. The other pillar of Kemetism, its equivalent to the Judeo-Christian Ten Commandments, is "negative confession," a declaration of forty-two laws, which according to the Book of the Dead, the soul is called to answer for at the hour of judgment, attesting that it has not contravened any of them.

Hermetic Texts

▲ *Matthäus Merian, "Opus Medico Chymicum," illustration from Johann Daniel Mylius,* Basilica Philosophica, *1618.*

The ancient Greeks believed that an Egyptian philosopher named Hermes Trismegistus had invented all of the sciences and jealously guarded the highest knowledge in the eponymously named hermetic works, which were mysterious and inaccessible and formed the basis of all occult knowledge. There was disagreement about whether he was a human or a supernatural being. In many respects his description dovetails closely with the Egyptian god Thoth and the Greek god Hermes, both of whom were credited with the invention of writing. To this legendary person, whose name can be translated as "thrice great Hermes" is also ascribed the invention of alchemy.

◀ *Hermes Trismegistus surrounded by his symbolic attributes, most importantly the caduceus.*

▲ *Jacopo Pontormo,* Portrait of Cosimo de Medici, *ca. 1518, Uffizi Gallery, Florence. During his time as duke, Cosimo commissioned the humanist Marsilio Ficino to translate the* Corpus Hermeticum *into Latin.*

Universal Correspondences

The significance of the term "Hermeticism" ("well hidden") is elaborated in the vocabulary of alchemy. The philosopher was believed to have invented an airtight tube that employed a secret seal and was therefore considered to be hermetically sealed. The alchemical and magical writings of Hermes Trismegistus, who was thought to have been a contemporary of Moses, were pored over for centuries by students aspiring to accomplish the "great work," turning base metal into gold.

The *Hermetic Books*, attributed to Hermes Trismegistus, form a heterogeneous collection of eighteen works written between the second and eleventh centuries CE. Some of them deal with practical matters, while others are more philosophical in tone. Of the former, the *Liber Hermes Trismegistus* stands out. It deals with astrology and its medical applications (connecting ailments to astrological influences), hermetic magic (with repeated invocations of Hermes) and alchemy, which not only sought to transform metals, but simultaneously to regenerate the practitioner spiritually. Among the noteworthy speculative treatises are the *Corpus Hermeticum*, the *Asclepius*, and the *Kore Kosmou* ("Virgin of the Cosmos").

The view of the world elaborated in these documents is based upon the doctrine of "correspondences," which asserts that all the elements of cosmos, both animate and inanimate, are connected by the myste-

« *As above, so below.* »

Emerald Tablet

▲ *The winged caduceus represents the principle of air, as well as Olympus, dwelling place of the gods.*

▲▲ *Heinrich Khunrath,* The Emerald Tablet, *drawing.*

rious action of divine energy. Humans are a part of this universal harmony, but their spirits are closed in by their bodies. For example, hermetic astrology explains that planetary demons cover the soul with vices, which adhere to it like barnacles, weighing it down, preventing it from rising to higher levels, and progressively drawing it deeper into their thrall. Hermeticism differs from Christian Gnosticism in that it teaches that salvation can be attained through the application of magical principles.

The Emerald Tablet

Part of the *Kore Kosmou* is the brief and cryptic *Emerald Tablet* (Latin: Tabula smaragdina), one of the most famous texts in Hermetic literature. According to legend its stanzas were composed by Hermes Trismegistus and found in his tomb engraved on a tablet made of precious stone. His followers believe that he placed it there himself before ascending into the heavens so that succeeding generations of seekers could be guided along the way. Until recently the only versions of the work known in the West were in Latin. However, an Arabic manuscript has come to light that turns out to be the oldest extant copy (twelfth century).

The Emerald Tablet contains in condensed form the whole art of alchemy. Its allegorical and obscure formulas were intensively studied by medieval and renaissance alchemists. Even Sir Isaac Newton made a translation of it. The work begins with the following claim: "Truth! Certainty! That in which there is no doubt!" And it continues

by establishing the correspondence between the microcosm and macrocosm: "That which is above is from that which is below, and that which is below is from that which is above, working the miracles of one." There is further advice for initiates, such as: "Separate the earth from the fire, so you will attain the subtle as more inherent than the gross, with care and sagacity." In conclusion the author leaves no doubt about his identity and wisdom: "And to this aspired Hermes, who was threefold graced with wisdom / And this is his last book, which he concealed in the chamber."

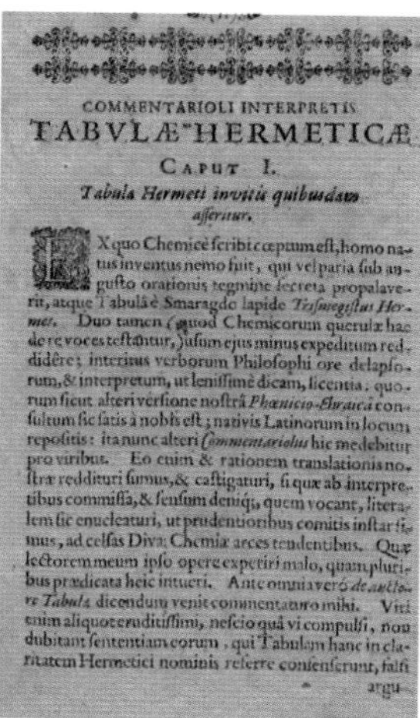

COMMENTARIOLI INTERPRETIS
TABVLÆ HERMETICÆ
CAPUT I.
Tabula Hermeti invitis quibusdam asseritur.

EX quo Chemicè scribi cœptum est, homo natus inventus nemo fuit, qui vel paria sub angusto orationis tegmine secreta propalaverit, atque Tabulâ è Smaragdo lapide *Trismegistus Hermes.* Duo tamen (quod Chemicorum querulæ hac de re voces testantur,) usum ejus minus expeditum reddidêre; interitus verborum Philosophi ore delapsorum, & interpretum, ut lenissimè dicam, licentia: quorum sicut alteri versione nostrâ *Phœnicio-Ebraica* consultum sic satis à nobis est; nativis Latinorum in locum repositis: ita nunc alteri *Commentariolus* hic medebitur pro viribus. Eo enim & rationem translationis nostræ reddituri sumus, & castigaturi, si quæ ab interpretibus commissa, & sensum denique, quem vocant, literalem sic enucleaturi, ut prudentioribus comitis instar simus, ad celsas Divæ Chemiæ arces tendentibus. Quæ lectorem meum ipso opere experiri malo, quam pluribus prædicata heic intueri. Ante omnia verò *de auctore Tabulæ* dicendum venit commentaturo mihi. Viri enim aliquot eruditissimi, nescio quâ vi compulsi, non dubitant sententiam eorum, qui Tabulam hanc in claritatem Hermetici nominis referre consenserunt, falsi argu-

▲ Commentary on the Emerald Tablet.

No Sacred Books

Hermeticism never constituted a true religion, nor did it offer an organized sect with a set liturgy. The earliest hermetic texts, which appeared in Egypt during its occupation by Rome, were not looked upon as holy. Its adherents banded together in small informal communities that developed magical and alchemical practices. The spiritual reflections of Hermes Trismegistus were considered to adorn the internal temple of each initiate.

Orphic Poems

▲ *Statue of Orpheus. Greek mythology recounts that Orpheus met his end when he climbed Mt. Pangeon to the oracle of Dionysius. There he was torn apart by maenads (female followers of the god) for calling his worship into question.*

No one knows whether a poet named Orpheus actually existed. Scholars cannot say for certain one way or the other. It may be the case that there was poet who lived in some remote time before Homer and Hesiod, and founded the Greek mystery religion named after him. Perhaps there were two poets of the same name who lived at different times between 1500 and 1000 BCE. There was certainly much poetry later in antiquity that was written in his name, but Orpheus remains shrouded in mystery and heavily laden with symbolic overtones.

> *O, ether, illustrious flower that shines with the light and splendor of the stars.*
>
> Orphic Hymn To Ether

The Singing Head

▲ *Relief of Orpheus and Eurydice, Amo Breker Museum.*

Legends say the no one ever could resist the power of Orpheus' music and poetry. Every species of animal gathered around him to listen; trees bent their boughs down close to him and rivers changed their courses. Thanks to his powers he was able to lead his wife Eurydice back from Hades, the underworld. In the end the women of Thrace conceived a violent love for the bard, and in their passionate fury tore him to pieces. But this did not put an end to his marvelous powers. His head continued to sing, and he was finally translated into the heavens, where he was converted into a constellation.

The apocryphal poems that were written in his name in different epochs were gathered together under the rubric of the *Orphic Hymns*. One of them, the *Argonauts*, recounts the heroic deeds the poet performed during his participation in the quest for the Golden Fleece. With his music he saved his companions from the fatally seductive song of the sirens and put the dragon that guarded the Fleece to sleep.

Dionysius, the Reborn God

Diverse theogonies, independent of Hesiod's well-known one, explain the origin of the gods according to the followers of Orpheus. They believed that the real creator of the universe was Eros. However, the central figure of the Orphic Mysteries was Dionysius (the Roman Bacchus),

◀ *Jean-Baptiste-Camille Corot,* Orpheus Leading Eurydice out of the Underworld, *1861, Museum of Fine Arts, Houston.*

▲ *Sebastian Vrancx,* Orpheus and the Beasts, *ca. 1595, Borghese Gallery, Rome. This is one of many classical paintings showing Orpheus entrancing animals with the beauty of his music.*

god of the delirious intoxication brought on by wine. Its adherents believed in immortality based on Zagreus (the first Dionysius), whom the Titans dismembered and devoured. Athena saved his heart, out of which was born Dionysius. Meanwhile Zeus reduced the Titans to ashes, from which emerged men whose divided nature reflects the evil of the Titans and the goodness of Dionysius. According to Orphism, which is impregnated by the duality of passion and resurrection, humans can be reborn and become like gods.

For the soul to become liberated, it is obliged to reincarnate again and again until it is able to wash away the original stain of the body that has imprisoned it. This degrading cycle of transmigration can only be interrupted through the agency of the *orpheotelestai* (Orphic initiators). They are the only ones capable of elevating the initiate to the divine realm. This being said, there are problems with attributing to Orphism the character of a true religion. It is rather a matter of an imprecise mystical tradition located on the margins of official cults, developed by wandering priests. Its secret ceremonies use the works attributed to Orpheus, the *Orphic Hymns*, which were composed in the time of Imperial Rome. Some of these were dedicated to Dionysius, but they do not provide an exact sense of the Orphic liturgy.

Declaration Of Innocence

The rites of the Orphic mysteries influenced those of Eleusis as well as

Dionysian celebrations that were known for their frenzied intoxication. But the Orphic doctrine did not encourage licentiousness, and in fact tended toward asceticism. Prayers invoked the gods, petitioning them for health, peace, and a fortunate death. Along the way initiates needed to lead virtuous lives with strict rules governing diet and dress. They were vegetarians and did not permit animal sacrifice. As with the Pythagoreans, eating beans was absolutely prohibited. They dressed all in white. At the hour of death the initiate was given certain written incantations that he would carry into the afterlife to help him avoid being reborn. With these formulas, known as "Orphic tablets," the deceased declared his innocence and his membership in the Orphic community. Only after making this declaration would the soul be eligible to be incorporated into the divine essence of Dionysius.

▲ *Gustave Moreau,* The Head of Orpheus, *1865, Musée d'Orsay, Paris.*

▲◀ *Orpheus' tomb in Thracian sanctuary in Tatul, Bulgaria.*

Avesta

▲ *The* faravahar *is one of the most prominent symbols of Zoroastrianism. It consists of a winged disk incorporating a human figure, possibly of the Persian king.*

Zarathustra is thought to have lived in the sixth century BCE, just as the Persians were beginning to establish their empire. His religious reformation accompanied the new monarchy's efforts to coalesce dispersed tribal loyalties and religious practices. At the same time as Ahura Mazda assumed the supreme celestial role, the Emperor Cyrus grasped the reins of earthly power. The religious ideas of the prophet, who is also known as Zoroaster, are set out in the Avesta, the sacred book of Zoroastrianism, a belief held by the Iranian people until it was overtaken by Islam in the seventh century of our era.

◀ *Fire Temple in Yazd, Iran. The city was an important Zorastrian center during the Sassanid Dynasty.*

▲ *"Tower of Silence," illustration from Cornelius Brown,* The Kingdoms of Queen Victoria. *This tower was a Zoroastrian funerary building. Cadavers were considered impure and were exposed to be devoured by animals.*

Ahura Mazda versus Angra Mainyu

The etymology of the term "avesta" is not firmly established. It probably comes from an ancient Persian dialect and signifies the same as the Hindu term "veda", that is, "knowledge." It is believed that Zoroaster himself wrote some parts of the work and that it was written down during his lifetime. The original manuscripts have been lost to warfare, pillaging and natural catastrophes, but its oral transmission by the priestly caste ensured that it was recopied later (at least in part) in the ancient Persian language known as Avestan.

Of the original Avesta only about one quarter survives. It is divided into five groups of texts. Of these the only one that has come down to us without extensive correction is the Videvdat ("Law of the Abjuration of the Demons"), an authentic Zoroastrian catechism. The beneficent god, Ahura Mazda, whose name means "Omniscient Lord," created the world and its two driving principals, Spenta Mainyu and Angra Mainyu, respectively Ahura Mazda's creative power and the power of evil: light and darkness. Angra Mainyu is a formidable opponent who will not be defeated until the end of time. In the meantime the struggle between these two powers defines the course of world history.

The Cunning of Evil

Ahura Mazda explains in the Videvdat how his work was sabotaged by his adversary: "I created the most beautiful place on earth filled

« We worship the Creator Ahura Mazda with our sacrifice . . . »

Avesta, Yasna

▶ *Representation of Zurvan, Zoroastrian creator god.*

▲ *Raphael,* School of Athens *(detail), 1509, The Vatican. Ptolemy and Zoroaster appear among the crowd of scholars and philosophers.*

with roses and birds with ruby plumage. Angra Mainyu then created insects to attack the plants and animals." Similarly with all of the wonderful things that the god of light had given to men, his opponent sowed lies in Muru, Ahura Mazda's holy city. In Niça, the city of prayer, he introduced doubt, and to Harju, the city of wealth, he brought idleness so that its citizens became destitute.

Angra Mainyu, whose name means "anguished thought," has at his disposal a retinue of demons who torment both gods and men. For example, he ordered the terrible god Vizaresha to stand on the Chinvat Bridge that the dead had to cross to reach the next world. This evil deity would shake the bridge so that souls would fall into the hellish abyss below and never reach the paradise that Ahura Mazda had prepared for them. Another of Angra Mainyu's main lieutenants is Aeshma, madness. This demonic power also appears in the Apocryphal Book of Tobit, with the name of Asmodeus. He is distinguished by his rebellious, destructive and orgiastic nature.

▶ *Relief shows the investiture of Papakan by Ahura Mazda, whose horse is stepping on the head of Angra Mainyu, the god of darkness.*

Perpetual Adoration

The section of the Avesta called Yasht ("Hymns") consists of twenty-one texts dedicated to the yazata (the venerated ones), entities that are owed worship, as well as others that adherents are permitted to worship. These include divinities from other traditions that were absorbed by Zoroastrianism, such as Mithras and Anahita. Some traditions believe that all supernatural beings on the side of good should be included in this category. Ahura Mazda is the chief of all the *yazata*, and Zarathustra is his prophet.

The following sections of the book provide details about Zoroastrian practice and beliefs. The Yasna is a collection of liturgical passages that are recited during ceremonies and include a series of songs (gathas) that are attributed to Zarathustra himself, since the prophet presents himself as a composer of religious hymns. The Visprad ("Prayer to All Patrons") contains invocations and prayers directed to the protectors of diverse categories of beings. The Khordeh Avesta ("Little Avesta") is a breviary of daily prayers that the laity should recite at various times (at dawn, on arising, to the moon, etc.).

Arzhang

▲ *Manichaean priests shown in a manuscript found in Gaochang, near Tarim, China.*

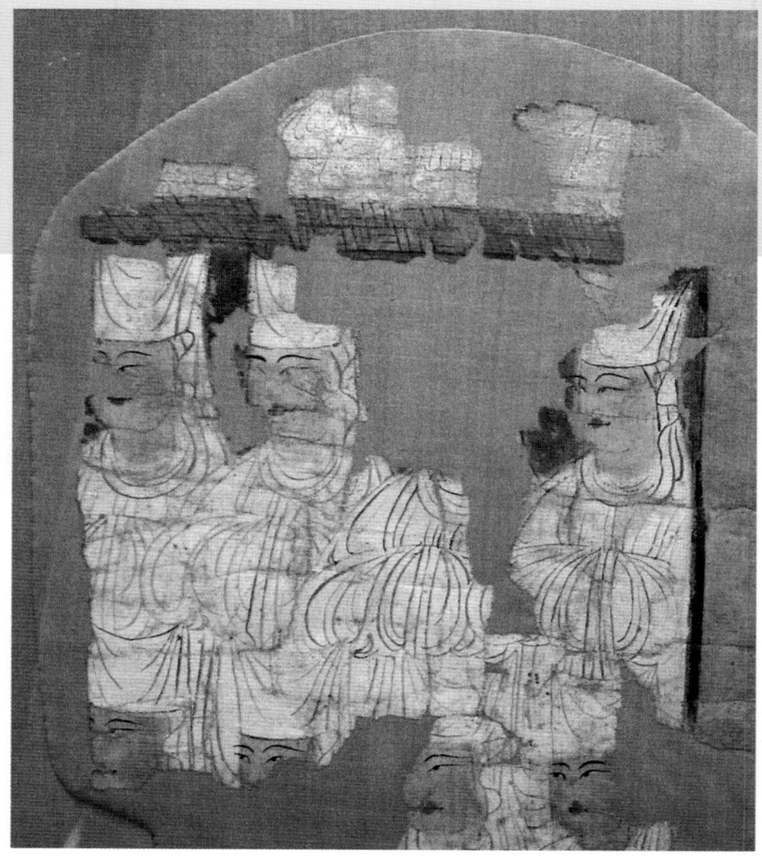

▶ *Manichaean* electae *from the same manuscript. The* electae *were priestesses who were entrusted with teaching the young.*

For Mani, or Manes, the founder of Manichaeism, the failure of Zarathustra, Buddha and Jesus was that they did not personally write down the revelations that were vouchsafed to them. To avoid that error, Mani wrote out his own scriptures in simple terms that could be easily translated without distorting his message. Further, he adorned one of his works, the Arzhang, with marvelous drawings that illustrated his ideas. Unfortunately this work, which earned him the soubriquet of "the painter," has been lost.

◀ *One of the lions adorning the Ishtar Gate in Babylon. Mani was born in the city in CE 216.*

Mani and His Heavenly Twin

▲ *Mani claimed that he had a celestial twin, who visited him when he was 12 years old and again at the age of 24.*

Mani was born in CE 216 to a noble family. His detractors painted him as a dangerous heretic, but we know that he was intelligent and extremely cultivated: learned in science, music, mathematics, medicine, geography, astronomy and above all art. However, his main interest, which he displayed even as a child, was religion and spirituality. He saw himself as a prophet whose message would supersede that of his predecessors: Seth, son of Adam, Enoch, Shem, son of Noah, Buddha, Zarathustra, and Jesus.

At four years old he entered into the Jewish-Christian sect of Elcasaites, who practiced sexual abstinence and fasting. Although he devoted himself to its practices and doctrine, he recounts that as he grew up, he felt protected by angels of light and inspired by gnostic visions. In this way he learned to revere the living souls hidden in all beings; he considered it impious to sacrifice animals or even to uproot plants, since this would destroy the particles of light imprisoned in matter. At the age of 12 he received a visit for the first time from his celestial twin, a luminous being who informed Mani of his destiny. His second visit happened at 24. It was at that point that his definitive revelation began. "The living Paraclete descended and conversed with me. He unlocked the secrets of the worlds and the generations. He revealed the mystery of light and darkness. The Paraclete revealed to me all that has happened and all that will happen."

Good and Evil, Eternal Enemies

Under the protection of the Sassanid king, Shapur I, Mani dedicated himself to elaborating his gospels. So that his message would remain clear and free from alteration, he invented his own alphabet. The later persecution of the sect resulted in the systematic destruction of all of his works. But thanks to discoveries in the twentieth century in the oases of Turfan, Medinet Madi, and Oxirrinco, his writings have been partially recovered. Today we know that the Manichaean canon included the Living Gospel, the Fundamental Epistle, the Book of Giants, the Book of Shapur, the Kephalaia and other tracts and books of psalms and orations. In addition he created the illustrated Arzhang, which the Copts call Eikon ("Images").

▲ *Heinrich Schmalz,* Zenobia's Last Look on Palmyra, *1888, Art Gallery of South Australia, Adelaide. Zenobia was the queen of the ancient city of Palmyra and a follower of Mani.*

From these texts it is evident that Manichaeism was closely related to Zoroastrianism, with the addition of Gnostic elements. It held that there were two eternal opposing forces: good and evil. Out of the conflict between them arose the first human couple, Adam and Eve, who had within them both principles. In order that the particles of light within each being return to heaven, the living spirit has sent Gnostic messengers, the last of whom was Mani. Once invested with the power of the new Paraclete, he could set about rebuilding the true Church of Jesus Christ.

◀ According to Manichaeism Adam and Eve were generated from the struggle between good and evil.

◀◀ Hans Holbein the Younger, Humiliation of Valerian by Shapur I. *Shapur was Mani's protector.*

> *«I have sown the seed of life from east to west ... None of the apostles did this.»*
>
> KEPHALAIA, MANI

From India to Extinction

To accomplish his mission, Mani did not content himself only with writing. Manichaeism was a well-organized church that aspired to be universal. Its founder preached in Persia, Media, Parthia, and traveled to India, where he met many adepts. While his followers spread as far as Egypt and gained success in converting people to the new faith, a new Persian king succeeded his old patron and began to lose confidence in the religion. A plot was organized by the established clergy and the mages, who were jealous of the upstart's increasing power. In the end Mani was imprisoned in Gundesapur, tortured and killed. His head was impaled on a spike at the gates of the city, an effective deterrent to sympathizers of the sect. Although Manichaeism had spread to the Roman territories of North Africa, and important figures such as St. Augustine communicated with its followers, it could not survive the combined force of imperial power and the early Christian Church. The religion disappeared in the fifth century.

▲ *Sandro Botticelli,* Saint Augustine, *1480. Augustine was one of the few Chruch Fathers who communicated with Mani.*

New Revelations

▶ Theosophy

The Secret Doctrine

▲ *Helena Blavatsky (1831–1891) was an indefatigable worker. She claimed that she received some of her ideas from the astral plane.*

In the last part of the nineteenth century, legendary Theosophist Madame Blavatsky roiled the waters of spiritual movements in Europe. Over a number of decades her enigmatic personality won the admiration of intellectuals, and her mystical ideas were the focus of long discussions and controversies in Bohemian circles and elegant salons. The mélange of occult sciences, Hinduism, and spiritualism that was propagated by the International Theosophical Society, which she founded, acted as a filter drawing in spiritual seekers, coloring modern thought and influencing Biblical studies.

There is no religion higher than truth.

Motto of the Theosophical Society

Intermediary of the Mahatmas

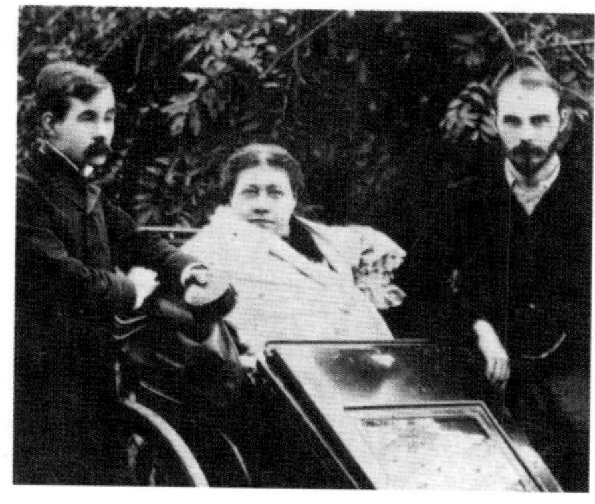

▲ *Blavatsky in London with James Morgan Pryse and George Robert Stow Mead.*

▲◀ *Blavatsky at home in 1887.*

The first reports we have of Helena Petrovna Blavatsky, born in the Ukraine in 1831, speak of an imaginative and daring young girl, who was an avid reader of works of Freemasonry and the occult found in the library of her grandfather. At a young age she learned to "produce" paranormal phenomena and received marvelous visions that her later critics claimed she invented. Through the course of her entire life she continued along the path she had set out upon in her youth. Once separated from her first husband, she traveled in Greece, the Balkans, Egypt, and England. She was a great supporter of Garibaldi's independence movement, and disguised as a soldier, she participated in the Battle of Mentana, where she was wounded and nearly died.

This experience opened her eyes as a medium. After her first trip to India — and Tibet as well, although some regard her reported contact with lamas as never having taken place — she declared that she had been chosen as an intermediary between humanity and a group of adepts, whom she referred to as "mahatmas," "Masters of the Ancient Wisdom." They communicated with her by means of written messages. In 1875, she founded the International Theosophical Society in New York City. Its stated purpose was to increase tolerance between different races and religions, encourage the study of antediluvian philosophies, and develop humanity's higher nature and latent powers.

▲ J. Krishnamurti and Annie Besant, Blavatsky's successor as head of the Theosophical Society.

▲▶ Blavatsky in 1884. She spent that year studying in Paris.

Fear, Admiration and Doubt

Madame Blavatsky's entrance upon the world stage coincided with an increasing interest in esoteric ideas, as shown by the enthusiasm for the Magnetism of Franz Anton Mesmer and the spiritualism of Allan Kardec, both of whom were quite popular at the time. Blavatsky was surrounded by an aura of mystery, and as with other proponents of the occult, she was greeted with a mixture of admiration and fear. In 1877, she published *Isis Unveiled*, her first great work. Two years later she settled in India to be closer to her mahatmas, and studied Parabrahma, absolute, immutable and unlimited consciousness, the connection between spirit and matter, the two fundamental aspects that constituted the universe.

Blavatsky interpreted the sacred texts of other religions according to her "internal inspiration," but critics began to accuse her of deliberate falsification of her experiences. They noted that her works plagiarized from writings published years before and insisted that her spiritualist manifestations were fraudulent. None of these criticisms deterred her or prevented her from writing her most expansive work, *The Secret Doctrine*, which eventually came to three volumes.

▶ *Theosophical symbol containing the Star of David, the swastika and the Sanskrit character om.*

▶▶ *Blavatsky in 1877, the year of the publication of* Isis Unveiled, *her first major work.*

Evolution of Humanity

▲ *Annie Besant arriving in Cardiff in 1924, for a meeting with Theosophists. She collaborated as Blavatsky's secretary on* The Secret Doctrine.

The first part of *The Secret Doctrine* purports to be a translation of a Tibetan text, entitled the *Book of Dzyan*, a work that has never been located. Blavatsky asserted that she discovered the book wrapped in palm leaves, treated with an unknown technology that rendered it waterproof and invulnerable to fire and air. This miraculous document contained a secret doctrine, the universal religion of the prehistoric world.

The second volume of her work describes the evolution of humanity through seven "root races." The first was pure spirit; the second, known as the Hyperboreans, lived in a land near the North Pole; the third dwelt in the continent of Lemuria; the fourth in Atlantis. The current race, the Aryans, are the fifth in the succession. They will occupy the earth for approximately one million years. After that the sixth race will arise. Their lives will be characterized by harmony and fraternal union. Finally a seventh race will evolve that will be illuminated by its closeness to God. According to Blavatsky, savages (such as Africans and Australian Aborigines) developed from the Lemurians and people of Atlantis. She considered Arabs and Jews as Aryans, but as "degenerate in spirituality."

The publication of these ideas laid Blavatsky open to charges of esoteric racism, which, united with accusations of fraud, diminished the credibility of the Theosophical movement. Its founder died alone in London, working on new volumes of *The Secret Doctrine.*

The Great Invocation

▲ *Shigatse in Tibet was the home of Djwal Khul until the Chinese invasion. Alice Bailey claimed that he dictated books to her telepathically.*

The initiatory adventure of Alice Ann Bailey followed in the footsteps of the great Theosophist, Helena Blavatsky. Bailey considered herself Blavatsky's disciple. She also spoke to the mahatmas, the hidden teachers of humanity. They informed her that the stage begun by Blavatsky had come to its conclusion and a new phase had begun. Bailey devoted her life to the propagation of this new message. She saw her leadership as preparing the way for a renaissance of consciousness that would result in the advent of the world teacher that all religions longed for.

◀ *Bailey taught that the New Age would arrive with God returning to earth with an army of illuminated beings.*

What Is to Come

▲ *Alice Bailey, disciple of Helena Blavatsky, was the author of* The Great Invocation.

This yearned-for avatar has been known by different names: Messiah, Maitreya, Krishna, Mahdi, Bodhisattva and others as well. His arrival at the head of the hierarchy of illuminated spirits will usher in a new era. These revelations established Bailey as one of the most important figures in the nascent New Age movement, which draws from many sources and approaches in furtherance of spiritual transformation.

In her *Unfinished Autobiography*, Alice Bailey (1880–1949) says that she was an Evangelical Christian until she encountered the Theosophical Society founded by Blavatsky. From that point her interest and activities in esotericism quickly burgeoned: the foundation of the Lucis Trust in 1920, the Arcane School in 1923, the publication of twenty-five books and her leading role in conferences, congresses, and groups. Above all, she maintained contact with her personal spiritual master, Djwal Khul.

Messages from Djwal Khul

Bailey claimed that the majority of her works were telepathically dictated to her, one of the best known and most widely commented upon examples of the phenomenon of channeling. The source of these messages was named Djwal Khul, nicknamed "the Tibetan," who described

▲ *Bailey was inspired by Patanjali's Yoga Sutra.*

himself as follows: "[I am] a Tibetan disciple of a certain degree, and this tells you but little, for all are disciples from the humblest aspirant up to and beyond the Christ Himself. I live in a physical body like other men on the borders of Tibet and at times (from the exoteric standpoint) preside over a large group of Tibetan Lamas, when my other duties permit." In this way he identified himself as one of the famous mahatmas that Madame Blavatsky had been the first to mention. Djwal claimed that he was a master of the fifth initiation, a disciple of the master of the second "root race," Koot Hoomi.

According to Bailey, at first the voice of Djwal Khul spoke to her dictating his message word for word. Later on, however, the fullness of his thoughts entered her mind, and she was able to transcribe them in a more fluent fashion. She finally became so completely identified with her master that there came a time when she could no longer tell what were her thoughts and what were his.

The teachings in Bailey's books are conveyed in a very simple style. They treat themes addressed by Blavatsky, such as meditation, reincarnation, karma, the spiritual energy of cosmic rays, and the functioning of the soul, which was examined through the lens of Patanjali's Yoga Sutra. She also devoted herself to analyzing the mysterious *Book of Dzyan* that her predecessor had presented in *The Secret Doctrine*.

◀ *Maitreya, Krishna, Mahdi, any of these can serve as the Teacher for the true seeker.*

> « *The mind reaches the state of yoga with practice and discipline.* »
>
> YOGA SUTRA

The Mantra of Light

The best-known work of Alice Bailey is The Great Invocation. It is a mantra or prayer transmitted by Djwal Khul. It is used in meditation groups often consisting of three persons. This triangular focus concentrates spiritual energy that can then be sent into the world to accelerate global spiritual development.

The invocation, which is repeated daily, goes as follows:

From the point of Light within the Mind of God
Let light stream forth into the minds of men.
Let light descend on Earth.
From the point of Love within the Heart of God
Let love stream forth into the hearts of men.
May Christ return to Earth.

From the center where the Will of God is known
Let purpose guide the little wills of men —
The purpose which the Masters know and serve.
From the center which we call the race of men
Let the Plan of Love and Light work out
And may it seal the door where evil dwells.
Let Light and Love and Power restore the Plan on Earth.

A Course in Miracles

▶ *According to its followers,* A Course in Miracles *offers a bridge to a higher truth that is actually real.*

Imagine that an atheist heard the actual words of Jesus Christ and decided not to believe them. This was the surprising case of Helen Schucman, who one day in September of 1965, heard a mysterious voice that said to her: "This is a course in miracles. Please take notes." Over the course of seven years she transcribed what the voice dictated to her, until finally it announced itself as Jesus Christ. *A Course in Miracles* is the result of one of the most remarkable examples of channeling that we know of, especially since, although Schucman considered the experience authentic, she never wholly endorsed its content. In fact, she retained some skepticism about it until the end of her life.

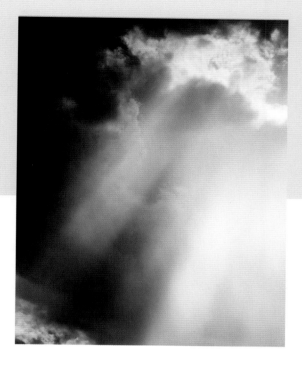

Channeling

The phenomenon of channeling occupies an important place in the thinking of the New Age movement. The experience is similar to watching television or listening to the radio, except in this case the transmitter is an immaterial being (angel, god, prophet). Its message concerns religious matters, and it is received involuntarily. The receiver often has only a limited understanding of the message. His or her function is primarily that of a transcriber. Experts attribute the experience as a little-studied manifestation of the collective unconscious, without discounting many instances of fraud.

▲ *The process of channeling is a kind of remote control. The receiver acts as a conduit for the message.*

The psychologist Helen Schucman (1909–1981) and her husband Bill, a psychologist as well, were not believers, although they had expressed some interest in esoteric ideas and in Christianity. Helen described the process of being an amanuensis for Jesus: "The Voice made no sound, but seemed to be giving me a kind of rapid, inner dictation which I took down in a shorthand notebook. The writing was never automatic. It could be interrupted at any time and later picked up again. It made obvious use of my educational background, interests and experience, but that was in matters of style rather than content. Certainly the subject matter itself was the last thing I would have expected to write about." The following day she would read her notes to her husband, who typed them up.

The Dream of Jesus Christ

▲ *According to* A Course in Miracles, *God sent the Holy Spirit to awaken Jesus Christ from his dream.*

A Course in Miracles was published in 1975. It entirely reinterprets the Gospels, as well as the passion and resurrection of Christ. God is seen as an impersonal mind that did not create the universe. Rather everything existent is an emanation of the Son. However, Jesus is not the only descendant, but rather the first to be aware of the fact. Jesus falls asleep and dreams that he is distinct from and as powerful as the Father. To awaken him, God sends the Holy Spirit. From that time on, it will be the voice of the Father within each of us. Jesus realizes that his sin was to separate himself from that which gave him life. Furthermore, this dream has arisen in humans, each of whom has the idea of being independent of God.

Throughout the many pages of the work, the traditional antagonistic dualisms of traditional religions (good and evil, God and the world, light and darkness) are replaced by the simple dichotomy of "real–unreal." Sin and guilt are not real. They are figments of a dream. Although the ego is real, it is a product of one's errant mind: a false substitute for the true self created by God. This confusion can be rectified by a miracle, which is defined as "a correction … that reminds the mind that what it sees is false."

> *Your task is not to seek for love, but merely find all the barriers within yourself that you have built against it.*
>
> A Course in Miracles, Chapter 8-vii 9.8

The Proper Channel

Of course, the idea of "miracle" undergoes a profound revision, distancing it from its traditional meaning. According to this teaching, a miracle can be defined as an expression of love, and as such it takes natural rather than supernatural form. A Course in Miracles asserts that sin, guilt, and the confusion generated by the ego can only be countered by love. Its basic message is to encourage knowledge of one's real self and the consequences of an ego-based life. This theme runs through all three parts of the book: "Textbook," "Workbook," and "Manual for Teachers."

Since its publication many groups have formed dedicated to the study of these texts, even though the author persisted in her atheism, never admitting the truth of what she had written down. An upsurge of interest occurred in 1992, following Marianne Williamson's endorsement of the teachings on Oprah Winfrey's television show.

Photographic Credits

a = above; b = below; d =right; i = left; c = center

DREAMSTIME: 12© Zasranka; 26© Rozdesign; 33© Centrill; 40© Pacza ni; 43© Markp; 44© Wellesenterprises; 45© Fotogenics; 46ai© Evergreenimps; 47ad© Desertsolitaire; 49a© Desertsolitaire; 50© Marisabel2005; 51a© Alysta; 51b© Randymir; 52© Stanisa; 53ad© Zugzwang; 57ad© Kamphi; 57bd© Carolyne; 59ai© Jasonbennee; 59ad© Joeygil; 60© Novell; 63cd© Noonie; 64© 123dk; 68© Basphoto; 69ai© Galoff; 69cd© Loraliu; 70ci© Radist; 73ad© Jurand; 73bd© Jasmina; 82© Hsandler; 85© Trajancorbel; 87a© Abbarich; 88c© Vadkoz; 89a© Photowitch; 90a© Photoguy707; 90b© Yoriy; 91© Boriail1; 96© Mazor; 97a© Oscar1319; 97b© Grobledo; 99a© Cammeraydave; 101© Jscalev; 102a© Tezzstock; 102b© Kshishtof; 103a© Zatletic; 106© Paulcowan; 107© Koscusko; 110a© Zensu; 111© Rueful; 112© Ebtikar; 113© Shariffc; 114ai© Distinctiveimages; 114bi© Ayazad; 116© Pooh1; 118bi© Dragang; 126© Gresei; 127d© Paulprescott; 130a© Suronin; 131ai© Samrat35; 131bd© Johnandersonphoto; 132© Jatinmax; 133© Videowokart; 134ai© Picstudio; 134bi ©Dreamshot63; 135a© Mschalke; 136© Ashwin82; 137a© Ashwin82; 137d© Thefinalmiracle; 138ai© Skutvik; 138ad© Samrat35; 138bi© Thefinalmiracle; 139bd© Taolmor; 140i© Hatric; 141a©Csld; 141b© Paulprescott; 142a© Poresh; 142b© Missbobbit; 144c© Shariffc; 145© Pazham;146ai© Dannyphoto80; 146ad© Elenaray; 147© Mudong; 148© Shanin; 149a© Dibrova; 149b© Nstanev; 150© Shanin; 151© Itpow; 152© Omkr;154ai© Dwights; 154b© Jaimaa85; 155©Joyfull; 156©Masterlu; 158 bi© Dimol; 159ai© Kaetana; 160i© Sofuzzz; 162b© Rgbspace; 163a© Mahesh14; 164© Jlye; 165ad© Shariffc; 166i© Chrisrawlins; 166c© Thefinalmiracle; 169a© Amabrao; 169b© Jeremyrichards; 171© Gardawind; 173a© Card76; 173b© Masterlu; 174a© Beatg; 174b© Taolmor; 178© Saviochote; 179© Plotnikov; 180ai© Holgs; 180ad© Studio; 180a© Chrisrawlins; 181ai© Suronin; 181d© Maxironwas; 182© Rsaraiva; 183© Surabky; 184© Volare2004; 185© Ginaellen; 186© Carlosmoura; 187ad© Mauro77photo; 187cd© Mauro77photo; 188© Starblue; 189© Mmero; 190ai© Martipas; 190ad© Razvanjp; 191© Bbbar; 192© Tneppl; 193ai© Stellapotography; 193ci© Fazztg; 194b© Fotosergio; 195ai© Cmfotoworks; 195bd© Woolfenden; 196i© Shariffc; 196d© Nsilcock; 197a© Shariffc; 198a© Volare2004; 198i© Wormold; 199a© Mcpics; 199d© Digitalpress; 200© Jarnogz; 201ad© Ooicl; 203ai©Ilgitano; 203ad© Kai815; 204© Hotduckz; 205ai© Zanskar; 205ad© Mark52; 206b© Aje44; 207© Dvincent; 208© Knighterrant; 209a© Seesea; 209b© Tc8888; 210ai© Songzier; 210ad© Bbbar; 211©Aneurysm; 212© Rcaucino; 213ai© Dimaberkut; 213ad© Szefei; 213cd© Leungchopan; 214ai© Chelovek; 214bi© Joyceqiu; 215ad© Tomboy2290; 215cd© Elenaray; 216© Carmentianya; 217ai© Marilyna; 217bd© Jayturbo; 218ad© Velusariot; 218bi© Photodesign; 219a© Pjworldour; 220ai© Sabobros; 220c© Bbbar; 221a© Yekaterina; 221d© Saipg; 222i© Rcaucino; 222d© Bbbar; 223ad© Szefei; 223bd© Hosouth; 226© Lieska; 227©Danherbertson; 228ad© Richliy; 228b© Taolmor; 229a© Casejustin; 229b© Genlady; 230ai© Lieska; 230b© Richliy; 231a© Lieska; 231bd© Lieska; 232c© Starblue; 232i© Dasar; 233bd© Christiansc14; 234 ai© Rodho; 234ci© Saniphoto; 234bi© Saniphoto; 235ai© Inerika; 235a© Artaniss8; 236© Dellyne; 237ai© Vanbeets; 237bi© Rssfhs; 239ad© Madartists; 240ai© Afonskaya; 240c© Mav888; 242a© Backgarden; 243b© Shariffc; 249bd© Rolffimages; 250a© Clintcearley; 251b© Aldaer; 253a© Fenghui; 254ai© Realrocking; 255d© Georgios; 256© Dreamshot63; 257a© Andreygorlov; 259a© Christophe.rolland1; 262© Nstanev; 263ad© Gnup; 264i© Andrewhoward; 265a© Noaphoto; 266© Tashka; 267a© Furzyk73; 267b© Hudis; 268a© Gamemon; 268b© Haak78; 269i© Gnup; 269d© Sensitive2light; 272a© Tund; 276d© Lorna; 277i© Krisgun01; 280a© Cheech95; 290© Gmv; 291ai©Jgroup; 292ad© Jumpingsack; 293ai© Ecobo; 308©Holgs; 309©Sanshams; 310© Omkr; 311©Bbbar; 312© Frenta; 313© Allein; 314a©Baloncici; 314b© Thecult; 315© Kolfambus; 316© Loveliestdreams; 317ai© Elnur; 317bd© Kaspiic; 318a© Madartist; 318b© Enruta; 319ad© Mike_ Kiev; 319bd© Valuavitaly; 320© Krisdog; 321© Wowbagger; 322c© Hyside; 323ai© Woodooart; 324© Dmyla; 325ai© Filmspiegel; 325ad© Markwaters; 326© Littlemacproductions; 327© Engel; 328© Eric 1513; 329ad© Mauro 77 photo; 329ai© Pstit; 330© Khz; 331a© Littlemacproductions; 331b© Loveliestdreams; 332© Azpworldwide; 333a© Keetten_ Predators; 333d© Friday; 334a© Ronfromyork; 335a© Nejron; 336a© Crazy80frog; 336b© Kristijanzonar; 339© Niserin; 340© Mjuncal; 341ai©Alvinhow; 341ad© Ensiferrum; 341b© Summersea; 342b© Krisgun01; 342ai© Alfonskaya; 343a© Realrocking; 343b© Linqong; 344© Kunaldaswani; 345a© Ladylyonnesse; 345b© Nmint; 346ad© Nicousia; 347a© Vilevi; 347c© Picsfive; 347b© Yakobchuk; 349© Potawa; 350© Chunche; 351b© Leesniderphotoimages; 355ad© Silverv; 356ad© De-Kay; 356ai© Mattwatt; 357cd© V0v; 358© Justinmetz; 359© Sanjab; 363© Prometeus; 364a© Ponitail 14; 364bi© Innovari; 365ai© Prometeus; 365ad©Jgroup; 367a© Oxanam; 369ai© Spaxia

WIKIPEDIA COMMONS: 37aBY Nina-no; 56BY Ondrej Zvacek; 65BY Fred J (http://commons.wikimedia.org/wiki/User:Fred_J); 117aBY Nicholas JB; 117bBY Nicholas JB; 118BY Nicholas JB; 119BY Nicholas JB; 123adBY Marco Abrar; 129dBY Ddalbiez; 130iBY Hanz Stieglitz; 167BY Vaikunda Raja; 168BY Hari Singh; 244BY Tom@HK; 291BY Bot Multichill; 295aBY Polimerek; 295bBY Kelson; 299aBY G. dallorto; 310BY Davin7; 346BY Пrate.
AGE: 348
CORBIS: **100**; **119c**; **175**; **246**; **247**